The Organization of Interests

Terry M. Moe

The Organization of Interests

*Incentives and the Internal Dynamics
of Political Interest Groups*

The University of Chicago Press
Chicago and London

The University of Chicago Press, Chicago 60637
The University of Chicago Press, Ltd., London

© 1980 by The University of Chicago
All rights reserved. Published 1980
Midway Reprint edition 1988.
Printed in the United States of America

Library of Congress Cataloging in Publication Data

Moe, Terry M.
 The organization of interests.

 Includes bibliographical references and index.
 1. Pressure groups. I. Title.
JF529.M59   329′.03   79-13238
ISBN 0-226-53353-0

To My Brother, Rick

Contents

Acknowledgments

I would like to express my appreciation to several people. Robert B. Kvavik stimulated my interest in political groups and, even more importantly, was an unfailing source of advice and support throughout my graduate years at the University of Minnesota; I owe him a great deal. Frank J. Sorauf was the first to encourage me to pursue the kinds of ideas now contained in this book; he also urged me to launch my own empirical study of group membership, something that I was not eager to do but that broadened my horizons considerably. W. Phillips Shively made many useful comments on the approach and content of my work and was especially helpful in keeping the analysis within limits; without his advice, I might have continued writing forever.

Mancur Olson, Jr., as the reviewer of an earlier draft, offered extensive and thoughtful suggestions for revision. While I did not always follow his suggestions, the book has surely benefited from his careful attention, and I am deeply appreciative.

The Political Science Department at Michigan State University gave me some time off from teaching in which to complete my work, and my colleagues have been a constant source of intellectual stimulation and encouragement. The departmental secretaries—Iris Richardson, Karen Albrecht, Karen Underwood, and Linda Salemka—expertly (and sometimes cheerfully) handled the mounds of paperwork I generated over the past few years, and I am grateful for their help.

Finally, I want to thank my wife, Debra Moe, for her patience and understanding, and for the sacrifices she made so that this book could be written.

It is now a commonplace observation that interest groups are important and even necessary components of democratic politics. Groups of various descriptions are ever-present in the legislative process, acting as agents of influence, channels of representation, sources of information and expertise, and communicators to specialized sectors of society, to name only several of their legislative roles. Much the same can be said of pervasive group activity in the executive branch of government, only more so; for in administrative arenas, especially in the European and Scandinavian political systems, many groups have, in effect, become officially recognized partners with government in the formulation and administration of public policy. They are not only accepted and valued participants, but, in some of their roles, are indistinguishable from government itself. Groups are even active participants in the judicial process—pursuing their goals through test cases, amicus briefs, and like means of shaping judicial outcomes.

Groups also carry on a variety of important activities that are less directly related to policymaking. They are integral participants in electoral politics, for instance, affecting who will be elected and how they will behave once in office. They have a hand in mobilizing people for politics, transmitting political information, shaping political attitudes, and integrating individuals into the political system as a whole. While groups are participants in policymaking, then, they also play a part in conditioning the broader political context in which policy is made, interpreted, and carried out.[1]

In view of the variety of roles that interest groups play at all levels of the political system, it is surprising that so little of a systematic nature is known about the groups themselves. We have only a rudimentary understanding, for example, of how these groups arise from the plurality of interests in society, how their organizational structures are developed and maintained over time, and by what internal processes their political goals are determined. These are the kinds of questions that help shape our notion of what interest groups are and provide a theoretical foundation for explaining why interest groups do what they do in politics.

The bulk of the work on interest groups is not concerned with probing these "deeper" aspects of group behavior.[2] Most studies focus on what groups *do* in politics and, if only implicitly, direct their theoretical attention to questions of how group activity can be made to fit into more general theories of politics, with special reference to the determination of public policy. These efforts tell us a great deal about the diverse dimensions of group politics, and it is largely from such sources that the political salience of interest groups has been documented. But they have rarely been balanced by complementary work that takes the groups themselves as the phenomena to be explained.

Any semblance of balance is primarily due to two bodies of research, studies of small groups and studies of larger voluntary associations—which, with a few exceptions, derive from the research efforts of sociologists and social-psychologists, not political scientists.[3] Understandably, theoretical questions fall along a broad spectrum of sociological and psychological concerns, and attention is normally not directed to interest groups, nor to the distinctly political aspects of goals, issues, interests, motivations, or environment. What these literatures have to say about interest groups, then, must usually be inferred from works carried out for other purposes, leaving the political scientist with an assortment of loosely related findings and a largely incomplete picture of the subject matter.

One result is that, until recently, there has been little coherent basis for confirming or challenging long-held pluralist notions about the nature of interest groups. Among these are the familiar beliefs that groups arise on the basis of common interests, that they are maintained through member support of group policies, and that group policies are an expression of underlying common interests. These and related notions are, in effect, a loosely structured theory of interest groups and have served in that capacity for some time, offering something that the existing empirical work has been decidedly unable to provide—a simple, intuitively pleasing framework for making sense out of a complex set of phenomena. Thus, when political scientists have found it necessary to explain the nature of interest groups, or when they have sought a broad explanation for group political activity, they have conventionally relied on pluralist theory for the answers.[4] With its central tenets virtually taken for granted, pluralism has been the major theoretical force shaping what we "know" about interest groups.[5]

The pluralist tradition suffered a dramatic setback, however, with the appearance of Mancur Olson's *The Logic of Collective Action*.[6] Applying a simple rational model to an analysis of interest groups, Olson is able to supply answers to basic questions about the foundations of group activity, answers that stand in direct contradiction to prevailing pluralist notions. Most importantly, he flatly discounts the core pluralist belief that interest groups arise on the basis of common interests, demonstrating that "If the members of a large group rationally seek to maximize their personal welfare, they will not act to advance their common or group objectives unless there is coercion to force them to do so, or unless some separate incentive, distinct from the achievement of the common or group interest, is offered to the members of the group individually on the condition that they help bear the costs or burdens involved in the achievement of the group objectives."[7]

Olson arrives at his unconventional conclusions by structuring an analysis around two key components. First, in what was at the time a novel and innovative move, he points out that when individuals have a common interest in achieving a political goal, the latter characteristically takes the form of a collective good. That is, once the goal is achieved, its benefits can be enjoyed by each individual in the group, regardless of whether or how much he has contributed toward that end. Recognizing that this should have an inhibiting effect on the willingness of individuals to pursue their common interests, Olson introduces the collective good as a key theoretical tool for reconceptualizing and explaining this aspect of collective behavior.

Second, the analysis is premised on a number of simplifying assumptions, the most basic of which are certain idealized propositions about individuals—that they are rational, perfectly informed, and economically self-interested. This simple model is then applied to a group context which, from the perspective of traditional pluralist thought, is ideally suited for the emergence of interest group activity: all individuals are assumed to be in perfect agreement on the desirability of achieving a given political goal, viewed as a collective good. The analysis subsequently centers on the question of how much and under what conditions individuals will contribute toward the collective good, thus "pursuing their common interests" by supporting interest group activity.

In this way, Olson develops what might best be labeled an economic theory of interest groups. This is appropriate in the sense that his rational modeling approach is a characteristically economic mode of analysis. But it is also appropriate because, in view of his assumption that individuals are economically self-interested, the theory is most usefully applied to economic interest groups—as opposed, say, to groups of a religious, ideological, or social nature. Thus, by referring to Olson's work as an economic theory of interest groups, we are reminded that it is a theory of limited scope, although it is limited to precisely those groups that, in virtually all Western democracies, happen to be the most numerous, active, and politically powerful.

With special reference to economic groups, then, Olson develops a logical argument that undermines the presumed pluralist link between common interests and collective action, showing that, with certain identifiable exceptions, political goals will not be sufficient to induce member support of interest group activity. Indeed, given his model of the individual's calculus, the crucial facilitators of group formation are not collective goods at all, but "selective incentives." These are benefits that can be conferred upon contributors and withheld from noncontributors—insurance policies, news publications, discounts on goods and services—anything at all that individuals may value and that can be selectively conferred or withheld. Thus, the question of whether interest groups will emerge, and how well they can recruit members and contributions, depends upon their ability to supply members with benefits that are essentially nonpolitical. It decidedly does not rest with the policy preferences of members, nor with the group's political appeals; and, in fact, groups may be quite large and well funded even if most members disagree with group goals.

Olson's work is the most promising step yet taken toward a theory of interest groups. His rational modeling approach, unlike the loose set of pluralist ideas, allows for a coherent theoretical structure from which conclusions can be logically derived. Moreover, the concepts around which his theory is built—collective good, selective incentive—are particularly well suited for capturing the essence of how interest groups emerge and what goes on inside them. These analytical advantages, along with the unconventional nature of the model's conclusions, underline the attractiveness of Olson's line of inquiry.

His theory is not very comprehensive, however, even as an economic theory, and it does not really tell us very much about interest groups. This is partly intended, since Olson's focus is limited in the main to the formative stages of group activity prior to formal organization, and he does not make an effort to move toward a more elaborate examination of organizational structures and processes. But it is also due to the fact that his theory is premised on highly restrictive assumptions about individuals. These assumptions are hardly unusual in modeling exercises of this kind, and they do allow for a clear, manageable analysis; yet they operate at the same time to shut out certain perceptual and value considerations that are potentially important influences on individual behavior and, ultimately, on organizational behavior as well. The result is a perspective on group membership that provides limited insight into the foundations of interest group activity and runs the danger of being misleading in certain respects.[8]

In this book, I will expand upon Olson's model of the individual's calculus and, with that as a basis, develop an organizational analysis of interest groups. In part 1, the purpose is to develop a logical analysis from first principles, one which is simple enough to clarify the nature of individual and organizational behavior, yet elaborate enough to address questions that are obviously important to a more comprehensive understanding. This involves a balancing act of sorts, an effort to reap the analytical advantages of simplicity without at the same time ''simplifying away'' those organizational aspects of interest groups that need explanation.

Chapter 1 supplies an introductory discussion of the nature of the task and the basic elements of the analysis. At this point, we need only note that the analysis is broken down into three areas of theoretical interest—the individual's decision to join, organizational formation and maintenance, and internal politics.

The decision to join is initially approached by setting out Olson's original model and showing how its dramatic conclusions about group membership are derived. By dropping the assumption of perfect information and allowing individuals to base decisions on their (imperfect) perceptions of the objective situation, we arrive at a more general model from which Olson's "nonpolitical" perspective no longer follows. It is replaced by a broader perspective that links the decision to join with varying individual perceptions and indicates that members may join for political reasons if they think their contributions "make a difference" in providing some of the collective good. While the collective good–selective incentive distinction remains a crucial one, both nonpolitical and political inducements now have central logical roles to play in explaining group membership. (The assumption of economic self-interest, however, is retained.)

This revised model of the membership decision is incorporated into a larger organizational framework by introducing a leadership component (the "political entrepreneur"), allowing for basic types of participants (for example, staff personnel, outsiders), and imposing certain simplifications on the organization and its environment. Organizational formation and maintenance are then approached by singling out the strategic options available to the political entrepreneur with respect to basic organizational dimensions—communications, the administration of selective incentives, the administration of collective goods, member bargaining, and environmental relationships—and by recognizing the costs and benefits associated with his various options. In supplying individuals with membership inducements, for example, should he set up his own "business" operations to produce selective incentives, should he rely upon outside means of producing them, or should he place much greater stress on collective goods and thus on developing the organization's political structure? Should he hire staff to perform organizational tasks, or should he rely primarily upon active members to do so? We will find that there are distinctive kinds of advantages and disadvantages associated with these and a range of other organizational options and that the entrepreneur's approach in building and maintaining the organization will be shaped accordingly. We will also find that the basic organizational dimensions are closely interrelated—there is a crucial overlap, for example, of the structuring of communications and the administration of political and nonpolitical benefits to members—and these interconnections, too, will shape the entrepreneur's organizational approach.

The analysis of internal politics assumes that the entrepreneur makes all policy decisions for the group. The central question becomes How is influence over his decisions distributed among individuals? This leads to an analysis of various bases for influence and the extent to which these are available to different types of participants—all of which has implications for group democracy and representativeness. We will find that some members count much more heavily than others in internal politics and that many members, particularly those who join purely for nonpolitical reasons, may have no basis at all for having an impact. Influence, moreover, is not restricted to elements within the membership; it is also available to staff members and outsiders, and these participants may play crucial roles in the determination of group policy. "Internal" politics, then cannot simply be understood with reference to leader-member relationships, nor even with reference to internal participants. We will also find that these matters are closely intertwined with the same factors that shape organizational formation and maintenance and that a systematic analysis of organizational foundations is a prerequisite for understanding the nature of internal politics. The bases for membership (in particular), the structure of communications, administrative mechanisms for the provision of benefits—these and other organizational characteristics have a direct bearing on the distribution of influence and on the ultimate content of group policy.

These three steps constitute what I will call an analysis of "material associations." The label is a reminder that the entire analysis to this stage is premised upon the assumption that individuals are economically self-interested. The final task of part 1 is to relax this simplifying assumption, allow for additional types of individual values, and, by retracing our steps, suggest how our understanding of interest groups is affected as a result. The purpose here, however, is not to provide a comprehensive analysis of the full range of individual values—this is clearly impossible—but simply to pursue a more complete analysis which, in taking maximum advantage of the assumption of economic self-interest, is not in the end entirely constrained by it. In carrying this out, we will see that the decisional relevance of these supplementary values can have far-reaching consequences for all the basic organizational dimensions. Above all, they have the potential for enhancing group representativeness, threatening organizational stability, and producing a more dynamic organizational context in which group goals and individual political preferences are more centrally determining factors than in material associations.

The final product is a logical framework that, because of the central role it ascribes to economic self-interest, is most usefully applied toward an understanding of economic interest groups, just as Olson's is. But, in building upon Olson's pioneering work, it yields a perspective on interest groups that is quite different from the original. Most obviously, it deals in an integrated fashion with a wider range of organizational behavior—investigating basic organizational dimensions, clarifying the nature of their interconnections, exploring the interrelated roles of major types of participants internal and external to the group, and linking the membership decision to a variety of organizational consequences. In the process, and perhaps most importantly to the political scientist, it highlights the close interdependence of group maintenance and internal politics and pursues an organizationally grounded understanding of the group's political goals—how they emerge, their correspondence to member preferences, their consequences for group survival.

But it also differs from Olson's analysis in a more fundamental sense, for, in relaxing his original assumptions, we are led to a perspective on group membership that has ample room in it for politically based membership. Because of the logical roles of imperfect information and values other than economic self-interest, rational behavior is not inconsistent with the pursuit of common interests. Olson's original model, in fact, can be viewed as a special case of this expanded model of membership, and his unconventional nonpolitical perspective can be understood to hold only under certain informational and value conditions. Under other conditions, distinctly different conclusions about group membership are entailed—and the pluralists, after all, can be quite right (and logically justified) in stressing the political bases of membership. The logical analysis of part 1, then, fits the Olson and the pluralist expectations within a broader framework, indicating how both the nonpolitical and the political bases of group membership can be explained and mapping out their implications for basic organizational dimensions.

What it does not do, however, is tell us what perceptions and values individuals actually bring to bear in their real-world membership decisions and whether they join for nonpolitical or political reasons. These are empirical questions. The logical framework can tell us what kinds of organizational implications to expect, given different bases for membership; but, to put the framework to use in deriving a detailed perspective on groups, empirical research is needed in order to give the logical analysis content and direction.

In part 2 I will take a step toward this end by evaluating empirical evidence on the bases for membership. Given the very real data constraints in the area, I will focus on a simple but crucial issue—the relative salience of political and nonpolitical inducements. The analysis will consist of three parts. First, I will present the available evidence within a broader context by outlining the background of theory and research that, over the years, has had a major impact on the way the membership decision has been understood and "documented." This will include a detailed discussion of the pluralist position and an evaluation of the empirical work on small groups and larger voluntary associations, which have served, in an indirect way, to bolster pluralist convictions about the political bases of interest group membership. Once this background is set out, I will consider research that has been undertaken directly on economic interest groups (labor unions, business associations, farm groups). These studies, while providing limited insight into the more subtle aspects of organizational incentive structures, clearly stress the primary importance of nonpolitical inducements for membership. Third, I will present some new data, collected from a survey of the members of five economic interest groups. These data confirm the basic findings of the other studies of economic groups. But they also suggest that the informational and value conditions conducive to politically based membership are prevalent, and that it is very common for politics to play a consequential role in member decisions to join.

The evidence suggests, then, that Olson is largely correct in his attack on pluralism: group goals are almost certainly not the key to group membership, and economic interest groups do appear to rest in great part upon nonpolitical foundations. On the other hand, the analysis also suggests that Olson's original model is inadequate for understanding the actual bases of member support, and certainly for drawing any inferences about organizational consequences. Political goals simply appear to have much greater inducement value for members than his theory leads us to expect. Thus, while the pluralist perspective is politically biased, Olson's perspective overemphasizes the nonpolitical—and each, as a result, can encourage misguided expectations about interest groups as organizations. The upshot is that a more comprehensive theoretical framework is necessary if the various political and nonpolitical bases of support are to be accounted for, and if their organizational implications are to be mapped out. The empirical analysis of part 2 thus helps to underline the utility of the logical analysis developed in part 1, as well as to indicate how important some of its components are likely to be.

Part One

The Logic of Interest Organization

One

Elements of the Analysis

In recent years, rational models of individual choice have taken on increasing prominence in disciplines outside economics, and particularly in political science. In the process, they have been applied to vastly different subjects—ranging from voting behavior to bureaucracy to international relations—and these efforts, understandably, have involved a variety of assumptions about decisionmakers and their decisional contexts. What these models have in common, however, is that they all make three distinctive assumptions that are central to the notion of rational choice: they assume that each individual is rational, that he premises his decisions on specified types of information, and that he evaluates his alternatives on the basis of specified kinds of values. These assumptions supplement each other, telling us what it means for an individual to make a rational choice in any situation. Together, they place theoretical constraints on the process of choice, guaranteeing that individuals within the model will behave in a regular, predictable manner.[1]

Our analysis of interest groups, then, will proceed from underlying assumptions about rationality, information, and values. It is the purpose of this chapter to explain more specifically just what assumptions will be made, as well as the role they will play in an analysis of individuals and organizations.

The Individual

The assumption of rationality is typically among the least unrealistic assumptions a theorist is called upon to make. For our purposes, a rational actor can be understood simply as an individual who, in choosing from a perceived set of alternatives, arrives at a transitive preference ordering of all alternatives and chooses the best one. This assumption simplifies matters somewhat. It tells us that each individual in the model will order and choose among alternatives according to the same general rule. It does not tell us, however, precisely what choices any given individual will make, since, in applying the rule, he will be led to different rational choices depending upon what information and values he brings to bear. To say that an individual is rational, then, is to say very little.

This worth stressing, because all too often in social science there is confusion about what the concept of rationality implies. Basically, the problem arises from a tendency on the part of some writers to overlook the distinctive contributions of the separate assumptions and to lump them together indiscriminately under the rubric of rationality. It is not uncommon, for instance, to find the concept of rational man equated with the classical notion of "rational economic man"—an omniscient decisionmaker motivated purely by economic gain. Perhaps even more frequently, the assumption of rationality is simply merged with one of the others. When this happens, rationality may be construed to imply that rational men have perfect knowledge, or that rational men must have economic or selfish motives. Political scientists sometimes claim, for example, that voters are irrational because they act on inadequate information or because they do not vote on an issue basis. And sociologists sometimes contend that organizational personnel cannot act rationally because they possess limited abilities to gather and process information or because they are motivated by social pressures rather than economic rewards.

In point of fact, rationality implies none of these. Rational individuals may be grossly ignorant of the objective context, and they may be motivated by the most altruistic of values. In constructing a model, these are simply additional matters of choice for the theorist, who has considerable latitude in deciding what assumptions to make about information and values. His decisions are designed to supplement the prior assumption of rationality, but they are not determined by it.

With this in mind, we can move on to consider the question of individual values. Any rational model is incomplete until it contains some kind of assumption on this score; rational behavior is, after all, goal-directed behavior. The individual evaluates each available alternative according to its net effect upon his value system and chooses the alternative that is most valuable by this measure. Efficiency and optimality take on concrete meaning, and rational behavior takes on direction, only when the value structures of individuals have in some way been specified.

But how should they be specified? Empirically, we know that people have complex systems of values that cannot conveniently be expressed in terms of a few clearly defined goals. To carry out an analysis of individuals as they "really are," we would somehow have to take into account such disparate considerations as money, altruism, ideology, loyalty, status, power, love, acceptance, security, religion, and so on. To achieve a high degree of rigor and precision, moreover, we would have to arrive at determinations of their relative salience and interconnections, as well as find some conceptual tools for comprehending and representing units of these intangible quantities.

Economists have conventionally dealt with these difficulties by focusing on production, consumption, and other distinctly economic activities of individuals, and by proceeding on the premise that, at least within these spheres of activity, individuals are economically self-interested. This has meant, when all is said and done, that economists have characteristically been able to employ money as a yardstick of value. And there are obvious advantages to this. It does away with qualitative distinctions among values, the need to measure intangibles, and the problem of establishing their interconnections. In place of these, the theorist is left with a single measure of value—one that is readily observed, easily quantified, and ideally suited for bringing a host of mathematical techniques to bear on questions of economic importance.[2]

For obvious reasons, social scientists in other disciplines often have not found these same motivational assumptions to be appropriate in their own areas of interest. This is certainly true for organization theorists. Indeed, particularly since the decline of classical management theory, they have made a concerted effort to get away (far away, it seems) from an economically oriented perspective. Their theories and research have extended prominent roles to such things as personality characteristics, social norms and pressures, needs for security and acceptance, and desires for status, with economic inducements viewed as one of many incentives that seem to explain organizational behavior. It is generally acknowledged that organizations can only be understood adequately as contexts of *mixed* motivations.

Within the organizational literature, the major decision-making analyses are accordingly very different from those found in economics.[3] The analytical advantages of the economic approach are purposely foregone, and an effort is made to build the analysis as clearly and systematically as possible under the circumstances.[4] This is accomplished with the help of various simplifications. One of the most important is that individuals are not understood in terms of a vast array of distinct motivations but, rather, in terms of broad value typologies or relatively small numbers of "significant" values. By such means, the notion of mixed motivations is conceptually reduced to manageable proportions.[5] The analysis is then developed in a less rigorous, less formal fashion that allows the theorist to consider, without complicated attempts at quantification, the implications for organizational behavior of qualitatively different motivations. The result is a more comprehensive and probably more satisfactory understanding of organizations than could have been attained otherwise, but at the cost of a less elegant theoretical structure.

In this book we will strike a middle course between the economic and organizational approaches to decision making. This is possible because the analysis is not proposed as a theory of organizations generally, nor even a theory of interest groups, but is developed with special reference to economic interest groups—in which, presumably, economic self-interest is often especially important. Given this somewhat restricted purpose, we need not pursue a balanced analysis of mixed motivations, with all the difficulties that that entails. The analysis will be unbalanced by design. We will assume from the outset that each individual is economically self-interested and develop most of the analysis on this basis. The remaining, "noneconomic" values are introduced as the final step, at which point the earlier steps will essentially be repeated, albeit in much less detail; the theoretical roles of these values will be understood, in the process, by showing how their motivational relevance alters (or fails to alter) the expectations already derived.

The third component of the model is the informational assumption. Given that the individual is a rational decision maker with specified values, we are only in a position to understand his choices if we know something about the information upon which he acts. Different information can easily lead him to different rational choices, even in identical decision contexts.

The first thing to note is that he needs information along several dimensions. At least implicitly, he must somehow arrive at perceptions of: the available alternatives, the possible consequences associated with these alternatives, the link between each alternative and the set of possible consequences, the value of each relevant combination of consequences, and the value of each alternative. Information on these questions goes to make up the individual's "definition of the situation," which, comprised of both descriptive and evaluative elements, places a structure on all essential aspects of the decision context—what alternatives and outcomes are to be considered, how they are related, and how valuable they are to him. This allows him to make a decision; for once he has arrived at these conclusions, he knows all he needs to know for the construction of a preference ordering of alternatives and for a rational choice among them.

The theorist interested in understanding the individual's behavior can therefore do so in either of two ways—by knowing the individual's preference ordering of the alternatives involved or by knowing how he arrives at his definition of the situation in any given context. The second approach is more comprehensive, since it allows the theorist to "connect" the individual with the decision context, and, in the process, to derive the relevant preference ordering. It also requires more knowledge on the part of the theorist, however, because he must determine what information is taken into consideration by the individual and precisely how it is used.

The traditional response to these problems is to solve them by assumption. More specifically, the conventional response is that of the economist, who commonly assumes that consumers and entrepreneurs are totally informed of the objective decisional situation, that they can properly combine all relevant information, and that they can make the calculations necessary for arriving at an optimal choice. In this way, the theorist posits that there is only *one* "reality" that is perceived and processed identically by all decision makers. This greatly simplifies the theorist's task by assuming away psychological, physiological, and other limiting factors that, empirically, are causes of varying definitions of the situation. For purposes of analysis, the objective and the subjective are merged.

The less traditional response is to reject such restrictive assumptions. The most persuasive reason for doing so is simply that they often do not allow the theorist to account for the behaviors in which he is interested. This is frequently the case for individual behavior in organizations. Major works on organizational decision making have consistently emphasized that definitions of the situation vary, sometimes markedly, across organization members and that these variations have important effects on the range of organizational behaviors that theorists want to explain.[6] Understandably, they have not been willing to assume away these informational variations by adopting the strict rationality approach, since this would require that they overlook what, from all indications, is a major determinant of organizational behavior. Instead, their efforts at theory construction have been concerned with questions of why such variations occur and what consequences are associated with them.

This alternative approach, then, purposely does not assume that rational individuals are perfectly informed. In attempting to understand the forces that shape an individual's definition of the situation, it reintroduces the subjective element and explicitly recognizes that there are limits on what individuals can know and do in their efforts to arrive at optimal choices. The model's actors still make rational decisions, but they do so on the basis of their imperfect perception of the objective situation, and subject to a number of limitations on their information and skills. Thus, in a world of "bounded rationality," different individuals may have markedly different definitions of the situation. In principle, there may be as many different "realities" as there are decision makers.

The analysis of this book is premised on a model of bounded rationality. Questions of how interest group members, potential members, and other actors form their definitions of the situation, and with what effect, will play a central role in our attempt to come to grips with the basic determinants of associational behavior. As suggested above, there is a trade-off involved in adopting this approach; while we are now able to consider a wider range of behavior, we are left with a more complicated model from which it is more difficult to derive conclusions.

These complications cannot be eliminated, but they can be dealt with in a manageable fashion. By and large, this will be done by assuming that all individuals carry out their computations in the same way (as outlined in chap. 2), regardless of what information they use; and by focusing on those types of misinformation—for example, overestimates and underestimates of the costs and benefits of political success—that prove to be significant in any given context. In this way, we can suggest how various kinds of informational conditions affect individual behavior and, in the process, how behavior is altered when the perfect information assumption is violated.

The Organization

Ultimately, we are interested in moving from an analysis of isolated individuals to an analysis of organizations—and this, in turn, involves a host of new problems, deriving from the inherent complexity of the organizational context. The conventional economic approach to these problems, just as to those associated with individual decision making, is to solve them through restrictive assumptions. Organizational behavior, for instance, might be understood from a game-theoretic standpoint, with member strategies and organizational solutions derived (if logically possible) from assumptions which drastically simplify the organizational context.

Our approach will be quite different. We are concerned with some of the most crucial characteristics of actual interest organizations— leadership, member participation, the role of staff, and internal politics, among others—and we cannot radically simplify the organizational context without omitting precisely those aspects that we are interested in examining. What we can do, though, is operate within a more elaborate framework that includes important dimensions of organizational behavior in simplified form. In doing so, we will be structuring the analysis in various ways, the most basic of which are outlined below.

A leadership component will be introduced, in the form of the entrepreneur; this serves to simplify the organization's leadership structure, reducing it to a single decision maker about whom we can make certain assumptions.[7] A number of other types of participants will also be introduced. The organization may contain staff personnel and lobbyists in addition to the entrepreneur and group members; and individual members may participate so as to occupy distinctive organizational roles—that of the communications middleman, for example, or the subgroup member. The organization's environment, in turn, will be characterized in terms of three important types of outside actors— governmental officials, officials from nongovernmental groups and organizations, and rival entrepreneurs.

The focus of attention will be shifted from individual members to the entrepreneur, an approach that has been used to good advantage in major works on organizational decision making.[8] An analysis of group formation, maintenance, and internal politics will then largely be developed from a leadership perspective by inquiring into entrepreneurial options and strategies under varying conditions and suggesting how these are ultimately reflected in organizational structures and processes. This does not mean other participants are omitted from consideration, for they are the raw materials out of which the organization is built, and the entrepreneur must design his own decisions with reference to the behavior of others. But the shift to a leadership perspective does allow us to pull things together by viewing the organization from a single standpoint.

The organizational analysis will be carried out in a looser, less formal manner than the initial analysis of individual decision making, since to do otherwise would require a much more idealized organizational context than we are interested in examining. We will develop the analysis by, in effect, "placing" participants in comparatively realistic organizational contexts. Given what we know about their decision-making characteristics and how their choices are affected by various informational and incentive conditions, we can proceed to outline the general dimensions of their organizational behavior. In this way, we can build a comprehensive perspective that indicates the general nature of formation, maintenance, and internal politics, but that refrains from idealizing the organization any more than is necessary.

Conclusion

Ultimately, then, after following a somewhat unorthodox path, we are able to arrive at an analysis that allows for both bounded rationality and mixed motivations at the individual level and that extends in application to the organizational context. In these respects, it has a great deal in common with other analyses of organizational decision making, or at least those that attempt to be comprehensive; and, as a consequence, it reflects the same kinds of problems and drawbacks.

These difficulties are due, at bottom, to an inherent tension between the need for analytical convenience and the desire to be comprehensive and realistic. Analytical convenience is facilitated by the individualistic assumptions of perfect information and economic motivation and by a radically rarified organizational context—or perhaps, as in Olson's analysis, by omitting the organizational context entirely. Comprehensiveness and realism are enhanced by the assumptions of imperfect information and mixed motivations and by an empirically grounded version of the organizational context.

Economists are fortunate on this score because, in many cases, the nature of their subject matter allows them to opt for the most convenient methods of analysis. But organization theorists are not nearly so fortunate. When the formal approach to theory is chosen, the results are often of restricted relevance, with little to say about the wider range of interesting organizational behavior.[9] A profitable trade-off is difficult to make without a substantial sacrifice in convenience. As a result, organization theorists have had to seek a satisfactory compromise—foregoing formality and rigor, but nevertheless simplifying individual decision making and the organizational context as much as a "satisfactorily complete" analysis will permit.

We have been similarly constrained by the nature of the subject matter and have also adopted compromise solutions. Even though this analysis is premised on a rational choice model, then, it will turn out to be quite different from those usually found in economics. It should also be understood, however, as being different in at least one important respect from most analyses of organizational decision making: it strikes a compromise that gives up less in terms of analytical convenience, but more in terms of comprehensiveness and realism, than is usually the case. Specifically, by taking advantage of the assumption of economic self-interest, we are able to ground the organizational analysis upon a fairly formal treatment of member decision-making and to view the inherently complicated organizational context from a much more manageable perspective—although the final product tells us less, as result, about noneconomic interest organizations. This reduction in scope is a price we pay for moving in an economic direction.

This approach is best viewed, then, as a hybrid of sorts. It borrows from both the economic and organizational approaches to decision making, capturing some of the advantages as well as some of the limitations of each.

Two

The Decision to Join

Because interest groups are comprised of members, it is only reasonable to begin an analysis of interest groups by asking why individuals choose to become members in the first place. What explains an individual's decision to join? Before *The Logic of Collective Action* first appeared, this question seemed to have a simple and obvious answer: people join groups because they agree with group goals. Indeed, the answer seemed so simple and so obvious that the question itself was not considered particularly interesting, and it was rarely the subject of inquiry. Olson changed all this. He did so by structuring his analysis of group membership around a theoretical concept that was essentially new to political scientists, but whose analytical value was recognized early on by writers in economics and public finance. This is the concept of a collective (or public) good.

For our purposes, this concept can be defined very simply. Any good can be viewed as a collective good for some set of individuals if, once it is supplied by one or more individuals in the set, it is automatically available for consumption by *all* individuals in the set.[1] A little reflection is enough to suggest that collective goods are widely sought and supplied in the political system. A public park is a collective good, for instance, because it can be enjoyed by everyone interested in using it, not just those persons who pay taxes and "supply" the park. Expenditures on national defense operate automatically to protect everyone in the nation, even though many individuals make no contributions at all.

These examples help to suggest why collective goods have such an intriguing theoretical role to play. In the first place, collective goods like public parks and national defense are often expensive to supply, while the average individual tends to gain an amount which, by comparison to the good's cost, is exceedingly small. If we think that an individual will typically be unwilling to contribute (pay) more than he stands to gain, then any contribution he could feasibly offer would constitute only a tiny portion of the total funds available to cover the necessary costs. It would appear to be a drop in the bucket, with little likelihood of making any noticeable difference in the good's supply. This should often serve as a major inhibitor of individual contributions. After all, if one persons fails to pay taxes, the national defense will not be impaired, nor will the public parks shut down. Moreover, this restraint on contributions is reinforced by a second factor that derives from the nature of the collective good itself: once it is supplied, the individual can enjoy the benefits even if he has shouldered none of the cost burden. As long as financial sources are found for public parks, national defense, and other collective goods, the individual can freely take advantage of them—without voluntarily throwing his money away on contributions that would, at any rate, have had no real impact in and of themselves.

This oversimplifies matters somewhat. But it should be clear that, when a collective good is at issue, the interesting question is why an individual would voluntarily want to pay something toward its supply. Olson's achievement is that he brought the analytical importance of collective goods to the full attention of political scientists. In effect, he shows how an "economic" concept can be transformed into a "political" concept, yielding a new and dramatically different perspective on the incentives for political action.

He does this by reconceptualizing the pluralist contention that individuals will act on the basis of common interests. He points out that, when individuals have a common interest in pursuing political goals—tax relief, civil rights legislation, farm subsidies, or minimum wage laws, to name only a few—these goals are typically collective goods for the "group" of individuals in question. If some of these people were willing to contribute toward the formation of a lobbying organization, and if this organization were successful in realizing the commonly held goals, all affected individuals would ultimately receive the benefits—noncontributors and contributors alike. This, along with the frequently high expense of political success, will clearly influence the willingness of individuals to contribute in the first place and thereby to "pursue their common interests." Thus, if we are to understand the conditions under which individuals will contribute toward interest group activity, the relationship between contributions and collective goods emerges as the fundamental consideration.

The Olson Theory

Olson's approach is straightforward. He proceeds by adopting a rational choice model and applying it to a group context which, from a pluralist standpoint, is ideally suited for the emergence of collective action: all individuals are taken to agree on the desirability of achieving a given political goal, viewed as a collective good. The question becomes: how much will rational individuals be willing to contribute toward the supply of a collective good that they have a common interest in obtaining?

Assumptions and Basic Conclusions

Olson is surprisingly vague about some of his assumptions, and a casual reading of his argument can easily lead to confusion about how conclusions are logically derived. This is particularly so with respect to individual values, since his intermittent reference to social pressure, ideology, and even altruism can leave the mistaken impression that a full range of values has been entered into the theory's premises. Because of such ambiguities, we will supplement Olson's explicit assumptions with others that are implicit in his analysis. The resulting set of assumptions, listed here, will be referred to as the Olson model. (*a*) Each individual is rational, perfectly informed, motivated by economic gain, and an independent decision maker. (*b*) The collective good is infinitely divisible.[2] (*c*) The marginal costs of providing the collective good are positive and increasing. (*d*) The marginal benefits of obtaining the good are positive and decreasing.

On the basis of assumptions corresponding to those presented here, Olson develops a mathematical analysis that justifies his conclusions about collective action. Given the task at hand, however, it is more instructive to forego a mathematical treatment and set out the elements of his argument diagrammatically.[3] Figure 1 consists of various margi-

nal cost and marginal benefit curves expressed as a function of the level
of collective good, X, supplied. For purposes of illustration, the
"group" is assumed to have N "members," N minus two of whom
derive equal benefits from increments of the collective good and have
identical marginal benefit curves MB_i. The other two group members, j
and k, are assumed to derive much greater benefit from the good, as
shown by MB_j and MB_k. The group marginal benefit schedule, MB, is
the sum of the curves of the N members. The MC curve expresses the
marginal costs of supplying the collective good, and it is the same for
everyone. It represents all the costs that are involved, organizational
and otherwise, in achieving each additional increment.

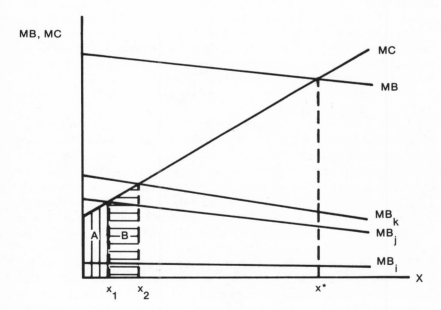

Figure 1

Each individual, in deciding how much to contribute, must take into
account how much it costs to supply each increment of the good, how
much he stands to gain from each increment, and how much of the
good has already been supplied (if any). Because he acts independently, he does not try to "game" his decision, nor does he enter into

any cooperative agreements. This being so, he will contribute up to the point where the marginal costs of providing the good are equal to the marginal benefits he derives. At this level he is maximizing his net benefits. Assuming none of the good is as yet provided, it is to k's advantage to supply x_2, to j's advantage to supply x_1, and to everyone else's advantage to contribute nothing. Based on their incentives to contribute, we will refer to j and k as "Large Members" and to the rest as "Small Members," as does Olson.

What is the total contribution? Although j and k have an incentive to contribute amounts A and $A + B$, respectively,[4] the total contribution is not $2A + B$. This is where the "prevailing level of supply" factor comes into play. For if k contributes first—which he might do, since he is not gaming the situation—then the new level of supply becomes a fact which, by assumption, is immediately known by j. Acting rationally, j will then ask himself, How much should I contribute given that x_2 has already been provided? The answer is that he should contribute nothing: at x_2, the costs to j of providing more of the good are greater than any benefits he will derive. Hence, in this case only x_2 will be provided, and even though everyone gains when the good is made available, k will have paid the entire cost.

If, on the other hand, j contributes first, then x_1 of the good is provided for the group and k must ask himself: How much should I contribute given that x_1 is already supplied? His optimal solution is to contribute an amount B sufficient to move the group from x_1 to x_2. In this case, j and k split the cost of x_2 while again the other members pay nothing. But in either case, and thus regardless of who contributes first, only x_2 is provided, the Large Members pay for all of it, and the Small Members get a "free ride"—illustrating what Olson calls "the exploitation of the great by the small."

This outcome is suboptimal for the group. We can see this by viewing the group as a "superindividual" with marginal benefit curve MB. Such an individual would contribute beyond x_2 until x^* is reached. At each point between x_2 and x^*, the gains to the group as a whole outweigh the costs. Because there is an aggregate surplus, it is clear that our superindividual could distribute the costs and benefits among members so that each gains at least as much as he is required to pay. When the group moves from x_2 to x^*, then, everyone can be made at least as well off as before.

Such a move cannot occur within the model because it requires some sort of coordination, which violates the assumption of independence.

As the situation stands, group members have no incentive to provide themselves with anything more than x_2. The group must remain at a level of provision that is "too low," with the cost load shared unevenly. Moreover, when individuals are added to the group (and k remains the largest member), the suboptimality increases. As N grows, the group's MB curve increases and pushes x^* farther out, thus widening the gap between x^* and x_2.

One final point: if all individuals in the group are Small Members, then no one will contribute and none of the collective good will be supplied. This conclusion is obvious enough, but it is especially important from Olson's perspective, because he makes the empirical argument that the Large Member phenomenon is very rare and thus many interest groups cannot turn to this source for any political support whatever.[5]

Bargaining and Selective Incentives

These aspects of the theory paint a bleak picture indeed. Yet interest groups are not necessarily doomed to failure or even to inadequate resources. This is because there are two basic mechanisms for circumventing, at least to some degree, the problem of contributions.[6]

The first is member cooperation through bargaining. This mechanism violates the assumption of independence, but it can be viewed as a "solution" of sorts if its relevance is allowed to turn on an empirical point—that the likelihood of effective bargaining varies with group size. In very large groups, the costs of communication and coordination tend to be prohibitive; each individual tends to see his own participation as unnecessary to a successful bargain; and, not least, each individual will get the benefits anyway if he lets the other members do the cooperating. As the group gets smaller—in particular, as it gets small enough to enable face-to-face interaction—members can become personally acquainted, aware of each other's interests, and in a position to predict and react to each other's behavior. It is more likely, then, that they will recognize their mutual dependence and calculate accordingly.

Small groups thus are different from large groups, in that they facilitate certain behavior—strategic behavior—that Olson's model assumes away. Even in very small groups, however, there remains a major obstacle to the success of bargaining agreements: as long as members are economically self-interested, and as long as they are bargaining over the supply of a collective good, the free-rider incentive is inherent in individual decision-making, including bargaining activities. Each member knows that if the *other* members (or some of them) do the cooperating and contributing, then he will get the benefits anyway. This makes bargaining agreements more difficult to arrange and constantly threatens the cohesion of any agreements that are actually arrived at. Additionally, the free-rider incentive should work to the disadvantage of Large Members, just as it does in the absence of bargaining, since they have an incentive to contribute even if the others do not, and they stand to lose a great deal if they hold back.

In sum, even for small groups in which bargaining occurs, the free-rider incentive continues to inhibit contributions and encourage the exploitation of the great by the small. The theoretical importance of bargaining is not that it solves the contributions problem, but that it holds out the possibility that small groups will be able to supply themselves with more of the collective good than independent behavior would lead us to expect. In view of this, Olson correctly suggests that his model is more usefully applied to large interest groups. It is here that individuals are most likely to make their decisions independently, and here that his theory's pessimistic conclusions are most likely to be borne out. Thus while bargaining is not actually incorporated into the model, its empirical relevance serves to qualify the model's range of applicability.[7]

There is another mechanism for increasing member contributions, however, that is entirely consistent with the original assumptions. This is what Olson calls a "selective incentive." Through the introduction of this crucial concept, he explains how large interest groups are able to attract financial support even when composed entirely of Small Members who calculate independently.

Selective incentives are private benefits which, precisely because they are private rather than collective in nature, can operate selectively on the membership as a whole: they can be conferred upon those who contribute and withheld from those who do not. For goods of this sort, there is no free-rider incentive. If a person wishes to obtain selective incentives, he cannot do so by waiting for others to shoulder the costs. He will have to "qualify" to receive them, which, in practice, ordinarily means paying dues and becoming a formal member.

This greatly expands the group's potential pool of inducements, for members will purchase anything of material value as long as they expect net benefits on the exchange. Information services, pension plans, group insurance—these are but a few of the most common selective incentives to be found in actual interest groups. Legal coercion is sometimes used as well; in these instances, the laws may be such that individuals are faced with fines, loss of employment, or loss of business if they do not join.

Herein lies the key to success for large groups. While the collective good itself is insufficient to induce member support, individuals who choose to pay for selective incentives are nonetheless contributing funds to group coffers, and leaders can use these funds to supply some of the collective good. Thus, even if no one has an incentive to supply any of the good at all, some of it may be provided as a by-product of the sale of selective incentives.

The Olson Theory: Concluding Comments

By recognizing that common interests typically take the form of collective goods and by making certain assumptions about individuals, Olson is able to arrive at basic conclusions about collective action. These he summarizes as follows:

> If the members of a large group rationally seek to maximize their personal welfare, they will *not* act to advance their common or group objectives unless there is coercion to force them to do so, or unless some separate incentive, distinct from the achievement of common or group interest, is offered to the members of the group individually on the condition that they help bear the costs or burdens involved in the achievement of the group objectives. . . .
>
> In small groups there may very well be some voluntary action in support of the common purposes of the individuals in the group, but in most cases this action will cease before it reaches the optimal level for the members of the group as a whole. In the sharing of the costs of efforts to achieve a common goal in small groups, there is however a surprising tendency for the "exploitation" of the *great* by the *small*.[8]

Olson's logic has quite a bit to say about politics. Above all, it subverts the traditional pluralist notion that common interests give rise to collective action, demonstrating that there are certain obstacles inherent in the situation that inhibit the average individual from "doing his part." Indeed, the irony is that the only way vast numbers of individuals can be induced to contribute their share is to offer them something different from, and perhaps entirely unrelated to, the group's goals.

This result has implications for a host of pluralist notions, because once the motivational connection between common interests and member support is undermined, a good part of the pluralist perspective on politics is called into question. For instance, Olson's analysis contradicts the notion that the effectiveness of a group, or at least its resource base, is a function of its degree of support in society. Widespread and enthusiastic agreement on a political goal may give rise to no contributions at all for its organizational sponsor—while other groups, enjoying far less support, may be better financed and more effective as a result of selective incentives, or perhaps the presence of a few Large Members. Thus, in terms of the impact on public policy, a political pluralism of groups may severely distort the underlying social pluralism of interests.

To take another example: we can see that a group's formal membership is not a valid indicator of its political support. This is particularly true of mass-based groups that successfully organize large numbers of average individuals. In such groups—like the Farm Bureau, the Chamber of Commerce, or Common Cause—Olson's theory points to selective incentives, not political goals, as the explanation of large size. Formal membership indicates that the group is successful at selling selective incentives, not that it is politically popular. Indeed, since selective incentives need have nothing whatever to do with the group's goals, there is no guarantee that any dues-payers even agree with those goals. What could be further from pluralist preconceptions?

A Revision: Imperfect Information

Olson's theory is a major contribution to the study of interest groups. It contradicts traditional ways of thinking about political groups, their connection to the social system, and their roles in politics. Moreover, it does this by employing new concepts—collective good, selective incentive—which, while previously accorded almost no systematic attention in political science, are clearly of the greatest relevance for political behavior and promise exciting new directions for theoretical inquiry.

Yet Olson's model is not the only way of constructing a rational theory of interest groups, nor are his dramatic conclusions the only ones implied by the assumption of rationality. What rationality "entails'' depends upon the nature of the other assumptions operating in conjunction with it, and, when these are allowed to vary, different rational models are created along with different sets of conclusions. We have already shown this to be so for the assumption of independence. In this section, we will see that the same sort of thing happens when the assumption about perfect information is relaxed.

Olson assumes that individuals are perfectly informed about marginal costs, marginal benefits, and the amount supplied by others. We can now drop this restriction and assume instead that individuals are imperfectly informed, that they arrive at estimates of each curve, and that their rational choices derive from these estimates. The question becomes: under what perceptual conditions will they have an incentive to contribute?

The most general relationships between perceptions and incentives are apparent if we mentally allow the curves in figure 2 to undergo basic shifts (and disregard any effects of attitudes toward risk). Consider individual i, who, given his present perceptions, is like Olson's Small Member in that he has no incentive to contribute. It is obvious from the

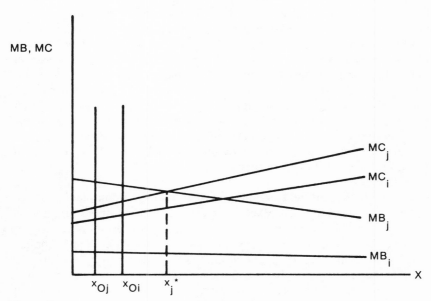

Figure 2

figure that any upward shift in his estimated gains from the collective good, as well as any downward shift in the amount he thinks additional increments cost, enhances the likelihood that his marginal cost and benefit curves will intersect at some point to the right of x_{oi}, the amount of X he expects others to supply. When this occurs, he has every incentive to contribute—and the amount he wants to contribute will then vary inversely with any changes in his estimate x_{oi}. Now consider individual j, who, like Olson's Large Member, has an incentive to contribute as things stand. Because his marginal cost and benefit curves already intersect to the right of x_{oj}, even the slightest changes in his estimates will alter his rational choice. The amount of the collective good he chooses to supply, $x_j{}^* - x_{oj}$, will vary directly with his estimated marginal benefits, inversely with his estimated marginal costs, and inversely with the amount of X he expects others to supply. And his contribution will adjust accordingly.[9]

The actual estimates people rely on and the way their perceptions are determined are, of course, empirical questions. The point to be stressed here is a logical one: that behavioral expectations are contingent in specific ways upon perceptions. This yields a perspective on interest groups that is very different from Olson's. Above all, whereas Olson claims that the vast majority of individuals can have no incentive to contribute toward collective goods, the revised model implies that anyone can have an incentive to contribute, depending upon his subjective estimates of the relevant quantities. Generally speaking, an individual is more likely to contribute the higher his estimate of marginal benefits, the lower his estimate of marginal costs, and the lower his estimate of the total level of supply. These estimates in effect lead him to think that his contribution will make a difference in bringing about net personal gains. They lead him, in other words, to have a perception of personal efficacy. The efficacious individual can have a rational incentive to contribute whether or not his efficacy is justified by the objective context.

It follows that interest organizations, even in the complete absence of selective incentives, are better able to recruit members and amass contributions to the extent that these estimates are characteristic of individuals in their sectors. Individuals will then join and quit for political reasons and, accordingly, a group's size and resource base should tend to be more strongly linked to its underlying political support. Thus, perceptions of efficacy among members and potential members suggest an organizational setting that may be roughly consistent with pluralist expectations and is certainly more conducive to political action than Olson's theory would imply.

Additionally, we should recognize that a model in which information about costs, benefits, and the level of supply is assumed to be less than perfect intrinsically contains a new tool for group leaders: some of that information can purposely be manipulated in order to attract members and contributions. This is all the more potent a device given that leaders are in an ideal position to possess (or claim to possess) such information, while the average individual has very few facts on which to base his estimates, other than what the leaders say. Thus, leaders need not simply leave the estimation process to chance, but can play an active role in shaping how individuals arrive at their decisions.

The Role of Efficacy: An Empirical Aside

It might be claimed that Olson's model is the "central tendency," since individuals are as likely to underestimate as to overestimate their true efficacy, and that this modification of his theory is uncalled for. Two basic responses are in order. First, it is an empirical question whether individuals are as likely to underestimate as to overestimate, and there is some basis for believing that overestimation is actually more common. There is now a good deal of research, for example, to indicate that efficacy plays a role in explaining individual involvement in various types of political activity—even when, as in voting, the objective likelihood that the individual's contribution will affect the outcome is infinitesimally small. Why should membership in interest groups be any different? Empirical work also indicates that subjective efficacy is not entirely derived from factors intrinsic to the decisional context itself. In many Western democracies, and certainly in the United States, individuals tend to be socialized to political efficacy by their experiences (e.g., childhood schooling experiences) within the prevailing political culture. They thus come to specific political contexts with certain "efficacy predispositions"—which, in coloring perceptions of the objective context, enhance the likelihood that they will think that their contributions make a difference. In democratic nations, then, perceptual errors by potential members may not be anywhere near randomly distributed about the true cost, benefit, and level of supply curves. The vast majority of individuals may well tend to err in the direction of greater efficacy. This expectation is only reinforced by the informational roles that leaders doubtless play in shaping perceptions.[10]

Second, even if individual estimates are distributed randomly, those who sufficiently overestimate their efficacy will have an incentive to join for political reasons because of it. Depending upon the size of the sector, this could translate into large numbers of people who join in support of group goals; and, especially if selective incentives are not too valuable, it is perfectly possible that most of any given group's formal members (as opposed to those individuals who might have joined but did not) are attracted because of its goals. Thus, even if Olson's model is the central tendency (and it probably is not), informational variations are still basic to an understanding of group membership—and, as we will see in the next three chapters, they play major organizational roles as well.

Conclusion

In this chapter, we began with Olson's model of the individual's decision to join, relaxed the assumption of perfect information, and arrived at a more general but still quite simple revised theory. From this perspective, the key to group membership does not rest solely with the congruence of member interests and group goals, as the pluralists contend; nor does it rest with the singular role of economic selective incentives, as Olson claims. Instead, we find that both group goals and selective incentives can serve as membership inducements for ordinary members, regardless of their economic size. (For an extended diagrammatical analysis that takes both types of inducements into account rather than just the collective good, see appendix A.)

These inducements come into play in different ways. Selective incentives are direct member inducements which the individual receives in exchange for his contribution; in deciding whether to buy, he is concerned with whether his gain from selective incentives exceeds their cost. If an individual is to be attracted purely on the basis of group goals, by contrast, he must perceive that his contribution makes a difference for the group's political success, resulting in net gains for himself. As a modification of Olson's analysis, this efficacy requirement opens the door for the inducement value of group goals; but it also represents a condition which many individuals may not satisfy even if they place very high value on the collective good itself. Thus, the introduction of imperfect information does not eliminate the "Olson problems" intrinsic to the individual's collective goods calculus. But it does imply a wider range of (perceptual) conditions under which these problems are overcome.

Selective incentives therefore retain their basic advantage over group goals as member inducements, but this advantage is now of less significance than Olson's original model contends. For any given group, the relative salience of the two types of inducements can vary depending upon the perceptual characteristics of potential members and upon the value of the selective incentives supplied. Some groups may be able to form by offering nothing more than political goals with which enough individuals agree. Other groups may have to supplement political goals with selective incentives in order to attract sufficient support. And still others may find that their goals have no inducement value at all, and that they can form only by relying entirely upon selective incentives. While we have a logical basis for highlighting the importance of selective incentives, then, both types of inducements play special roles in attracting members to the group—and both will take on distinctive organizational roles in the analysis that follows.

Three

Organizational Formation
and Maintenance

While we have so far been concerned with how common interests can be pursued by unattached individuals, what we want is a theoretical treatment of organized interest groups. Unorganized groups, after all, cannot really "provide themselves" with selective incentives, and collective goods are not simply "supplied" when contributions are sufficient. These things to not happen by themselves; some person or set of persons arranges for them to happen. Moreover, interest groups commonly have leaders, administrative structures, mechanisms for communication and representation, and avenues for member participation.

In this chapter, we will use our analysis of the decision to join as a basis for developing a broader analysis of interest groups as organizations, with special emphasis on their formation and maintenance.[1] We will begin by introducing a new and particularly useful concept, that of the political entrepreneur.

The Political Entrepreneur

The political entrepreneur is a hypothetical individual who exploits profitable opportunities by providing, or promising to provide, services that are designed to attract support from individuals who might find them of value. If the basic terms here—profit, services, support—are broadly interpreted, it is easy to see why the familiar entrepreneur-customer relationship might usefully be applied to a host of interesting situations involving leaders and constituents. Legislators, presidential candidates, party and group leaders, revolutionary figures—all these and more can be approached from an entrepreneurial perspective.[2]

In developing an entrepreneurial perspective on interest groups, we will assume that the entrepreneur is boundedly rational and (for now) economically self-interested and that he is both the administrative and political leader of the group. Administratively, he takes action to enroll members, to design, sell, and distribute packages of benefits, to set up an administrative structure, and, in general, to manage exchange relationships with other participants in such a way that the group survives with an adequate surplus in excess of costs. His political role, if and when it is to his advantage to play this role, is to lead the group in attempting to realize goals within the political system.

In all his organizational activities, he will act rationally to maximize his own material surplus, premised on whatever information he may possess about the objective situation and the possible actions of other individuals. It is this surplus-maximization motive that underlies his role in the formation and maintenance of an interest group. His behavior is obviously shaped, then, by the fact that an ongoing and successful association generates a material surplus, which he controls. In addition, though, he may personally derive benefits from the collective goods and selective incentives that the organizational structure enables him to provide. And he may even use his leadership position to extract side payments from other participants, both inside and outside the group.

Because the solvency of the group enterprise makes all these benefits possible, ensuring group survival is the fundamental task of the entrepreneur. In this chapter, we will be concerned with the question of how he can go about performing this task successfully. We can begin by noting that the political entrepreneur's situation is analogous to that of the economic entrepreneur in simple theories of the business firm. In broad outline, the requirements of survival are the same in both cases. The entrepreneur can be viewed as investing capital in a set of benefits (collective goods and selective incentives) that he offers to a market of customers (potential members) at a price—the cost of joining the group (dues) plus any extra fees that may be attached to particular services. Potential members buy the offered package of benefits, and thus join the group, only if the value of the benefits is expected to be greater than their price; and they will remain in the group as long as this continues to hold true. The entrepreneur, on the other hand, will continue to provide those benefits only as long as he expects to receive a sufficient return on his invested capital, which, at a minimum, means that he must expect to cover the costs of his own operations; if returns do not exceed costs in the long run, the association must fail unless subsidized from the outside. Complicating factors (such as legal coercion) aside, there are thus three necessary conditions for associational emergence and survival: an entrepreneur must offer potential members a set of benefits, some of these potential members must be willing to buy, and the costs and benefits involved must be such that both the entrepreneur and the members continue to expect a net gain on the exchange.

But while the group survives by virtue of mutually beneficial exchange relationships between the entrepreneur and group members, these relationships do not simply emerge from the uncoordinated interactions of individuals. It is the entrepreneur's task to initiate exchange relationships and to maintain existing ones on terms that are most nearly optimal in view of his own interests. To understand the processes of group survival, then, we must understand how he goes about doing this. In this regard, the essential point is that there are alternative strategies available to him. There are many ways to organize a group and many ways thereby to derive a surplus, leaving the entrepreneur with a range of possible actions from which to choose. Most obviously, he might choose to emphasize either collective goods or selective incentives, or perhaps both. Which he chooses to stress will determine the kinds of individuals that respond, the contributions forthcoming, the actions required, and so on, all of which bear directly upon his own surplus, the survival prospects of the group, and the manner in which the organization must be structured. Similarly, there are different marketing strategies available to him. He may offer a given set of incentives across-the-board to all potential members, for example, or he may formulate a variety of incentive packages, aiming them differentially at subsets of potential members. His problem is to search for the best strategic options, given the inevitable limitations on his own information, skills, and resources.

Because these and other aspects of entrepreneurial strategy are, at the same time, mechanisms of group formation and maintenance, it is useful to develop the organizational analysis with reference to the strategic options of the entrepreneur. We can do this in a manageable way by singling out several dimensions of his organizational behavior that are crucial to group formation and maintenance, as well as broad enough to facilitate a sufficiently comprehensive analysis. These are communication, administration of selective incentives, administration of collective goods, member bargaining, and environmental relationships.

Communication

In a world of bounded rationality, there is no guarantee that individuals will possess even the most basic information about the proposed exchange relationships; members may not have perfect knowledge of the selective incentives or collective goods offered and may even be unaware of the entrepreneur's existence, while the entrepreneur may lack information about who and where potential members are. His situation is analogous to that of the business firm whose products are virtually unknown to the consuming public. In order to sell his products—and thus in order to enlist new group members and retain old ones—he must somehow contact customers, inform them of the benefits he has to offer, and establish the terms of the exchange. In doing so, communication becomes a cost. As with any other cost, he has an incentive to communicate as cheaply as possible and, hence, to use the most efficient means available for obtaining and exchanging information with clients.

Efficient communication involves more than simply finding potential members and acquainting them with the benefits offered. Notably, once these basic steps are taken, the entrepreneur may be able to shape member perceptions in desired ways by carefully choosing the types of information—or misinformation—he transmits. As the analysis in chapter 2 suggests, for example, he might be able to turn individual ignorance to his own advantage by claiming that collective goods are more valuable or less expensive to supply than is actually the case, or by claiming that the prevailing level of contributions is lower than it really is. In general, the entrepreneur's success depends not only on his contacting and informing potential members, but also on their willingness to buy—and he may find that he can influence their decisions by providing them with false, misleading, or ambiguous information. For the entrepreneur, such tactics are an integral part of the game. He is concerned with his own surplus; the method and content of communications are simply means to his material ends and are utilized accordingly.

His ability to put communication to good use will also depend in great part on what he knows about members. He must, of course, have some information about who and where they are. But he must also have an idea of what their economic interests are and thus some grasp of the economic circumstances in which they find themselves. This kind of information is crucial for a well-designed package of incentives, one that meets with the best possible response from the potential membership. He also needs information about what members know—that is, what information they already possess. With data of this sort, he can assess the nature of their perceptions, the likelihood that different types of potential members will join, the kind of convincing that may be necessary, and so on, and he can design his communication efforts accordingly. Because he needs to know certain things *about* members, then, as well as to transmit information *to* them, it is important that the flow of information be two-way.

With these considerations in mind, we can move on to ask about the process of communication. How does the entrepreneur go about communicating with his clients? There are a number of methods he might choose, but, for our purposes, it is useful to classify them into two types. First, he can attempt to establish *direct contact* by use of the various communications media available to him—newspapers, radio, telephone, the postal system, personal contact, and so on. When the potential membership is large, however, this method may be quite inefficient as part of an organizing strategy, not only in purely financial terms, but also in terms of the entrepreneur's time, energy, and talents. It would be very difficult and highly costly, after all, were he to try to make direct personal contact with hundreds or even thousands of potential members, and his problems increase if the clientele happens to be geographically dispersed or difficult to identify. Use of the mass media can correct for these, but there are inefficiencies involved here as well. Because of the blanket coverage afforded by the media, the entrepreneur may be led to communicate (and to pay for communicating) with many individuals who are not potential members. This is a waste of resources. Additionally, his media appeals may not be persuasive, personal, intensive, or specialized enough to convince the desired numbers and types of persons to join.

Some of these problems might be minimized through the use of "direct mail" techniques. With this approach, group literature is mailed only to those individuals who are preselected on the basis of data—on their occupations, memberships in other groups, contributions to political candidates, etc.—indicating that they are particularly likely to be responsive to entrepreneurial appeals. Even here, however, the costs and inefficiencies can be formidable. Reliable data must somehow be collected or purchased, an administrative apparatus must be funded, and a variety of mailing costs must be incurred for each person on the list. And, while the response rate is likely to be higher than with blanket appeals, it is also likely to be quite low in absolute terms. The economic risks of this approach, especially for large constituencies, can be substantial.

There are good reasons, then, why the entrepreneur would not want to rely exclusively upon direct contact in attracting people to the group, unless the clientele is fairly small or some other special condition obtains. On the other hand, direct contact appears highly useful as a method of communicating with members, persons who have formally joined the association. They are less numerous than the general clientele, more easily identifiable, and can be reached without diffuse appeals to a general population.

A common means of communication is the associational newspaper or newsletter, which is sent out at regular intervals to all members. For several reasons, this simple link between entrepreneur and membership can play a crucial role in maintaining the association. In the first place, the entrepreneur can use the newspaper to advertise the benefits he has to offer. He can acquaint members with the various selective incentives, explain their value, and try to increase the perceived value of group membership. In the process, he might be able to create a market for some selective incentives where none existed before—by advertising new services, for example, or by arguing on behalf of new techniques or methods of production requiring new inputs. His influence on member calculations is likely to be particularly important, however, in respect to collective goods. While selective incentives can usually be immediately purchased, experienced, and evaluated, information on collective goods is much more remote and, significantly, it is difficult to obtain except through the entrepreneur. By emphasizing the number, value, and type of political goals he seeks, the effectiveness of his political methods, and the need for funds (none of which is necessarily close to the truth), he can endeavor to increase the levels of contributions and political support. He is especially likely to be successful with low-information members who depend heavily upon him for the "facts."

Important as it is, this "advertising and propagandizing" employment of direct communication is only one aspect of its utility. There is another aspect of equal importance both to the entrepreneur and to the group—by structuring the content of communications in certain ways, the entrepreneur can turn the medium of communication into a selective incentive. He can do this by providing members with specialized information related in various ways to their economic well-being—information about their industry, government regulations, recent economic developments, new production techniques, labor or management relations, etc. Moreover, because such information is likely to appeal only to a select clientele, it probably cannot easily be obtained elsewhere; the general communications media must appeal to a more heterogeneous population and cannot regularly supply the kind of narrow, detailed information that is needed. Given the nature of the market, therefore, the entrepreneur may find himself sitting on a gold mine—in a position to establish a virtual monopoly over a commodity of value to a set of consumers.

Furthermore, the entrepreneur can take advantage of this role as "supplier of facts" to enhance the effectiveness of his own appeals, which need not be factual and which, if offered alone, might arouse the kind of healthy skepticism that sellers' pitches often evoke from buyers. In the course of providing detailed information of value to members, he can simply include advertisements and propaganda, presenting them as factual information or fact-based evaluations and making no clear distinction between them and other kinds of information relevant to members. In this way, organizational services can be clothed in the facts, with member perceptions influenced by the objective setting in which they are displayed. When engaged in informational activities, then, the entrepreneur might be much more successful by playing up his role as "supplier of facts" and pretending not to be the "seller of commodities" he also is.

When the membership is large, or when a large percentage of the potential clientele is brought into the group, the entrepreneur can take advantage of still another bonus: his communications link with members can become useful to other individuals, and he can charge them a fee in return for access to it. This is most obviously the case for individuals who supply specialized products to the group's members. By advertising their products via the entrepreneur's link to members, these outsiders can reach just the right portion of the population, their potential consumers. For some producers, then, advertising in (say) the association's newspaper represents a highly efficient advertising expenditure. By selling space for such appeals, the entrepreneur can cut down on communication costs and perhaps even turn a profit on advertising revenues alone. He might also offer advertising space to his own members, either at a price or "free" as a selective incentive. They might be suppliers for other members, for instance, or they might advertise certain goods in a want-ad section of the group's newspaper, typical of those carried in general circulation newspapers but guaranteed to reach the right audience.

In sum, direct contact is a critical entrepreneurial tool that can be used to his own advantage and to the advantage of organizational maintenance, especially with regard to relations between the entrepreneur and formal members of the group, his captive audience. More specifically, direct contact with members can be employed (a) to acquaint them with the full array of his services and to influence member evaluations of the costs and benefits of both selective incentives and collective goods; (b) to serve as a selective incentive, with information content taking on its own value for members; and (c) to raise revenue from sources outside (and perhaps inside) the association. In each case, the communications process is utilized to fortify the material foundations of the group. Moreover, in each case, effectiveness is enhanced to the extent that the entrepreneur can establish a virtual monopoly over certain kinds of information. The more control he has and the more efficiently he uses that control, the more the membership will depend on him for their perceptions of the economic and political world—and, indeed, the more costly it may become for nonmembers who refuse to purchase the informational benefits he has to offer. This does not mean that any given entrepreneur can actually attain this level of control, for there are organizational competitors, alternative channels of communication, and costs of communication that stand in his way. Because of such factors, some entrepreneurs may not find it worthwhile to establish regular communications links with members at all. What direct contact represents, rather, is a strategic option available for use to the degree that the situation permits.

The entrepreneur's second option is to use *indirect contact*, in which his messages are transmitted to members and potential members by other individuals who serve, in one of their capacities, as middlemen in the communications process. When using this method, the entrepreneur need contact only a relatively small number of these middlemen, each of whom can pass the information on to comparatively large numbers of customers, some of whom may be induced to relay the information to still others. In doing so, he can take advantage of knowledge, contacts, skills, and labor which, though he himself does not possess them, can be brought to bear in achieving his own ends. When employing indirect contact, for instance, he needs to have only a minimum of initial information about precisely who and where his potential members are; if he chooses active persons who know the constituency and if he persuades them to act as middlemen, he can shift the task of identifying and locating potential members to individuals who are particularly suited for carrying it out. Indeed, what is a complex task for the entrepreneur can prove to be a quick and easy one for persons who know what they are doing, since they may simply be asked to contact people with whom they are already acquainted and in frequent communication.

Furthermore, it is possible that such contacts will be more persuasive than if the burden is shouldered entirely by the entrepreneur. Middlemen are in a better position to make personal appeals and to shape their arguments to the specialized needs and perceptions of customers. Also, because they are focal actors in a communications process, they may be well informed about the problems and issues of relevance to clients, and hence in a position to provide them with the "right" kind of convincing evidence. And finally, if middlemen and their contacts are acquainted, there may exist a store of trust on which the middleman can rely, enhancing the believability of his arguments. Taking all these factors into consideration, then, the entrepreneur may be wise to have other individuals identify, locate, and contact his customers.

To facilitate this kind of contact, a communications network can be established in which communication flows are regularized between the entrepreneur and each middleman and between each middleman and particular sets of members and potential members. As for how the entrepreneur might set up such a system, there appear to be three principal methods. First, he might single out certain critically situated individuals—those, for instance, who have large numbers of contacts within the clientele or who are extremely well informed. For business associations, large firms would often meet both these criteria. The entrepreneur could then try to persuade them to play the desired role in the communications process. (The question of why they should comply will be discussed later.) The second method is that of using existing groupings within the clientele, whether these groups are formal or informal, and regardless of their raison d'être. In following this strategy, the entrepreneur's concern is to take advantage of whatever organization prevails. Where there is organization, there are typically links among involved individuals which can be used for communication purposes; if activists within these subgroups can be contacted and persuaded to go along, existing mechanisms can be relied upon to carry information between the entrepreneur and clients. A final means of setting up the structure is perhaps an obvious one from an administrative point of view: he can simply hire staff on the basis of expertise, sales ability, enthusiasm, or related criteria, and they can be sent out into the field to perform the tasks ascribed above to middlemen. Because staff personnel perform these tasks as part of their jobs, they can devote their working time toward these ends and, with experience, may become effective and professional. They must also be paid, however, and this will constrain the entrepreneur's willingness to rely upon them.

When employing indirect contact, then, the entrepreneur recruits middlemen by some means and takes the best possible advantage of their communications services. The resulting structure supplies him with channels of access to individual clients, whom he can reach with comparative ease, once given their general positions in the network. In principle, specialized information can thus flow quickly and efficiently through the system to desired recipients—without the costs of paper, stamps, and printing, without the preparation that impersonal media require, without blanket coverage, without the entrepreneur's having to commit himself on paper (which is instrumental if secrecy or bargaining is involved). Moreover, and this is particularly important, this kind of communications network can perform a feedback function. Middlemen can operate not only to relay information from the entrepreneur to clients, but also to transmit information from them—or about them—to the entrepreneur. Active communicators can thus serve as a critical means by which the entrepreneur collects data on his clientele—on their interests, their economic circumstances, their likely responses to certain appeals, and so on. He need not rely on surveys or questionnaires, on his own knowledge, or on costly "tests" of incentive packages. By structuring communications, he can seek to guarantee a continuous inflow of information, apprising him of prevailing circumstances and indicating likely directions of future change.

The structure of indirect communications, however, also involves a very special kind of cost, for, within this framework, the entrepreneur no longer controls the content of communications. He shares control with middlemen. They are the ones who contact the clientele, and there is no guarantee that the "pure" entrepreneurial message will be relayed, nor that their special talents and information will be employed to entrepreneurial advantage. These problems could arise because of mistakes, oversights, or information overloads. But they may result from the unavoidable fact that middlemen have their own interests and will follow the entrepreneur's game plan only as long as it is in their interests to do so. When interests diverge, they may purposely distort, subvert, or block entrepreneurial communications.

The entrepreneur's task is to see that this does not happen. Accordingly, individuals must be provided with appropriate incentives, incentives that induce them to become middlemen and to perform tasks as the entrepreneur wants them performed. In some cases, this can be brought about with no obvious "payments," because additional information and contacts are valuable to middlemen as well as to the entrepreneur; some members might agree to comply with entrepreneurial directives, then, simply because they expect net benefits from active participation in the communications process. On the other hand, some members may require concessions and favors, or even cash payments, in return for their services; significant among these are members who make their compliance contingent upon political payments asking, for example, that the entrepreneur pursue specific political goals or that he allow them to take part in making certain types of decisions. If the middleman's services are valuable and not easily replaced, it can be perfectly rational for the entrepreneur to capitulate to such demands. He is simply concerned with making a net benefit on the exchange.

In view of all these considerations, it is clear that both direct and indirect methods of communication have something to offer the entrepreneur—for a price. Their relative merits can now be briefly summarized.

Except in special circumstances, the various methods of direct contact cannot be major mechanisms of recruitment, but they are potentially critical mechanisms of maintenance. The uses of indirect contact are more generalized; indeed, as an approach to recruitment, this method involves just the right kind of information, skills, and linkages.

In establishing direct contact with members, the major benefits to the entrepreneur lie in his personal control over certain kinds of information, his corresponding influence over member perceptions (of his services, of the economic and political world), his use of information as a selective incentive, and his use of the medium to raise revenue from the outside. By employing indirect methods to contact members and potential members, he can take advantage of the information, contacts, skills, and labor of middlemen—who can form a network allowing for continuous outflows and inflows of information, carried within personalized channels of access to individuals and subgroups in the clientele. Thus, while there is a degree of overlap in the benefits these methods offer, they largely yield different kinds of advantages.

Their drawbacks are also distinctive. Outside of small groups, direct contact may require substantial costs, must usually be intermittent, lacks the personal touch, and cannot efficiently provide feedback. Indirect contact, which appears to minimize these, involves two basic kinds of costs. First, incentives must be supplied to middlemen, which may imply salaries for staff. Second, the entrepreneur becomes dependent upon middlemen to perform valuable communications functions, and they may selectively distort or subvert information, or even use their pivotal positions in an effort to extract political benefits from him.

Given these distinctive patterns of advantage and disadvantage, there is a rational basis for the entrepreneur to use the two general methods in combination, with each employed to do what it does best in terms of its net effects upon his surplus. Both have integral roles to play in the process of group formation and maintenance.

Administration of Selective Incentives

Because selective incentives may well prove to be the key to entrepreneurial success, particularly in large groups, an important entrepreneurial task is to set up an administrative apparatus for the production and distribution of valuable incentive packages to members. The types and costs of incentives, the ways in which they are combined and advertised, the extent of their attractiveness—these and other factors will help determine whether the group will survive or fail and, if it survives, whether it will be stable or unstable.

How does the entrepreneur go about supplying these incentives? When something tangible must be produced and exchanged, he has two options: he can set up production and distribution processes *within* the organization or he can rely on *outside* processes (e.g., by relying on established business firms). By following the first course, he is in some sense starting his own business enterprise, which requires that he invest a certain amount of capital. He might, for instance produce commodities specialized to member needs, perhaps selling them at a discount (or giving them away); provide group purchasing and group marketing opportunities; provide specialized information, perhaps via the newspaper, perhaps via the services of an expert staff of researchers; use his central location, contacts, and resources to solve special problems, complaints, or grievances that members may have.

There are any number of goods and services the entrepreneur might attempt to produce and sell. The significant point is that, in doing so, he gets any profits that are generated, while at the same time tying members into the group and gaining their contributions. This yields him two interrelated sources of income. In some cases, he may be able to "fit" his clientele so appropriately with incentive packages, and to supply them so efficiently, that greater business profits and increased member contributions go hand in hand—a formidable prospect which is enhanced by his use of the communications structure in controlling information and advertising his goods and services. Yet business profits and member contributions do not necessarily go up and down together; they may tend sometimes to cancel each other out. Since the entrepreneur is only concerned with his *net* surplus, however, he has some room to maneuver in combining the two. Most importantly, he might accept a loss on his business operations if it is more than offset by increased member contributions, or accept declining membership and declining member contributions if they are more than offset by business profits. The former possibility is familiar to us by now, since this is necessarily what happens when the entrepreneur offers selective incentives "free" to members in return for dues. The latter possibility is less obvious, suggesting one reason why the entrepreneur is not always interested in higher levels of membership. In either case, the entrepreneur is simply seeking a trade-off that works to his advantage.

For this reason, then, the entrepreneur will not have an incentive to structure the provision of selective incentives with an eye toward maximizing business profits. This is not what "efficiency" means for him. He is concerned with maximizing his surplus, and this is different than maximizing business profits. The ways he patterns personnel and resources within the group will reflect the entrepreneur's unique perspective on efficient operation.

It will also reflect his adaptation to a major element of his business environment—the tax laws. Although these laws can vary from one political jurisdiction to another, it is commonly the case that "nonprofit organizations" receive special tax treatment from the government and that member associations are frequently so classified by the responsible public agencies.[3] The entrepreneur might be able to take advantage of this in several ways, even though the organization as a whole may not qualify as nonprofit, due to its business components. First, he might set up his own business operations as entities that are legally separate from the association itself; thus, the profit-making activities of his businesses would not undermine the favored tax status of the association and its revenues. Second, money could be funneled back and forth between the association and the businesses to the advantage of both. As part of their costs of operation, for example, the businesses might purposely "pay" the association exorbitant rents for office space, fees for the use of staff, dividends, and so on—all of which might then receive favored tax treatment as associational revenues. On the other hand, if some of the entrepreneur's businesses were crucially in need of cost advantages over outside competitors, the association might "charge" much less for its services than outsiders must pay in the marketplace. Third, the entrepreneur may even be able to structure his profit-making businesses as (nominally nonprofit) "cooperatives" by returning some of the profits to share-holding members; in these cases, he would still be able to control the business operations and their surpluses (minus dividends), but the businesses would also benefit from favored tax treatment.

Tax considerations alone, then, could lead the entrepreneur to adopt a very complex organizational structure—to the point where the organization is legally divided into a number of separate entities, all of which he controls in an interrelated fashion. To keep matters simple, however, we will continue to treat the entire organization as though it were a unified structure, and we will continue to use the terms "organization," "association," and "group" interchangeably in reference to it.

The second way the entrepreneur can supply selective incentives is by relying on business operations *outside* the association. Outside business will often be eager to provide specialized products or to sell at a discount if a sufficiently large number of orders can be guaranteed. Indeed, they may even be willing to pay him for the privilege. The entrepreneur's task is to scan the environment for opportunities, taking note of his clients' interests and demands and attempting to satisfy them with appropriately priced benefits from the outside. Essentially, his role is that of a middleman between business and his clients; and, especially if there exists an efficient communications structure linking him to members and potential members, his resources and location greatly facilitate his ability to deal with both sides. Outside businesses, after all, do not ordinarily have easy access to a population of customers and, at any rate, would make different appeals to individuals than they would to organized groups, since the latter can represent pools of purchasing power. Thus, by coordinating the individuals in his clientele and by recruiting and dealing with interested businesses from the outside, the entrepreneur can bring about exchange relationships that probably would not occur otherwise.

The inside and outside methods provide an interesting contrast. When setting up his own business operations within the organization, he has major competitive advantages (favored tax treatment, ready-made communications links to customers), he gets any profits so derived, and he gets any increases in member contributions. Moreover, he is not highly dependent upon outside business firms; he controls the means and ends of production and can take direct action to augment his surplus. On the other hand, he must invest sufficient capital to create and maintain such operations, and he thereby must face the risk that his ventures will not prove successful, must incur sunk costs that will limit his flexibility in the future, and must enlarge the association's structure to include the necessary personnel and resources, thus requiring greater efforts at communication and control. The problems of the inside method are largely avoided when he relies on established businesses outside the association. Here, selective incentives can be supplied at levels of cost and risk that are comparatively low, with the financial and organizational problems shouldered by persons external to the group. As a result, this method can be used with greater flexibility in adapting to changing membership and environmental conditions; if one package of incentives fails to have the desired impacts, it is relatively easy for the entrepreneur to shift to another package. But, on the negative side, he also foregoes any profits that are derived on the sale of incentives (except for any side payments he receives from outsiders) and gives up a degree of control over their supply and price. In sum, then, the inside and outside methods have distinctly different kinds of implications for the entrepreneur's surplus. His task is to develop an overarching administrative strategy which, in using these general methods singly or in combination, promises him the best possible economic gains.

The supply of selective incentives does not always require the production and distribution of something tangible, however, and does not always require a reliance upon business operations. Indeed, the entrepreneur can actually get members to *supply themselves* with selective incentives. He can do this by setting up meetings, conferences, seminars, and the like, at which members can get together to exchange information, discuss problems, work out differences, or devise plans for concerted action. He might also create subgroups (e.g., committees) or cultivate existing groupings to encourage these interactions.

Member participation mechanisms of this sort, particularly if regularized, can be a source of benefits for both the entrepreneur and group members. Members are induced to participate in various events precisely because there are expected economic gains involved; and, if these events are properly arranged (in respect to time, location, frequency, etc.) they might be attended by members with little or no obvious material outlays. For his part, the entrepreneur has an incentive to generate member activities because they make membership status more valuable to the participants, serving to tie them into the group more securely. And he need incur few immediate costs in doing so. By using his central location and communications structure, resources not available to the average member, he can take steps to coordinate members in ways that they themselves find beneficial.

Administration of Collective Goods

The second side of the administrative structure is concerned with the provision of collective goods. This side is of special interest to political scientists, of course, because it is the organizational component most immediately connected with what interest groups do in politics. In this section's analysis, however, the political side of the organization is salient not because it is political, but because of its major role in group formation and maintenance. It is a central means by which the entrepreneur can go about ensuring the survival of the association and the maximization of his own surplus.

His structural incentives are shaped by three basic elements. First, whenever there are certain individuals whose membership and (perhaps substantial) contributions hinge upon the provision of collective goods, the entrepreneur must in the long run be able to show some success or at least some promise of success in supplying such goods if he wants to take advantage of their support. Second, the entrepreneur may want to pursue collective goods because they are of direct material benefit to himself (or to a nonmember who is willing to reward him for pursuing them), quite aside from member interests. Third, political activity may at times enhance his ability to supply members with selective benefits. To the extent that these incentives are present, the entrepreneur will have reason to develop the political side of the organization.

His approach in structuring the organization will be influenced not only by these incentives, but also by the alternative courses of action associated with success.[4] There are many such possibilities, of course. But there are several broad opportunities that, in principle, are available to all entrepreneurs and that directly affect the organization's ability to achieve collective goods. Most fundamental among these are access to critical governmental arenas, with those that are critical determined largely by the nature of the group's goals; lobbying with public officials, including activities ranging from political pressure to the simple presentation of views; the cultivation of contacts with allies (and sometimes even opponents) to facilitate coalition building, bargaining, information exchange, and mutual trust; the transfer of resources—campaign support, money, research reports, prepared speeches, transportation—to other participants.

In order to pursue these activities effectively, moreover, he must be organizationally equipped to deal with a basic fact of political life: he can only supply collective goods with the support of outside participants, especially public officials, and, because their support is not automatically forthcoming, he must be in a position to induce them over to his side. This means that he must be concerned with understanding the values and perceptions of other participants and with marshaling the kinds of resources necessary for influencing their decisions. Bureaucratic officials, for example, may place high value upon technical information, organizational assistance in policy administration, political support before legislative committees, and favorable publicity for agency activities. Legislators, on the other hand, may be more interested in campaign contributions, political information about constitutents or other legislators, favorable publicity in the constituency, and political support from "representative" interest groups.[5] The more the entrepreneur is able to offer these crucial participants, the more politically successful he is likely to be.

When he has incentives to seek collective goods, then, he will attempt to design the group's political structure with these "requirements" of success in mind. How can he go about doing this? At the heart of his organizational task is the question of personnel. He must recruit individuals who, because of experience, training, personality, or aptitude, can perform the kinds of political services that he needs performed. In particular, he might look for people who already have or who may be expected to develop personal contacts or influence in government, the media, interest groups, the membership; knowledge of member interests and the economic environment; knowledge of the political process; technical expertise; administrative expertise; interpersonal skills enhancing persuasiveness, trustworthiness, and the like.

The entrepreneur may himself possess a number of these desirable characteristics; and, especially if his resources or political incentives are restricted, he may decide to perform all political activities on his own. The group's political structure would then consist primarily of the political activities of the entrepreneur. Yet this is only the limiting case, and there are various ways in which he might rely upon the political services of others, among them professional lobbyists, staff personnel, and individual members. In all instances, of course, he must provide individuals with incentives to induce the services he needs, and his recruitment process will be guided by an evaluation of the costs and benefits implied for his own surplus.

A lobbyist, for example, can be valuable because he is a political specialist. It is his job to help interest groups achieve their goals within the political system, and hence part of his job is to develop the kinds of characteristics and resources referred to above. Precisely because they are common requisites of political effectiveness, these are the tools of his trade. The entrepreneur, for his part, can choose a lobbyist who, dollar for dollar, appears to offer the best promise of success—which, in turn, depends upon the specific goals in question, the governmental agencies, the affected groups, and so on. These factors will determine what contacts, information, channels of access, and resources are most likely to bring about the desired results, and thus what characteristics a "good" lobbyist should have. In addition to cost considerations, then, these are the kinds of things the entrepreneur will take into account in deciding whether a lobbyist is valuable enough to be incorporated, even if temporarily, into the political side of the organization.

To the extent that the entrepreneur would like to pursue more goals, to focus on more arenas, and to perform a wider range of functions, he may find his own activities inadequate even if supplemented by those of a lobbyist. When he finds himself in this kind of situation, one reasonable response is for him to hire staff personnel. This renders the organization more complex, enabling a division of labor in which employees specialize in one or several useful activities—carrying out research on legislative issues, for example, or maintaining contacts with agency experts. Because the political staff need not be concerned with selective incentives, member recruitment, and other nonpolitical aspects of group maintenance, they can concentrate their energies and talents in a way that the entrepreneur cannot.

Qualified individuals, whether lobbyists or staff personnel, do not necessarily come cheaply, however. And we must also remember that many members and potential members may not contribute for political reasons anyway and will not reward the entrepreneur for political success. Both these factors undermine his incentives to hire personnel for political action. Depending upon the nature of his membership and the cost requirements of political effectiveness, then, he may have to settle for a political structure that is simple, unsophisticated, and poorly funded. This may be his optimal structural design under the circumstances.

Yet there remains a third important way that the entrepreneur can seek political effectiveness, quite apart from hiring lobbyists and staff. As was true in his communications and selective incentives strategies, the entrepreneur can rely upon *members* to perform certain kinds of activities. And it is easy to see why he might have an incentive to do so. In the first place, certain members may have one or more of the desirable characteristics noted above; in particular, they can be used in political contexts—legislative committee hearings, for example—to supply evidence of member interests and prevailing economic conditions, or perhaps to perform functions calling for expertise. Members may also have important personal contacts that the entrepreneur can draw upon—contacts with legislators, administrators, or potential allies—that can be used to facilitate access to decision-making sites and to develop political support. Additionally, the entrepreneur can put participation to use by inducing members to write letters, sign petitions, make telephone calls, and so on, in an effort to convince outside decision-makers that his policies are important to a given constituency and representative of their interests.

Given that participation can be valuable to the entrepreneur, how can he induce members to participate? In the most obvious case, incentives will derive from member support of group goals, with individuals motivated by the benefits that will accrue to them if the entrepreneur is successful. This is not necessarily enough to get them to participate, however, since each individual is asked to "contribute" his participation toward a collective good, and the usual Olson problems may prevent him from doing so. The keys to his decision are the costs of participating in certain ways, the probability that his participation will make a difference to the outcome, and the benefits contingent upon success. Significantly, though, the costs of participation are often quite low, even negligible; writing letters, making phone calls, and signing petitions usually involve no cash outlays, and members may view them as imposing no (or virtually no) costs upon them. On the other hand, they may feel that their input carries at least some weight, particularly if it regards some specialized matter affecting a relatively small number of people or if it is directed toward a decision maker (e.g., a friend or a local legislator) with an incentive to listen. For these reasons, then, participation may not be very difficult to induce.

Moreover, politically oriented participation can be induced from members regardless of size and regardless of the reasons they joined the group. This is true because the decision to participate is different from the decision to join and pay dues. Even the smallest member may have an incentive to write his legislator about a political issue affecting his interests, while at the same time refusing to stay in the group and pay dues unless selective incentives are provided. In his efforts to stimulate participation for certain purposes, then, the entrepreneur can regard all members as potential participants. This does not mean that member size is an unimportant consideration, though. Larger members will ordinarily have a greater incentive to participate, since they stand to gain more from their participation "expenditures." And the importance of size is underlined when we take into account empirical conditions that will often prevail. Large business firms and large farms, for example, are much more likely than their smaller counterparts to have political contacts in strategic places, wealthy associates and allies, more accurate and detailed information, more resources to use in bargaining, and so on—and thus are likely to be more effective participants. This, too, gives them a greater incentive to participate.

There are other incentives for participation besides those deriving from member support of group goals. In fact, members may engage in "supportive" participation even if they do not support group goals or are indifferent. The entrepreneur, for example, might simply seek out and "pay" selected members to participate in certain ways, where payments may be in the form of cash or, perhaps more realistically, favors that the entrepreneur is in a position to extend. A second possibility is that a member may participate in order to make contacts, establish useful friendships, create alliances, regularize personal ac-

cess, etc.—in an effort to gain a personal foothold in politically important territory, with the expectation of pursuing political purposes that
may have no direct bearing on the group at all. Third, a member may
participate because the services he performs give him a degree of bargaining leverage with the entrepreneur; for when political activities
have a value to the entrepreneur, the individual who can supply or
deny him that value might be in a position to demand certain benefits in
return.

In sum, member participation is variously motivated. Some individuals may be active because of the collective good at issue. For
others, the collective good may only be the apparent object of their
participation and may actually have nothing to do with why they are
politically active. The entrepreneur's task is to shape and use member
participation as best he can, in view of the kinds of participation
needed and the incentives available for bringing them about. In doing
so, he has a number of options. He may, for example, rely on many
smaller members to perform inexpensive acts (e.g., writing their legislators), without expending resources trying to persuade them to
perform more costly ones; selected larger members may willingly undertake these. Moreover, the issues and public arenas involved will help
determine which members should participate and how. In one situation, goals may be pursued most effectively by having smaller members
(the "average affected individuals") testify before a legislative committee; in another, effectiveness may require private talks between
bureaucratic officials and a few of the largest members. Overall, the
entrepreneur will want to structure resource allocation in such a way
that different numbers and kinds of members can be induced to engage
in different types of participation, depending upon the issues and public
arenas.

Finally, it is important to note that, while we have viewed the administration of collective goods and selective incentives as taking place
on distinct sides of the organization, this has been only for convenience
of presentation. Actually, of course, the two are fundamentally related.
Selective incentives attract members and generate funds, both of which
can then be put to political use. Conversely, external political efforts
may yield greater tax advantages or monopolies over special types of
benefits (e.g., through "delegation" of public functions by governmental agencies) that can be used as selective incentives, or produce legal regulations that compel potential members to join. Internally, as we have seen, opportunities for political participation may

themselves supply members with selective incentives. Moreover, even members who join purely in response to the entrepreneur's political appeals represent an accessible clientele for the sale of selective incentives. Politically motivated members may subsequently purchase group insurance, for example, simply because it is convenient to do so, or because they are persuaded by the entrepreneur's constant advertising, or even because they place special trust in him as their political spokesman and feel safer buying insurance from him than an outsider.

Thus the political and selective incentive sides of the organization overlap in a variety of ways and are mutually conditioning. It is true that politics can be a by-product of selective incentives. But it is also true that the entrepreneur's ability to supply selective incentives is often influenced by his ability to achieve political goals, structure political participation, and attract members on political bases—and thus that selective incentives can be a by-product of politics. The entrepreneur's task, if he is to maximize his surplus, is to take these interdependencies into account in designing his organizational strategies. He must harmonize the two sides of the organization, taking best advantage of the pool of resources that they collectively offer.

Member Bargaining

The entrepreneur can also encourage group formation and maintenance by promoting bargaining relationships among members. In chapter 2 we noted that, as the group increases in size, it is less likely that bargaining relationships can have any impact on provision of the collective good. But then we were dealing with a model that lacked any central coordinating force, and now we have one in the form of the entrepreneur. This adds a new dimension to the interactions of potential contributors and opens up more favorable possibilities.

Because the entrepreneur is at the center of group-related activities, he can utilize the mechanisms he has developed for locating, communicating with, and bringing together particular individuals in his clientele. This is an advantage that no one else will likely possess and that would be lacking were there no entrepreneur. Furthermore, he is in a position to collect information on member interests and environmental conditions, to control information, and thus to influence member perceptions of each other and the benefits of cooperation. In the process, he may be able to convince some members of their mutual dependence, establish a degree of trust among them, and demonstrate how their resources can be pooled for mutual gain. His success will depend in part upon his personality—his persuasiveness, his bargaining skill, his insight into personal relationships. And success will, of course, depend upon such factors as member incentives and the size of the group. But the major determinant is his central position, with all that it implies in terms of resources and strategic advantage. It makes him a very special actor in the bargaining arena.

We need not dwell on the various ways he might encourage successful bargaining arrangments. Yet there is one method which, because of its structural implications, deserves to be singled out. According to this method, the entrepreneur seeks to enhance bargaining relationships by deliberately creating subgroups or by cultivating existing ones. These may take the form of committees, discussion groups, advisory panels, and the like; they may be divided, for example, along lines of interest or geography; and they may reflect varying degrees of formality. Their utilization, therefore, yields an elaboration of organizational structure, designed to increase and regularize interactions among selected members. By promoting member activities in subgroups, then, particularly if they continue over some appreciable length of time, he can employ structural means to enhance mutual understanding, trust, and cooperation. He is best off, moreover, if he does not focus his energies on all members equally, but concentrates instead on those members whose cooperation is likely to yield the greatest contributions. In other words, he should concentrate on larger members at the expense of smaller members and allocate his resources in such a way that larger members are encouraged to interact with each other. The entrepreneur's subgroup strategy is thus intimately linked with the activation of larger members, and this will be reflected in organizational structure.

While bargaining may sometimes prove important, we must remember that there remain major obstacles in the way of enduring bargaining agreements. The free-rider incentive is an ever-present problem, since individuals will always prefer that the costs be shouldered by others. And, once any bargain has been struck, changing interpersonal relationships and changing political or economic conditions always threaten a breakdown of cooperation. For these reasons and for others already suggested (e.g., group size), it is risky for the entrepreneur to depend to any great extent upon bargaining as a foundation for associational survival. In their effects on stability, other organizational mechanisms must be regarded as generally safer and more reliable.

Environmental Relationships

Until now, we have focused primarily upon relationships internal to the group, treating environmental actors only secondarily as their behavior became relevant. Yet it is clear that outsiders have very important roles to play in group formation and maintenance. In the provision of selective incentives, for example, outside business operations represent one means of supplying member services; and, in the provision of collective goods, public officials are in a position to facilitate or impede the realization of entrepreneurial goals.

This section will take a closer look at environmental actors and their connection to the organization. The analysis will be conducted with reference to three broad sets of environmental actors—governmental officials, officials from nongovernmental groups and organizations, and rival entrepreneurs—and, in each case, a few of the most basic organizational relationships will be singled out for attention.

Governmental Officials

It is already clear that, if the entrepreneur is to provide collective goods, he must be centrally concerned with establishing instrumental relationships with public officials and that this, in turn, has implications for his organizational strategies. There are other bases, however, on which governmental relationships can prove both beneficial and far-reaching in their organizational consequences. Here, we will look at three interesting cases in which this can occur. Each is noteworthy because it involves more than the simple pursuit of specific collective goods, to the point where the group becomes a favored participant in the political process.

The entrepreneur can enhance his political position immeasurably if he can get public officials in a given policy area or governmental unit (agency, legislative committee, city council) to recognize his group as the legitimate representative of a certain economic sector. His ability to do so largely depends on what he can offer public officials in return (information, political support, administrative cooperation). But once he gains their recognition, the entrepreneur becomes an official spokesman for a sector of society, at least at some level—even though he may have organized only a small percentage of potential members—and many of the obstacles to his political success are swept away. He is viewed by others as "belonging" in the political arena;

access, contacts, and useful lobbying relationships are virtually guaranteed. The most obvious consequence, therefore, is that he is more likely to achieve his political goals. Yet there is more to be said than just this. When the entrepreneur is officially recognized as a legitimate spokesman, other groups from the same sector are effectively denied the perquisites that go along with being favored; hence, he has a critical political advantage over entrepreneurs who may be competing with him to organize and represent the sector. Furthermore, he is doubly advantaged because his favored status makes membership in his group more valuable to politically motivated members and potential members, including those who belong to other associations. If the entrepreneur can gain favored status, then, he may see his own group's maintenance enhanced and, at the same time, the maintenance of rival groups damaged.

A related kind of favored relationship occurs when the entrepreneur is in a position to help administer public programs. Public officials are likely to find such a relationship advantageous to the extent that he can provide a ready-made organization for the implementation of specialized policies, technical or generally useful information enhancing effective administration, advice reflecting a genuine understanding of the sector, and the cooperation of group members. These make the government's job much easier and less costly and help to assure that programs will be carried out by persons well acquainted with the specialized matters involved. From the entrepreneur's point of view, this arrangement promises a range of benefits. First, a group that helps to administer programs will, as a result, have contacts and access that can be used to influence policy; in fact, government may encourage their input so that policies and policy administration can be jointly designed. Another advantage is that the implementation of policy can bring the group into contact with potential members; indeed, the government may, in effect, pay him to find out who and where these individuals are and to contact them. Thus, the government may enable him to carry out what amounts to an expensive identification and recruitment campaign—accomplished under the ostensive purpose of policy administration at the government's expense. Finally, because there is always some flexibility involved in the implementation on programs, the entrepreneur may be able to use this flexibility to his own advantage. Most notably, he might discriminate in favor of his own members—he could attempt to see that they have their requests processed more quickly, that they receive special attention, and, in general, that they find it easier to secure benefits. These amount to selective incentives which operate to increase the value of group membership. On the whole, then, by assuming an administrative role "on behalf of" the government, he can enhance both the political and nonpolitical bases of organizational maintenance.

The government is in a position to grant the group a third kind of favored status by legally requiring that potential members join the group if they are to qualify for certain benefits or opportunities. This is often referred to as coercion, but it is perhaps better viewed as a drastic restriction of viable alternatives. A worker, for example, may find that his legal options are to join a trade union or to look elsewhere for employment; since the latter may involve substantial costs, he may effectively have "no choice" but to join the union. From the entrepreneur's point of view, legal restrictions like this can be extremely rewarding. To begin with, group resources are swelled by the contributions of individuals who otherwise had insufficient incentives to join. Additionally, it is very inexpensive for the entrepreneur to tie in members when legal restrictions are working in his favor; he does not need to attract them with extra selective incentives or collective goods. Indeed, he should even be able to reduce his original incentive packages once the laws go into effect, since the members initially attracted by these inducements will similarly find their outside options constrained. Still another gain for the entrepreneur is that legal restrictions could enable him to establish a virtual monopoly over individuals in the economic sector. To the extent that he is able to do so, he will be in a good position to seek the other kinds of official favoritism discussed above—thereby further enhancing his prospects for group survival, political success, and material well-being.

Nongovernmental Groups and Organizations

Just as the entrepreneur has an incentive to use government to enhance his material position, so he also has an incentive to establish beneficial relationships with nongovernmental groups and organizations, ranging from voluntary associations to business corporations to nonprofit institutions. (For simplicity's sake, we can use the term *groups* in blanket reference to all these outsiders.) We have already considered one instance of such relationships in the analysis of selective incentives, noting that the entrepreneur can supply members with various inducements by relying upon outside business operations for their production and distribution. In this section, we will consider the more general coalitional options available to the entrepreneur, options which involve beneficial coordination between the entrepreneur and outside groups.

For any set of issues, the entrepreneur may seek out groups with similar goals in order to coordinate resources and activities. By this means, groups can pool their political contacts, channels of access, sources of information, and so on, as well as the talents and expertise of their personnel, to yield a greater fund of resources to draw upon, enlarged possibilities for the combination of resources into alternative strategies, and a division of labor and responsibility. In these ways, groups can eliminate duplication and direct their collective resources into the most productive channels for bringing success to their side of the issue. A united front may also have some political value independent of these considerations—public officials may view it as an important indicator of popular (or sectoral) support, or even consensus, and give their views more weight. When the costs of coordination are not too high, therefore, it is to the entrepreneur's advantage not to fight his political battles alone. Indeed, to take maximum advantage of outside support, he may find it instrumental to regularize coalitional relationships, developing patterns of communication and coordination that continue over time; in following this course, "ready-made" coalitions and strategies can be activated to deal with particular issues or problems when they arise, at virtually no additional expense to the coalition partners. Thus, in developing regular political relationships with outside groups, the entrepreneur can, in a sense, realize a double savings by gaining the benefits of combination and coordination while at the same time cutting the arrangement costs that such agreements entail.

The ultimate regularized coalition is the merger of two groups into one. Under the right conditions mergers will take place, but there are good reasons why this option will often be unattractive. First, a political coalition of two groups may be beneficial for one issue or issue area, or perhaps for several, but a permanent coalition could easily prove disadvantageous when the full range of political activities is considered. Second, the focus of each of the two entrepreneurs is on the maximization of his own surplus; and, in deciding whether to merge with another group, each must take into account all the political and nonpolitical implications, including (most importantly) questions of how authoritative decisions are to be made in the new group and how the general surplus is to be divided. Thus, while there may be certain political advantages to a merger, and while there may be other economies involved (e.g., in supplying selective incentives), a number of factors must fall into place for both entrepreneurs before a merger can occur.

In his coalitional relationships, the entrepreneur need not always seek out groups with goals similar to his own. He may sometimes seek out groups that are indifferent to the outcome or even on the opposite side of the question in an attempt to bring about a trade: their support on one issue for his support on another. By thus engaging in logrolling, groups can make mutually advantageous exchanges of support, accepting defeat or undertaking certain expenditures in one area in order to enhance the prospects of success in another. This is especially likely to occur when groups can play blocking or veto roles at various points in the political process, for then some kind of coordination can be a prerequisite for political gains on any side. To the degree that he does find logrolling beneficial, there are important implications for entrepreneurial "goals": the entrepreneur may concentrate considerable amounts of resources on the pursuit of goals which, in the absence of logrolling, would be very low on his list of priorities; and he may pursue goals that promise no immediate benefit for himself or for group members, and, in fact, are negative in their immediate effects. When logrolling is a part of the entrepreneur's political strategy, then, his behavior can prove a misleading indicator of his underlying interests.

In addition to these more ordinary interactions among groups, there is a special kind of coalitional relationship that should be discussed here: the entrepreneur may find that other groups are willing to subsidize his associational endeavors. Politically, outside groups may be interested in the survival of an association that can be counted upon to provide support, perhaps because of the entrepreneur's known goals, perhaps because he agrees to adopt certain goals in return for subsidization. This same strategy may be followed in order to assure that "hostile" entrepreneurs do not succeed in organizing the constituency. Subsidies may also be forthcoming for reasons that having nothing to do with politics; most obviously, outsiders might invest in the group enterprise in return for interest on the invested capital, a share of the profits, or a new market for certain goods and services. To the extent that outside groups find subsidization attractive, whatever their motivation, the entrepreneur need not cover costs in his exchange relationships with members. This can give him a great deal of flexibility, both in designing and experimenting with packages of selective incentives and in constructing an effective political structure. It also gives him important advantages over rivals seeking to organize the same sector and over nonsubsidized political opponents. If these advantages are used wisely over a sufficient period of time, the entrepreneur may be able to overcome the most serious obstacles to group formation and survival, consolidate his position, and become entirely independent of any subsidies whatever (including the "strings" that may go along with them). Clearly, then, the search for subsidies is an important entrepreneurial option, especially in the early period of group formation when the hazards and uncertainties are greatest.

For precisely the reasons outlined above, the entrepreneur has the converse option of being the subsidizer. Like the others, he may find it advantageous to provide financial assistance to groups in need of it—hoping to ensure political support, gain political influence, obtain a share of future profits, or otherwise leave himself in a better long-run material position.

Rival Entrepreneurs

Throughout this chapter, it has been imperative to refer to the importance of the rival entrepreneur. The basis of his importance is not difficult to discern: his goals—more accurately, those group-related goals that make him a rival—place him in competition with our focal entrepreneur; thus, because the nature of their pursuits brings them into conflict, the entrepreneur has an incentive to develop strategies that take rivals, or at least the threat of rivals, into account.

Though the implications can be significant, there is good reason for waiting until this point to discuss them in greater detail. We now have a basis for understanding a variety of factors internal and external to the group that have a bearing on its formation and maintenance and for understanding the ways that they enter into the strategic calculations of the entrepreneur. As a result, it is much easier to evaluate the nature of his relationship with rivals. This is especially important because there is a theoretical issue involved in this instance which, in the absence of the preceding discussion, may have led to some confusion about the role that rivals are to play.

The root of the problem is simply this. In conventional economic theories of entrepreneurial behavior, premised on assumptions of perfect knowledge and perfect competition, a greater than "normal" entrepreneurial surplus in one industry (sector) will stimulate additional entrepreneurs to enter until the level of surplus is reduced to "normal"; the myriad original entrepreneurs, behaving independently in a perfectly competitive economy, have neither the incentive nor the market power to retaliate. Thus, successful entrepreneurs will be beset by competition until the margins of their success are wiped out. Because our entrepreneurial model is in some ways closely analogous to models on which such conclusions are based, the implication seems clear enough: any successful group entrepreneur should find that rival groups spring up in his sector until his own surplus falls to some normal level.

In fact, however, we are not led to this same conclusion. On the contrary, there are a number of factors that operate to give the entrepreneur important advantages over his rivals. It is useful, therefore, to conduct the analysis below with two purposes in mind. The first, as with the other actors, is to suggest the nature of relationships between the entrepreneur and rivals. The second, an added dimension in this case, is to make clear why our expectations are not the same as those implied by well-known economic models.

We can simplify matters by looking at a hypothetical situation in which an entrepreneur who has established a successful, surplus-producing association in an economic sector is faced with challenges from rivals who are attempting to set up alternative associations in the same sector. Since the rivals are simply entrepreneurs who play special roles in the analysis, we will thus be examining a situation in which an established entrepreneur seeks to maintain his association in competition with unestablished entrepreneurs—and the analysis will demonstrate why it is that the established entrepreneur has substantial competitive advantages.

We can begin with a point that is at once obvious and quite important: in a world of bounded rationality, rivals may have little credible information about the level of the entrepreneur's surplus. Indeed, the likelihood of their having inadequate or inaccurate information is heightened by the fact that the entrepreneur has a degree of control over that information, as well as an incentive to suppress or distort it in such a way that rivals are discouraged.

Moreover, unlike their counterparts in a perfectly competitive economic world, rivals must compete with the entrepreneur for a limited number of potential members. As the proportion of organized individuals increases, and particularly as it approaches 100 percent, entrepreneurial rivalry approximates a zero-sum game—membership gains for one entrepreneur are membership losses for another. Thus, given whatever supply and demand factors prevail, there is a question in all sectors as to whether there are enough potential members to support more than one group (or more than two, more than three, etc.). In deciding whether to challenge an entrepreneur, then, a rival must reckon with the limited nature of the market; while a sector may appear to yield large surpluses in his absence, there is no guarantee that it will yield a large surplus, or any surplus at all, to an additional entrepreneur.

Another consideration is that, unlike the classic economic entrepreneurs, political entrepreneurs may derive their surpluses in various ways, not simply from the group surplus. As a result, the same group-related behaviors could yield substantially different overall surpluses for different entrepreneurs. In a business sector, for example, the entrepreneur may be a large firm that derives a surplus from both its business operations and its leadership of the group. In this case, the entrepreneur's lobbying activities may benefit him doubly—by tying in members who join for political reasons and by achieving goals of direct value to his business. An entrepreneur whose only source of surplus is the group surplus itself would thus have less to gain from the same behaviors. In general, some entrepreneurs will have an advantage over others, even if all provide identical benefits to members; and hence the mere existence of any large entrepreneurial surplus, even assuming its magnitude is known to potential rivals, is not sufficient to induce an organizational challenge by them. The nature of their goal structures must be taken into account as well.

While the above considerations are important, the most significant factors can be listed under the heading of market power. To the degree that the entrepreneur is established within a sector, he can fight back with weapons that are not available to the economic entrepreneur under perfect competition. These weapons may be so formidable as to virtually rule out any serious competition.

By means of his communications structure, the entrepreneur acquires critical information about members and potential members— who and where they are, what their interests are, the kinds of appeals they respond to, and so on. It is unlikely that rivals will possess such information, particularly in the early period of competition. Primarily for this reason, they cannot simply enter a sector to sell goods and services to potential members and expect to compete on the same footing as an established entrepreneur. Instead, they will commonly find themselves up against a competitor with an initial strategic advantage when it comes to identifying and contacting clients, offering them benefits that they value highly, making the right kinds of appeals, and, in general, securing members and contributions.

The entrepreneur may also have substantial control over certain kinds of information available *to* his members—on the uses of the group's services, on its goals, on its political successes, on economic conditions, and the like. By using information to influence member perceptions, the entrepreneur is in a position to influence market demand and, through it, the maintenance of the group. This is doubly disadvantageous to rivals. In the first place, they commonly cannot rely upon regular, systematic communication with a subset of the clientele unless and until they become established entrepreneurs themselves. Second, the entrepreneur's communications network represents an influence barrier that they must break through if they are to attract members away from him. Thus, by appropriately designing information available to members, the entrepreneur can use that resource to shield them from outside appeals and to make his own organization appear more attractive.

Another basis for entrepreneurial advantage is inherent in the selective incentive side of the administrative structure. First, the entrepreneur might eventually be able to supply members with selective incentives that are extremely expensive to produce, requiring considerable capital and high fixed costs. Competition on that basis would involve tremendous investment and risk for rivals, and the tendency would be for competition to diminish or for rivals to search for other benefits that might attract members away. In this way, the entrepreneur might be able to carve out an area of safety for himself—although he may forego this route for essentially the same reasons as his rivals. A second factor is the element of price control; in view of the types and prices of benefits offered by rivals, the entrepreneur can adjust the prices of his own selective incentives in order to compete most effectively. Following a classic monopolistic strategy, he can cut prices on those benefits offered by rivals, perhaps raising them on other benefits or simply absorbing short-run losses with an eye toward the long-run gains entailed by successful elimination of competition. The latter option is especially devastating when employed by an established entrepreneur with a sound material base upon which to draw; unsubsidized rivals may find their resources quickly drained if they insist on continuing the challenge. A third element is the variety of selective incentives that the entrepreneur can offer. By providing a number of different incentives for membership, the entrepreneur can make life difficult for rivals; the latter may be able to outdo the entrepreneur on one or more benefits (lower prices, higher quality), yet still be unsuccessful because of the other ways individuals benefit from membership in the original group. Finally, the established entrepreneur is in a position to see that members are supplied with special benefits that rivals, at least initially, cannot offer—namely, benefits deriving from member participation in meetings, conferences, committees, and the like. These are selective incentives that are available to individuals because they belong to an ongoing organization in which, over some period of time, member activities have been coordinated in ways beneficial to those involved.

The pursuit of collective goods is another means by which the entrepreneur can use his established position to gain an advantage over rivals. The entrepreneur can wield market power in respect to collective goods to the degree that he possesses the "requisites" of political success: access, contacts, expertise, information and resources, coalitional relationships, and so on. Since these commonly take time to develop, an established entrepreneur who has so elaborated his political structure is likely to face rivals who, in the early stages of competition, are at a disadvantage in pursuing political goals. In such cases, the entrepreneur is able to offer collective goods at a lower price because he is in a better position to achieve them efficiently. This holds most forcefully, of course, when the entrepreneur has successfully obtained favored status in the political process, for then he has a virtual monopoly over channels of access and the legitimate articulation of interests for his sector. Despite these potential advantages in the pursuit of collective goods, however, the entrepreneur is nevertheless vulnerable in another respect: rivals may be willing to pursue goals which, because of their net effects upon his own material surplus, the entrepreneur is not willing to pursue. This is likely to occur the greater the number and heterogeneity of politically motivated members and the more specialized the entrepreneur's own goal structure. As a result, even though rivals may initially be less efficient in their political activities, they may be able to attract away certain members by championing their specialized goals when the entrepreneur is reluctant to do so. On the collective good side of the equation, then, this tempers the entrepreneur's market power. Yet the important point is still that there is a basis for market power and entrepreneurial advantage. Once he decides which goals he wants to seek in the political system, the established entrepreneur has the potential for being a more effective participant than his unestablished rivals.

A final aspect of the entrepreneur's market power is his potential for relying upon outsiders for assistance. To the extent that he has developed mutual benefit relationships with governmental officials, for example, these officials may be willing to deny his rivals effective access to critical centers of decision making or to discriminate against them in others ways, in return for various kinds of benefits that the entrepreneur can offer. For similar reasons, nongovernmental groups and organizations may agree not to extend assistance to rivals or hinder their activities. This could prove critical when there are established outsiders who are initially willing to subsidize his rivals. Not only does subsidization give rivals an impetus to challenge him, but it also serves to undercut the various advantages noted above: a rival who need not cover costs is better able to weather price competition, to initiate costly recruitment and communication campaigns, to spend time and money developing political contacts, and, in general, to absorb substantial short-run losses in order ultimately to achieve a successful, surplus-producing association. To ward off this eventuality, the entrepreneur has a strong incentive to bargain with outsiders, offering them certain benefits or making certain promises in return for their nonsupport of rivals. Indeed, when subsidization is a generalized threat, established entrepreneurs from various sectors may even find it to their advantage to enter into "nonaggression pacts," the purpose of which is to solidify sector hegemony, maximize security, and minimize competition through a system of mutual understanding.

In sum, the established entrepreneur holds important trump cards that give him the edge from the outset in his competitive relationships with rivals.[6] Rivals are faced with a context in which the entrepreneur controls information about his surplus, the market of potential members is limited, some entrepreneurial goal structures are more likely than others to yield surpluses, and the established entrepreneur has several degrees of market power—in the form of information about the clientele, influence over member perceptions, the design and pricing of tangible benefits, the structuring of participation, the provision of collective goods, and the use of coalitional relationships with outsiders. These factors condition the nature of competition within an interest sector and, more fundamentally, determine whether there will be any effective competition at all. Because of them, rivals are not only less likely to be successful in their attempts to establish alternative groups, but they also have less incentive to initiate such challenges in the first place. For any given sector, therefore, these considerations work to inhibit the number of formal associations and to enhance the stability of existing ones.

We have focused here upon the situation in which an established entrepreneur is challenged by unestablished rivals. But the basic points can easily be generalized. When the entrepreneur is unestablished and competing with established rivals, the above roles are reversed and the latter entrepreneurs have the competitive advantages. When neither is established, it becomes a question of who can employ the various mechanisms of formation and maintenance to cultivate a position of advantage. And when both are established, they compete with each other in potential possession of the full arsenal of economic, political, and organizational weapons.

Any given entrepreneur, then, is most vulnerable during the period of group formation. If he is able to maintain the group over an appreciable length of time, certain advantages accrue to him by virtue of the resources and relationships that successful maintenance entails. These can be used to fortify and secure the group's position from challenges. Because this holds for all entrepreneurs, however, he faces his greatest threat from those who are already established; they, too, have privileged weapons to employ in the interests of their own survival.

Whatever his own position, the entrepreneur's task is to devise internal and environmental strategies that best take his rivals into account. The form of competition, or the prevention of competition, depends upon the prevailing context. With an eye to the power positions of the relevant participants, the entrepreneur may find that his best options lie in outright economic competition, in the use of governmental machinery and connections, in the assistance of outsiders, and, generally, in strategies designed to eliminate rivals. On the other hand, some contexts may encourage him to seek bargaining agreements directly with his rivals. He may find it possible to buy them off, for instance; or, if rivals are established and powerful, he may willingly enter into restraint-of-trade agreements in which the sector is consensually divided up among the participants. Though there is no universally best strategy, the basis for all of them can be found in the several factors we have discussed and in their variation. They shape the entrepreneur's relationships with his rivals, determining the elements of advantage and disadvantage that underlie competitive interactions.

Environmental Relationships:
Concluding Comments

This examination of the associational environment is premised upon a simplified depiction of environmental actors, and it is far from comprehensive. Nevertheless, it indicates very clearly that group formation and maintenance depend upon much more than the internal relationships linking the entrepreneur with his clientele. To be sure, outsiders generally have a different role to play in the entrepreneur's calculations. They are important actors primarily because they can facilitate or hinder those efforts of the entrepreneur that, in the final analysis, are directed at his own constituency. Thus, while he commonly does not extract contributions from outsiders, he is better able to profit from his clientele when he supplements his approach with advantageous external relationships.

In the entrepreneur's overall strategy of surplus maximization, then, an environmental strategy is an integral component with its own distinctive part to play. It is the full constellation of internal and external relationships that ultimately determines the group's survival, its economic and political activities, and the magnitude of the entrepreneur's surplus.

Conclusion

This chapter began by developing what we have called an entrepreneurial perspective on interest groups, which extends the analysis of the individual's calculus in chapter 2 by introducing a leadership component. At its simplest, this perspective allows an interest group to be approached in terms of exchange relationships between the entrepreneur and each potential member, with the former offering some combination of selective incentives and collective goods and the latter deciding on the basis of cost-benefit calculations whether to buy the benefits offered. An association comes into existence when potential members do, in fact, buy and thereby join the group. Unless subsidized from the outside, the association is maintained over time through the realization of net benefits by both the entrepreneur and the members.

For the most part, our efforts here have been devoted to filling in and elaborating upon this simple framework. This has been carried out by structuring the analysis around major entrepreneurial strategies of formation and maintenance: a communications strategy for obtaining information and using it to best advantage, an administrative strategy for the provision of selective incentives, an administrative strategy for the pursuit of collective goods, a bargaining strategy to encourage coordinated contributions toward political goals, and an environmental strategy to establish beneficial relationships with outsiders. In each case, the analysis unfolds through an examination of the strategic options available to the entrepreneur—alternative courses of action that take on significance in light of our prior assumptions about participants and in light of the organizational and environmental settings in which they may find themselves. The entrepreneur's task is to integrate these options in such a way that his resources are most beneficially allocated among them.

The substance of the analysis need not be summarized. One important point, however, can be stressed in conclusion: there is nothing here to suggest that economic interest groups are *primarily* political organizations. For his part, the entrepreneur derives a surplus by choosing among and integrating a variety of organizational options, only some of which are political. For their part, members may join, contribute, and participate for reasons that have nothing whatever to do with the group's political goals or activities. In the internal life of an economic interest group, the role of politics is problematical, its importance varying with a host of factors bearing on the incentives of individuals and the context in which they make their decisions.

Four

Internal Politics

For most students of politics, the major value of a theory of interest groups derives from what it can say about group goals and, in particular, how they are formulated as a function of member goals. This is understandable, given the perspectives from which interest groups are commonly viewed. Whether they are seen as active and sometimes powerful actors in the political system, as interest articulators, as legitimate (or illegitimate) participants in the democratic process, as agencies of representation, or as mediators between the social and political systems, the salient characteristic of interest groups is that they pursue goals that are presumed to stand in some relation to member goals.

From the traditional pluralist standpoint, the nature of this connection is easy to understand. Because members are presumed to join and quit on the basis of their agreement with group goals, the pluralist logic of membership ensures that group goals will reflect member preferences. Internal political processes are not of consequence in this respect, since, regardless of how group goals may change over time, member turnover (the exit of dissenters, the recruitment of supporters) will guarantee the group's representativeness in the long run. From our analysis of the individual's calculus, however, these conclusions certainly do not follow. Members may join and quit for a variety of reasons that have nothing to do with politics, and it is possible for groups to be large and prosperous even if most members disagree with group policy. The connection between group goals and member preferences remains an important question—one that can only be answered by looking inside the organization itself and asking how its goals are formulated. To understand the nature of group representation, we must understand the nature of internal politics generally.[1]

The By-Product Theory

Olson does not attempt to analyze internal politics. He does, however, contribute to an understanding of group goals by means of his "by-product theory of large pressure groups." We can begin our examination of internal politics by briefly taking a look at what the by-product theory is and how it is derived.[2]

The by-product theory is not a theory in and of itself, but is derived from Olson's basic model. It strictly applies only to what Olson calls a "latent" group, a group in which there are no Large Members and which is too large for any successful bargaining arrangements to take place. Very simply, the essence of the theory is as follows: (a) members of latent groups can only be induced to join through the operation of selective incentives, yet (b) the sale of selective incentives yields a surplus (in successful groups) that can be used by group leaders for lobbying and other expenditures on collective goods; it follows that (c) these political activities are by-products of the operation of selective incentives—they have nothing to do with why members join, but are made possible because members join; therefore (d) the leaders of latent groups may pursue any collective goods they wish without fear of losing member "support," since contributions are independent of political considerations.[3]

What the by-product theory asserts, in other words, is a disjunction between member goals and group goals. There is no necessary connection between the two in latent groups. As long as members are tied into the group by means of selective incentives, it is to their advantage to continue contributing even if they disagree with associational policy and even if the group is entirely unsuccessful in achieving goals they agree with. The leadership can pursue an independent course without fear of losing either members or their contributions and is set free of member pressure in respect to political issues and activities.

While Olson does not do so, it is possible to develop a more general by-product theory applicable to all economic groups. The above analysis need only be supplemented by the following: when there is at least one Large Member, or when bargaining is successful, the model implies that (*a*) one or more Large Members, or a set of cooperating individuals, have joined wholly or partially because of collective goods; (*b*) their membership in the group and, thus, their support in the form of contributions depend upon whether those collective goods are provided; and therefore (*c*) group leaders must take action to see that these goods are supplied or risk losing these members and their contributions; assuming that leaders want to avoid these consequences, it follows that (*d*) in the pursuit of at least some collective goods, leaders will have an incentive to represent the interests of these people, especially when they make substantial contributions.

When the by-product theory is supplemented in this way, then, Olson's model has implications for goal formulation in material associations generally. Whatever the group, members who join for selective incentives are in the weakest political position; group leaders are not induced to represent their interests because they will continue to contribute anyway, regardless of the group's policies and activities. The only members that leaders have an incentive to represent are those that join out of an interest in collective goods, for their contributions are rationally contingent upon political considerations. These individuals, who may be Large Members or cooperating Small Members, are thus the only ones in a position to influence associational policy. They are, in other words, the politically important members of the association.

An Entrepreneurial Perspective
on Internal Politics

The by-product theory is based on a highly rarified depiction of the internal associational context. Not only is there no explicit recognition of leadership, but no attention is paid to the various factors involved in formation and maintenance, nor to the salience of external actors; and, not least, information is assumed to be perfect. These constrain what the by-product theory has to say about internal politics.

·From an entrepreneurial perspective, internal politics revolves around the entrepreneur. This follows from the fact that the entrepreneur controls group policy and, in particular, controls the group revenues—the surplus (if any) as well as the resources allocated toward the production of a surplus. It is he who ultimately decides what group policies will be, how revenues will be spent, and who is to have access to them. His decisions then determine the relative emphasis upon political and nonpolitical goods and services, the nature of political goals, the methods of seeking such goals, and so on. If individuals within the group are to play a role in determining the group's policies, they must center their efforts on the entrepreneur. Somehow, they must prevail upon him to make choices that they feel are in their own best interests.

Given this perspective, the fundamental question of internal politics becomes How can individuals have an effect on the entrepreneur's policy decisons? In part, an answer lies with the entrepreneur's goal of surplus-maximization. From this we know that the formation, maintenance, and political activities of the group are merely his instruments for material gain. He is not in business to represent individuals, to respond to their specialized interests, or to provide them with channels of political access. He is in business for himself only and will disregard individual policy preferences whenever he finds it advantageous to do so. On the other hand, just as he will disregard individual preferences in some cases, he will also respond to their preferences if he expects to be better off as a result. The entrepreneur is not automatically unresponsive simply because he is "selfishly" interested in material gain. Rather, he is selectively responsive, with his pattern of selection determined by economic costs and benefits.

This is the key to individual policy roles: in order to play a role in internal decision making, an individual must be able to make it worth the entrepreneur's while to respond. And this can be brought about only after two basic prerequisites have been met. First, the entrepreneur must perceive that the individual is in a position to have an effect on his material surplus; and second, the entrepreneur must perceive that this effect is contingent upon his responding to individual preferences in certain ways. Once these are satisfied, anyone, whether he is inside or outside the group, can influence the entrepreneur through the operation of anything of material value. The greater the contingent value, the greater the entrepreneur's incentive to respond.

The task at this point is to extend these basic conclusions about internal politics into a more elaborate analysis that builds upon the work of past chapters. This will be carried out with the help of three simplifications. First, the association will be viewed as a bargaining arena consisting of all participants, including staff personnel and outsiders, and each individual will be viewed as having a bargaining position vis-à-vis the entrepreneur. The analysis will then focus on the nature and determinants of the bargaining positions of various participants. The use of bargaining terminology, however, does not mean that all individuals actually engage in bargaining interactions, that they calculate strategically in their decision to join, or even that they communicate any of their preferences to the entrepreneur. When we say that an individual has a bargaining position, we mean that there is some identifiable basis on which he *could* bargain with the entrepreneur over group policy. We are really talking about potential sources of influence.

Second, we will separately consider the bargaining positions available to three classes of participants—members, staff personnel, and outsiders. Because we are primarily concerned with the connection between group goals and member preferences, however, more emphasis will be placed on the membership itself and on the determinants of member bargaining positions. It is here that the third structuring element is helpful: we will recognize five major sources of bargaining strength potentially available to members for use in internal politics. It is instructive to think of these as deriving from roles that a member might occupy as an individual contributor, a supplier of services, a rival entrepreneur, a subgroup member, or a subgroup leader. Since all group members are individual contributors, it is useful to take contributions as the most basic determinant of bargaining strength. The other roles reflect important factors that give members added bases for influence.

Finally, it should be stressed that this chapter's analysis will be bound inextricably with all aspects of the work that has gone before. We will find, above all, that processes of internal politics are closely tied up with processes of organizational formation and maintenance, and it will quickly become clear that a prior analysis of formation and maintenance is necessary for an adequate understanding of internal politics.

Members

Individual Contributors

Contributions can yield power only if the entrepreneur believes they are contingent upon the political decisions he makes. Assuming the individual's contributions are indeed seen as contingent, they can be employed in two ways, as sanctions and as rewards. While these can be construed as two sides of the same coin—sanctions being negative rewards, rewards being negative sanctions—it is useful to treat them differently. In one case, the individual has already contributed a certain amount, he has a stake in the presumed goals of the group, and he can threaten to withdraw some of his material support if the entrepreneur does not perform as expected. This is a threatened sanction, implying a loss for the entrepreneur. In the second instance, the individual is simply offering to contribute a certain amount if the entrepreneur promises to adopt new or supplementary policies justifying the contribution. This is a reward, implying an element of gain for the entrepreneur should he agree to certain changes or additions.

We can begin by taking a look at all individuals who have been induced to make contributions to the group, and ask What sanctions are available to them as a result? For any given person, the answer depends upon whether some portion of his contribution is motivated by political considerations and upon the amount of the contingent portion—and, importantly, we know that all contributors are not equal in these respects. In the first place, when we consider those persons whose contributions are at least partially political, it is clear that there may be great disparities in the amounts they have an incentive to employ in sanctioning the entrepreneur. The contingent amount wielded by one member may far exceed the amount wielded by another. In the second place, only certain individuals can claim that any part of their total contribution derives from political inducements anyway, and they are the only ones who have an incentive to withhold financial support or leave the group for political reasons. Because they perceive the economic returns from their contributions as fluctuating with the entrepreneur's political choices, their gains from contributing could easily diminish or disappear should the entrepreneur adopt undesirable goals, and they would have every incentive to follow through on the sanctions they threaten. This is not true for the remaining members, who are simply dues-payers offering their contributions in exchange for selective incentives. For these individuals, the direct benefits of membership outweigh the dues costs, independent of group goals, and they would suffer a net loss were they to drop out (or pay less than dues) in response to the entrepreneur's political choices. Thus, while some of these members might threaten to use their contributions as sanctions, they have an economic incentive not to follow through on that threat.

The pattern of stratification within the group, then, is shaped by the underlying factors that explain why and how much individuals will contribute. And these, of course, are the same factors that played central roles in the analysis of the individual's calculus in chapter two.

Size. Because a member's economic size is an objective measure of how much he stands to gain from the collective good, both the contingency and amount of contributions should vary positively with size. The larger a member is, the stronger his bargaining position is likely to be.

Imperfect information. Generally speaking, the contingency and amount of contributions vary with certain kinds of member estimates—higher estimates of benefits, lower estimates of costs, and lower estimates of the level of supply. These influences do not erase the importance of economic size, since a member's estimates should tend to reflect his actual size in some systematic fashion. But they do mediate and qualify the impact of size on member bargaining positions, and this has implications for internal politics. The most important implication by far is that smaller members, acting on the basis of certain kinds of estimates, may rationally make their contributions contingent upon politics, and thus may drop out or vary their contributions in response to (or anticipation of) entrepreneurial choices. Precisely because they are misinformed in certain ways, they have an economic basis for affecting group policy.

Selective incentives. Members of all sizes find that their bargaining positions, and thus their bases for participating effectively in internal politics, are shaped by the value of selective incentives. Individuals joining for selective incentives find themselves tied into the group with no sanctions to wield. Individuals joining at least partially for political reasons find that they have nonpolitical inducements for staying in the group and for maintaining their contributions at a given level. Overall, for any member: when selective incentives are entered into cost-benefit calculations they function as a kind of cement that keeps individuals and their contributions within the group, lowering sanctions available for political purposes.

Bargaining. When individuals are able to coordinate their decisions, the contingency and amount of their contributions will be affected, and so will their bargaining positions. This is most likely to occur in small groups, in subgroups of larger associations, and among larger members—although smaller members, too, may be able to augment their bargaining positions in this way. (This is a special kind of power base, and it will be given more detailed consideration under the heading "Subgroup Members and Subgroup Leaders.")

Given this analysis of the sanctioning power available to contributors, it is a relatively easy matter to consider the other side of the coin, rewarding power. It is easy because essentially the same factors are involved; the individual still derives bargaining strength from the contingency and amount of his (proposed) contribution, which, in turn, depend upon size, information, selective incentives, and coordination with others. The difference lies with group goals. Sanctioning power comes out of a situation in which individuals have joined on the basis of prevailing group goals and propose to decrease their contributions in response to undesirable goal changes. Rewarding power, on the other hand, derives from a situation in which individuals propose to increase their level of contributions if new or supplementary goals are adopted. In essence, sanctioning power operates to maintain the status quo, while rewarding power operates to change it.

Because both of these make up an individual's bargaining position, it is not enough to know how incentives are structured with respect to prevailing group goals. Even if the latter remain constant, individual bargaining positions will vary over time as new political issues emerge. An individual who has little interest in prevailing group goals, for example, may, at the same time, have a stake in a newly salient political issue. Thus, while he possesses no sanctions to wield in internal politics, he may have a degree of rewarding power that can be employed to change or expand the group's goals. Similarly, a larger member may wield severe sanctions on the basis of prevailing goals, but find that he has only weak rewarding power with reference to certain types of new issues.

It is misleading, then, to think of an individual as having *a* bargaining position or to think of the membership as rigidly stratified into those who have influence and those who do not. Both individual bargaining positions and the overall pattern of stratification can change with internal variations in size, information, selective incentives, and bargaining, and they can also change as political issues rise and fall in salience. All of these factors can produce a degree of fluidity in internal politics.

These are important points. Nevertheless, they do not imply that fluidity is the rule or even of real significance for the ordinary group, at least in the short run. It is a theoretical possibility which can occur if circumstances permit; but circumstances may often dictate otherwise. Most obviously, there is every reason to believe that larger members will tend to maintain more or less permanent bargaining advantages over smaller members. Large business corporations and commercial farms, for instance, are characteristically affected by a wider range of issues, due to the functional and geographical scope of their operations; and they should typically have a greater economic stake in issue outcomes, due to the dollar volume of their transactions. Accordingly, they are more likely to make contingent contributions than smaller members and to contribute greater amounts. While these bargaining advantages may be weakened (or strengthened) by variations in other factors, they are nonetheless a structuring element that lends a pattern to internal politics. A balanced perspective on internal politics must recognize both the structure and the fluidity of bargaining positions.

Suppliers of Services

The individual can gain a degree of leverage when he is able to perform valuable services. The explanation is by now familiar. On the one hand, an individual who is supplying services can threaten to withdraw some of these values if the entrepreneur fails to respond to his policy preferences. And, on the other hand, an individual who is in a position to perform certain services can offer them to the entrepreneur in return for decision-making advantages. Thus, services, like contributions, can be a source of sanctions and rewards to be employed in internal politics.

Just how much they add to an individual's bargaining position depends upon their value, of course, but also upon two basic considerations bearing on their contingency. First, can the entrepreneur secure these same services elsewhere? If he cannot, then the total value of services can be made contingent upon his responding, and the individual's rewards and sanctions take on their full value. If he can, however, then the individual's ability to extract concessions is obviously limited; the entrepreneur has other means of obtaining these same values, and he will make concessions to the individual only up to the point where it becomes profitable to purchase these services from someone else.

Second, to what extent does the individual have an incentive to vary his performance of services in response to the entrepreneur's political choices? If the individual is a communications middleman, for instance, and performs these services because of economic gains, opportunities for making contacts, and the like, then he will lose these benefits if he stops operating as a middleman. Although he may control services of value to the entrepreneur, then, he may have difficulty using these for bargaining purposes because, group policy aside, he has an economic incentive to continue performing them anyway. To gain maximum bargaining advantage from the performance of services, his performance incentives should be connected to group policy—so that, should the entrepreneur adopt undesired policies, the individual would have less to gain from the continued performance of services. In its most extreme form, this would be the case if the individual gains nothing from the performance process itself, but engages in these activities only because he expects political concessions from the entrepreneur in return; he would then have every incentive to vary his level of performance depending upon the expected political payment.

This connection between performance inducements and group policy is not absolutely necessary, though, and the individual may also have an incentive to vary his performance even if he gains a great deal from the performance process itself, independent of politics. This can occur if he is able to continue engaging in the same general kinds of service activities that generate benefits for him, but to vary the way in which he performs the services. A communications middleman could continue to carry out communications activities with the same set of members and with the same frequency, for example, but deviate from entrepreneurial directives by distorting messages and introducing negative information about the entrepreneur. Without really altering the values generated for himself, then, he might be able to lower substantially the values produced for the entrepreneur. Because this strategy can be used for greater influence (and greater expected gains) in internal politics, he may easily have an incentive to vary his performance along these lines—even though his basic inducements for participating may not be at all political.

In order to gain a solid influence position from services, then, an individual must have the incentive to vary his performance with entrepreneurial responsiveness, and he must control values that are not easily available elsewhere. Within these parameters, there are any number of services a member may employ for influence purposes. Anything of material value will do, although the net value of a service may vary over time, and different contexts may call for special kinds of services. The services below illustrate some of the activities in which a member might be engaged and the kinds of resources he might draw upon.

Obviously enough by this point, he might serve as a communications middleman, transmitting information from the entrepreneur to members, or, perhaps, collecting information from or about members and transmitting it to the entrepreneur. From the entrepreneur's perspective, such services can be of substantial value in identifying and locating clients, acquainting them with the benefits of membership, shaping their preferences, adapting organizational benefits to changing member needs, and so on—all of which are basic to the survival and prosperity of the association. Moreover, the middleman may augment these informational functions by taking an active part in recruiting members, since he is especially well situated for doing so. Whatever his chosen tasks, the middleman's ability to put them to use in internal politics depends upon his success at carving out a distinctive area of competence, so that the entrepreneur must turn to him if he wants the services performed. This may be accomplished over time by building up a network of contacts, developing a close acquaintance with clients and their needs, and becoming an integral component of the communications process. Middlemen who are able to establish themselves in this manner may be difficult to replace or circumvent, at least in the short run. They are also in a position to retaliate against the entrepreneur by transmitting unfavorable information to clients, an especially damaging prospect if much information is commonly channeled along this route.

An individual may derive bargaining strength from the possession of specialized information or skills. He may, for instance, be able to obtain accurate, detailed, comprehensive information about aspects of the economy or the political system, information that could help the entrepreneur in both his internal and external relationships. He might also have an area of expertise—law, statistics, economics, or some other technical area—in which advice or analysis might be sought. Or he may possess valuable organizational experience, useful to the entrepreneur in structuring the association, designing packages of benefits, or retaining members. These are resources that individuals can make available to the entrepreneur at a price—decision-making responsiveness.

Individuals may supplement their bargaining positions through services of a political nature. Some may have achieved access to certain decision-making arenas in government, giving them a capacity to facilitate the entrepreneur's political activities. Others may have contacts with outsiders, whether governmental or nongovernmental, whose assistance can prove valuable in attaining desired ends. Still others may possess resources because their opinions are given weight by governmental officials. Depending upon the issues and arenas involved, these members may be able to use their pivotal positions to facilitate the entrepreneur's political success and to extract concessions from him in exchange. Similarly, they may be able to inflict costs on the entrepreneur who fails to respond—not simply by refusing to cooperate, but by purposely working at cross-purposes to him, using environmental connections to frustrate his efforts and inhibit his chances of success.

By being in a position to perform various services, then, members can augment their bargaining strengths. This is one way that smaller members can gain a measure of influence in internal politics, even if their contributions give them no initial sanctions or rewards with which to work. In principle, services could operate as an equalizing force. Yet this seems unlikely. In the first place, larger members can draw upon services to enhance their strengths still further. And, empirically, larger members are usually in a better position to do so. Big corporations, for example, tend to have more extensive contacts with government and other outsiders, better information, their own experts and research personnel, and so on. Thus, it is likely that, while this source of strength is in principle available to all members, it actually operates to emphasize any existing "influence gap" that separates the large and the small.

Rival Entrepreneurs within the Group

Another role available to the individual member is that of the rival entrepreneur, through which he can attempt to exact benefits from the entrepreneur by threatening to set up an alternative group. The sanctioning power here could be substantial, implying for the entrepreneur a loss of members and funds, a loss of potential clients, a decline in political influence, and threats to group maintenance, among other things. The more credible a rival's threats, and the greater the material damage implied by his carrying them out, the stronger his bargaining position. For the entrepreneur, then, a central question becomes Is the rival in a position to supply selective incentives and collective goods, and can he do so in such a way that the new group will attract the contributions sufficient for maintenance?

In the last chapter we discussed the entrepreneur's strategic considerations with respect to rivals who are outside the group and found that the established entrepreneur has important advantages over them in organizational competition. Were we to review the details of that analysis, it would be clear that he possesses similar advantages over those insiders who play the rival role; his control over information, market power, structured relationships with outsiders, and other resources that go along with "being established" give him significant means of dealing with organizational threats, whether they come from within or without.

In certain respects, however, inside rivals are actually in a better position to challenge the entrepreneur than outside rivals are. The entrepreneur will tend to have fewer inherent advantages over them, and, as a result, will tend to be more vulnerable to threats from the inside. Some of the reasons for this can be briefly suggested.

An insider, by virtue of his activities in group affairs, is better able to gain information about the entrepreneurial surplus and thus about the potential rewards involved in starting a new group.

By participating in the communications structure, an individual can gain valuable information on the identity, location, and interests of members and potential members. He can thereby determine to whom his appeals should be made, what benefits they desire, and what appeals are likely to work.

Participation in the communications structure also gives him an opportunity to shape the information going to members. This may mean altering or selectively filtering entrepreneurial communications, introducing unfavorable information about the established group, or introducing favorable information about a possible new group. He can thus attempt to disrupt entrepreneurial efforts to influence individual perceptions, while at the same time undertaking his own efforts at influence.

Knowledge of interaction networks within the membership may allow him to offer a new group in which beneficial patterns of interaction are maintained. Entire subgroups can be appealed to on this basis, for example, because their wholesale shift in group membership would preserve this source of member benefits. Outside rivals may, of course, adopt the same strategy, but they are less likely to have the necessary information on interactions internal to the group.

By participating in group-related political activities, the inside rival can develop the contacts, access, knowledge, and skills that facilitate success on precisely the types of goals generally desired by members. Political activity thus leads to the acquisition of resources, which can then be employed in the construction of an alternative group.

By taking part in internal politics, perhaps in conjunction with communications activities, the rival can come to understand the nature of political divisions within the group and can champion those who are disaffected with entrepreneurial policies, particularly large contributors (or potential large contributors).

In these and other ways, a rival who is inside the group is in a better strategic position than one who is not. But this does not necessarily mean that the entrepreneur is seriously threatened by rivals, for he still has major weapons to use in combatting them. Furthermore, he always has the option of simply expelling rivals from the group, forcing them to operate (if at all) as outsiders. Indeed, having perceived that a member is emerging as a rival, the entrepreneur may choose to expel him well before he has a chance to acquire dangerous levels of information, knowledge, skills, or contacts.

These last points, together with the earlier analysis, tell us something about which members are most likely to endure as inside rivals and to use this role for influence purposes. In the first place, all members are not equal in respect to the resources and incentives necessary—those who perform communications or political services have access to important resources; larger members are more likely than smaller members to be suppliers to these services and to possess resources of their own; and larger members stand to gain a greater surplus from entrepreneurial activities. Thus, larger members, and especially disaffected larger members, are more likely to emerge as inside rivals. In the second place, the entrepreneur will tend not to expel rivals to the extent that they are valuable members of the group—and larger members who perform services are likely to be the most valuable of all. His gains from expelling them may be far overshadowed by the concomitant losses of contributions and services. At any rate, he still has an arsenal of weapons at his disposal that can be employed to minimize a rival's threats, so expulsion must be considered the extreme option.

In sum, the rival entrepreneur is one role an individual may be able to use in enhancing his bargaining position, and insiders are in a better strategic situation than outsiders. For most members, though, this role probably is not a feasible source of bargaining strength. On the one hand, the established entrepreneur has economic, political, and organizational resources that inhibit competition and, on the other hand, only members who are already strong (due to contributions, services) can generally emerge as effective challengers. Thus, the role of rival entrepreneur, which is a possible source of supplementary strength for any member, tends to reinforce the "influence gap" between the strong and the weak.

Subgroup Members and
Subgroup Leaders

While the analysis so far has tended to treat the membership as atomized, we have allowed for the existence of member subgroups and have suggested several ways in which they might prove theoretically important—for example, by affecting the level of contributions (through bargaining) and by facilitating communications. We can now give more detailed attention to subgroup phenomena, asking how members can assert themselves collectively rather than individually in their relations with the entrepreneur.

A subgroup is a set of individuals whose interactions are regularized or coordinated. These interactions must (by assumption) be motivated by economic self-interest: members participate in patterned relationships, or agree to coordinate their actions with others, because they find it economically worthwhile to do so. There are no social incentives operating, no peer-group pressures, no feelings of responsibility or obligation. There are, however, a number of different economic bases on which individuals may interact, giving rise to qualitatively different kinds of subgroups. Subgroup relationships may be motivated, for instance, by agreement on general political goals, the exchange of information, the discussion of common problems, or the coordination of political tactics or resources.

There are also various ways in which subgroups can emerge. First, regularized interactions may exist prior to group membership and persist after individuals join, as when a formal unit of one association transfers into a new one. Second, subgroups may be created by the entrepreneur. In his efforts to increase the level of contributions, for example, he may create subgroups by encouraging bargaining relationships among contributors; and, in his efforts to provide selective incentives, he may set up subgroups for the exchange of information and the discussion of common problems. Third, in view of the potential benefits of subgroup formation, individual members may willingly undertake the structuring of interactions and incentives. Certain members are, of course, in better positions than others to perform these functions successfully, or even to recognize the opportunities for beneficial organization, since information, contacts, and other resources are unequally distributed. Communications middlemen are in highly favorable positions, as are members who participate actively in other ways. Fourth, in some cases there is no single organizing force to explain the existence of a subgroup; it simply emerges over time as members find, in incremental fashion, that certain kinds of interactions are materially beneficial and could be successfully maintained.

Many of these subgroups may be constructed on bases that are entirely nonpolitical. But once interactions among individuals have been regularized, whatever the motivations of participants and organizers, there always exists a potential for political coordination. This is because interaction brings people into contact, increases information about mutual interests and pursuits, and facilitates the development of trust—all of which can lead to various kinds of concerted action, including political action. What this means, then, is that nonpolitical subgroups—e.g., those based upon the exchange of economic information—represent contexts of interaction which, under the right circumstances, can give rise to political subgroups. This is especially interesting when we consider its consequences in light of the entrepreneur's strategies of formation and maintenance; for when he structures member participation, when he encourages members to perform political functions that he finds valuable, and when he sets up communications networks, he may inadvertently be laying the basis for the eventual emergence of political subgroups. The very structuring mechanisms that enhance his ability to maintain the association may give rise over time to subgroups that challenge his decisions about group policies.

While politically oriented subgroups can emerge in various ways, the question remains: How are they able to influence entrepreneurial decisions? To some extent, subgroups derive influence in the same ways that individuals do. It all depends upon the rewards and sanctions available to them. Like individuals, they can (collectively) manipulate their contributions and services, act as rival entrepreneurs, or threaten to drop out of the group. Yet subgroups are also special participants in internal politics. In one sense, they are special because they are favored; not only can they control greater amounts of contingent resources, but there are also certain kinds of rewards and sanctions available to them that are not at the same time available to isolated individuals. In quite another sense, though, subgroups are special because they are disadvantaged; they are plagued by problems with which individuals do not have to cope. These points of similarity and contrast are clarified when we consider more specifically what factors underly the bargaining positions of subgroups.

Cohesion. This is the factor of primary importance, since it is agreement among individuals that makes concerted action possible in the first place. However, cohesion is a variable characteristic, both in respect to the number of matters on which members agree and, perhaps more importantly, in respect to the solidarity of their agreement, where the latter is a measure of the extent to which members are willing to maintain their arrangement despite the presence of threats, costs, and other inducements to break away. The more cohesive the subgroup, the greater its ability to mobilize and integrate member resources and the greater its basis for political success within the group.

It is precisely the pivotal role of cohesion, however, that throws up obstacles to effective subgroup participation in internal politics, for cohesion is inherently difficult to achieve in a material association. There are two main reasons for this. The first is that the cementing and behavior-orienting functions of social norms and pressures, loyalty, friendship, obligation, ideology, and other nonmaterial incentives are not operating; there can be no noneconomic basis on which the subgroup is "knit together," shielding it from the fragmenting effects of purely economic self-interests. The second reason is that, once again, the free-rider incentive inhibits individuals from pursuing their common interests through collective action. For the subgroup just as for the association, the economically self-interested member will have an incentive to make others pay the costs of achieving the agreed-upon goal—since, if they are the ones who do the cooperating, he will get the benefits anyway. As a result, members are less likely to enter into agreements with others and, even if they do, they are more likely to abandon their participation when faced with threats and costs.

These obstacles need not be prohibitive. In very small subgroups, of course, a clear recognition of mutual dependence and the development of familiarity and trust can enhance the likelihood of coordinated action. But there is hope even for larger subgroups. Cohesion may be promoted by enterprising action on the part of individuals within the subgroup. Those in favorable communications positions, for instance, may be able to use their information about members (e.g., by bringing the right people together at the right time), or their control over information to members (by shaping their perceptions), to construct a basis for agreement. Larger members may stand to gain so much from coordinated action that they are willing to make side-payments to others in exchange for agreement—which is one way that selective incentives may operate in the subgroup. And rival entrepreneurs may be able to stimulate cohesion by offering realistic opportunities for a new group, should things "go wrong" in internal politics. Thus, by employing the resources and skills available to them, active members of the subgroup may be able to deal with obstacles to cohesion and facilitate agreement.

Another cause for hope is that the individual costs of agreement, the costs of holding up one's part of the bargain, may be extremely low in relation to the potential benefits. This is likely to occur when members agree to offer or withhold certain services that the entrepreneur needs, their verbal support in governmental arenas, or their cooperation in other ways. When agreement requires so little from the individual and when the strategy appears promising, he may willingly consent. When these approaches are called for, then, larger subgroups will have some basis for playing a role in group decision making.

On balance, however, cohesion must be viewed as a real and continuing problem. While there are ways that some degree of cohesion can be established, they only partially overcome the obstacles to collective action and are likely to work most effectively in small subgroups. For all subgroups, though, the struggle to establish cohesive agreement is the foundation of their political position within the association. In shaping the role of subgroups in internal politics, cohesion is at once the key to power and the major stumbling block.

Financial significance. When individuals agree to increase or decrease their contributions in a coordinated fashion, the subgroup's bargaining position is clearly augmented. This is most easily brought about when members have already joined for political reasons. But even members joining for selective incentives may sometimes find, after bargaining with others, that they have an incentive to make their contributions contingent. A number of "independently nonpolitical" members, for example, may find it rational to pool their resources, make them contingent upon group policy, and bargain as though they collectively constitute a larger member—once they agree to coordinate their decisions in certain ways. In this fashion, a subgroup may threaten sanctions and offer rewards when it is irrational for any individual to do so alone. Such outcomes hinge, of course, on solutions to the kinds of cohesion problems discussed above.

Assuming cohesion is sufficiently strong, the subgroup gains leverage with the amount of contributions it controls; and its strength is therefore enhanced as the size of the subgroup increases, as the number of larger members increases, and as certain resources (like control over information) can be applied in structuring individual incentives. In the limit, a subgroup can be so important financially that a calculated decrease in contributions, or, indeed, its secession from the association, renders the established group unable to cover the costs of maintenance, leading to organizational failure. In cases approaching this limit, the subgroup's position may be strong enough to enable it to gain control of the association's policies in certain issue areas. And even when the limit is not closely approached, threats and rewards may give the entrepreneur adequate incentive to respond.

Control of services. Subgroups can augment their bargaining strength by manipulating services of value to the entrepreneur. When its members play important communications roles, when they control contacts, access, expertise, and skills, or when they are instrumental on the selective incentive side of the organization—then by pooling these services and by formulating rewards and sanctions on the basis of their combined value, subgroups can attempt to assert influence. In this respect, subgroups differ from individual participants because they have a greater pool of resources upon which to draw.

The truly distinctive characteristic of subgroups is that their members need not simply pool their services, but they may also coordinate and integrate them, producing a whole that is more valuable than the sum of its parts. The communications efforts of single individuals can be transformed into the systematic recruitment of new members. Individual contacts, information, and skills can become integrated lobbying campaigns. Conversely, individuals may agree not to cooperate with entrepreneurial efforts to get them to participate in various ways, perhaps leading to concerted acts designed to frustrate or defeat his purposes.

Along these same lines, a special resource that subgroups can trade upon is their representativeness—for this characteristic is commonly given substantial weight by public officials in democratic systems. If a subgroup can claim to represent a certain kind of economic agent, a certain kind of member, or perhaps a cross section of the associational membership, its support or opposition on a political issue may prove crucial to entrepreneurial success. By simply aggregating opinions, a resource of very low cost to individuals, a subgroup can wield rewards or sanctions in internal politics.

As far as the employment of services is concerned, then, the subgroup has a range of possible options. What is especially interesting about them is that, generally speaking, they do not require much on the part of the individual. Even if members are not willing to manipulate their financial contributions in any way, they may agree to undertake certain low-cost acts, from signing a petition to facilitating political access, as part of an integrated subgroup strategy.

Ease of secession. The threat of secession is any group's cardinal bargaining chip because it involves multiple and potentially serious losses for the entrepreneur. Should a subgroup actually withdraw, he loses all of their contributions and services, he loses a degree of representativeness in his political activities, and he may subsequently be faced by an augmented opposition that makes representational claims of its own. Yet the threat is also restricted in its credibility, since, for most members, the incentives to withdraw may be difficult to bring about.

The problem, at bottom, is that individuals belong to the association because they are obtaining (or expect to obtain) net benefits on the exchange. While they may collectively threaten to drop out in response to a policy dispute, each individual will find that he loses these benefits if he follows through on that threat. This will have little effect on members who join for policy reasons, since policy changes can lead to an evaporation of their benefits and, hence, to an incentive to drop out. For those who join for selective incentives, however, this will not be the case. And, even assuming that they agree (for strategic reasons) to make such threats in the first place, they have an economic incentive not to follow through if and when their bluff is called.

The difficulties of secession are eased when subgroups have sources of benefits available to them. One opportunity arises when members derive some portion of their benefits from interactions with other subgroup members. When this is true, subgroup members can take these benefits with them if they secede as a unit. If most subgroup members agree to cooperate, therefore, they can maintain a pool of benefits for themselves should they secede and, at the same time, deny these benefits to any recalcitrant subgroup members who refuse to go along, thus reducing the value of organizational membership.

Another factor working to ease secession problems is the existence of alternative groups into which the subgroup may transfer. These groups are primarily of value to politically motivated members, serving as alternative vehicles for representation and the pursuit of political goals when the entrepreneur's activities prove unsatisfactory. On the other hand, competing associations will generally not suffice to attract away members who join for selective incentives, since, unless these members were previously unaware of organizational alternatives, they must have found that such groups offer them fewer net benefits than the association to which they already belong. If this were not the case, they would have changed groups earlier. While the availability of alternative sources of selective incentives lowers the risks and losses associated with the secession threat, then, these members ordinarily do not benefit from secession and have an incentive to resist that course of action. The major exception occurs when subgroups take benefits with them upon secession. In this case, the individual must lower his evaluation of the original group and raise his evaluation of the competing group, perhaps giving him an incentive to secede *if* the others do. An interesting possibility, in fact, is that policy-motivated members may serve as "prime movers" of subgroup secession—by threatening to transfer and hence to deny other members any benefits generated within the subgroup, they may stimulate a wholesale transfer into the new association. Here, competing associations become important because of their effects on these "prime movers," and the effects are mediated through them to other individuals initially unwilling to make the transfer.

A final consideration enhancing subgroup secession is that they may be able to exist on their own as separate associations or to initiate broader groups that could survive. Following this course, active individuals within the subgroup, performing collectively as a rival entrepreneur, must be able to supply subgroup members with selective incentives and collective goods of greater value than those already supplied by the entrepreneur. They are in a better position to do so, of course, if valuable benefits are generated internally. Additionally, they are more likely to be successful if the subgroup is fairly homogeneous in comparison to the rest of the association. In such cases, rivals might be able to offer increased benefits to subgroup members by specializing selective incentives and collective goods to fit their more homogeneous needs. The entrepreneur is vulnerable to the extent that his own packages of benefits are broad and general. In the final analysis, however, they must face the same problems as any internal rival; the established entrepreneur, because of organizational, economic, and political resources he may possess, will tend to have formidable weapons to employ in frustrating their designs. Thus, the formation of a new group will commonly be a final resort in internal politics.

In general, then, the threat of secession is not an easy one to make credible, especially when the subgroup contains members who join for selective incentives. Although there are several factors that may facilitate subgroup secession, these tend only to mitigate the basic obstacles to withdrawal, and they represent conditions upon which all subgroups cannot hope to rely successfully. In view of the problems involved, the secession threat is most likely to be employed with any weight at all by small groups of politically motivated members, particularly if they are large contributors.

Now that we have considered how subgroups can develop bargaining positions for use in internal politics, we should devote some attention to the relationship between the bargaining positions of subgroups and those of their constituent members. When subgroups are capable of playing a role in internal politics, what are the implications for the bargaining positions of individual subgroup members? The answer is that individuals will have their bargaining positions supplemented in at least one of two possible ways, depending upon the nature of their role within the subgroup. The first is available to virtually all subgroup members: each individual is in a better position to have a political impact because he has agreed to coordinate his actions with those of other members. This is a kind of "collective power" that derives from the fact that the individual is not acting alone. It is important to note that members who have no influence basis as isolated individuals—and many smaller members may fall into this category—can gain a measure of influence in this way. Collective power, however, is a very special kind of supplementary power for the average subgroup member; it can only be employed in conjunction with other participants, and it is therefore of restricted utility. It is power of a different sort than that possessed by politically motivated contributors, say, or by members who perform valuable services—since their power involves rewards and sanctions that can be invoked by one person, in light of his own best interests, without the necessity of coordination with others. A further qualification is that the collective power conferred by subgroups is not equally available to all association members, since certain types of members are more likely than others to participate. Specifically, larger members, communications middlemen, members who control valuable political services—and generally, members who are already powerful as individuals—are in the best position to form cohesive subgroups for political purposes. They have the incentives and resources that facilitate successful coordination in light of common goals; they are more likely to be sought out by others interested in coordinated action (because they have more to offer); and fewer of them are required to achieve a given political effect.

The second type of power is partially derived from the collective power of the subgroup, but it is not ordinarily available to all consenting participants. It is available only to those individuals who play pivotal roles within the subgroup. These are roles involving functions that must be performed if the subgroup is to be an actor in internal politics—initiating and organizing member interactions, speaking for the subgroup in internal politics, formulating detailed positions, plotting strategies, pooling and coordinating resources, and so on. When individuals participate actively in some or all of these ways, they have a degree of control over the subgroup itself. More than the other members, they shape the amount of subgroup power, the nature and extent of its employment, and, indeed, whether there will be any cohesive agreement at all. By taking on leading roles in the subgroup, then, they are better able to use the subgroup for their own ends. Though, like the others, they are participating in the wielding of collective power, they have a wider range of individual choice by virtue of their control over the vehicle of collective action. We can call such individuals subgroup leaders.

There is no guarantee that anyone will be disproportionately active in performing these functions. In very small subgroups, participants may share these roles more or less equally, with control dispersed among the several members. But as the subgroup gets larger, equal participation by all members in its various aspects tends to become unwieldly and disfunctional, and it is increasingly likely that specialization will occur. Moreover, certain kinds of members possess resources, skills, and incentives that "qualify" them for these roles. Large contributors, especially if disaffected, have more to gain from concerted political action than others do and should be more likely to play initiating and organizing roles. Members who control information can be instrumental in identifying, locating, and shaping the perceptions of subgroup members. These members, along with rival entrepreneurs and members who control important services, may also be invited into subgroups by other, less advantaged members, and rewarded by being offered leading roles as spokesmen, strategists, and so on. In general, the greater an individual's basis for influence outside the subgroup, the greater his chances of playing a leading role within it—and, thus, the greater his ability to gain power not available to the average subgroup member.

In sum, subgroup participation can augment individual power in two ways, delineating two types of participants, subgroup members and subgroup leaders. Subgroup members are better able to achieve their political goals by virtue of their agreement with others and the resources that can be marshaled toward agreed-upon ends; theirs is a collective power with very limited individual flexibility. Subgroup leaders can enjoy this basis of influence, plus the greater measure of influence they derive from whatever control they have over the goals, strategies, and survival of the subgroup itself. Furthermore, we have also seen that, while these avenues of influence are open to all members of the parent association, they are more open to some members than to others. In particular, individuals with independent bases of power are more likely both to be members of effective subgroups and to be subgroup leaders. Participation in subgroups, then, turns out to be an influence base that overlaps with the other major determinants of individual bargaining positions. Although it offers real opportunities to the less powerful members of the association, its advantages tend to accrue disproportionately to those who are already favorably positioned in internal politics.

The Membership:
Concluding Comments

In this section, we examined the bases of member influence by singling out several roles, potentially available to all members, that represent major determinants of member bargaining positions—the individual contributor, the supplier of services, the rival entrepreneur, the subgroup member, and the subgroup leader. In each case, analysis involved an evaluation of how the relevant resources could be employed, along with an elaboration of various factors that conditioned the member's ability to take advantage of that basis of influence. In the process, it became clear that these roles are related in certain ways and that the factors conditioning one source of influence often have effects on other sources as well. Member size, to take the most obvious example, appears to have an impact on all of them.

But while the determinants of member influence are often complicated, the overriding point about internal politics is quite simple: members *can* play a part in goal formulation, even though the self-interested entrepreneur has sole authority to establish official group policies. There is thus a "democracy" of sorts within the group. It is not a system responsive to numbers, and it does not assign equal weights to individuals who seek to participate. Rather, the influence of a member is a function of economic rewards and sanctions, with the entrepreneur responding selectively to members on this basis. Even without a representational structure, then, and without any other formal rules governing decision making, there *is* a link between member preferences and group goals—one that works to the advantage of some members and to the disadvantage of others.

It is interesting to note, moreover, that the nature of this link would be essentially the same even if the group had a formal representational structure. Were the election of leaders and other trappings of formal democracy imposed upon organizational decision making, group policy would remain economically responsive to bargaining strengths, rather than democratically responsive to voting strengths. For an analysis suggesting why this is so, see appendix B.

Staff

Organizational staff may perform a variety of valuable tasks, ranging from routine maintenance chores to more consequential tasks of a political or organizational nature. In principle, of course, these same tasks could be performed by members or by the entrepreneur, and perhaps they are in many associations. What is distinctive about the bureaucrat is that, while he is an insider and part of organizational structure, he performs these tasks as part of his job; he is paid a wage or salary to do so and is supplying a service in return for direct material compensation (although this need not be his only motive—we are making no assumptions about his goals).

If he is to have any role in internal politics at all, this is the key to the role he will play, for it is his job that affords him opportunities for accumulating and wielding an assortment of valuable weapons. This is largely due to specialization. The bureaucrat may, of course, come to the association as a specialist, hired precisely because of the particular resources and skills he possesses. But whether or not this is the case, he will tend to acquire knowledge, information, contacts, and skills simply through the continual performance of his assigned tasks; moreover, he may have a strong incentive to acquire these, since they will enhance his ability to do his job successfully. Over time, then, a staff person tends to become a specialist in certain activities and thereby possesses specialized resources and skills that other individuals do not.

The nature of his resources and skills will depend upon the nature of the activities in which he engages. If he performs communications functions or is assigned to organize, recruit, or administer to members, he will acquire information about the clientele and control certain kinds of information transmitted to them; he will develop contacts with members, especially the active ones; he may develop expertise in the formulation, sale, and distribution of selective incentives; or he may become a specialist in legal and technical matters related to the association. On the other hand, he may be assigned tasks of a political nature, which could lead him to establish personal contacts with political figures, knowledge and information about political issues and participants, lobbying or negotiating skills, and so on. Generally speaking, then, it is what an individual does as an employee that determines the specialized resources and skills he will acquire. These, combined with the resources and skills he brings with him to the association, shape his opportunities to play a role in internal politics.

There are three basic ways that he can have an impact on group decision-making, each of them deriving from his job-related activities. First, he can attempt to transform his specialized resources and skills into rewards and sanctions. The essence of this strategy is that the individual can threaten (at least implicitly) to quit, to perform fewer services, or to perform the same services less efficiently unless the entrepreneur responds to given policy preferences. Success depends upon the net value of his services, which, in turn, reflects the relationship among the resources and skills he can bring to bear, the tasks he is assigned to perform, and the material compensation he receives. Moreover, since the entrepreneur always has the option of dismissing an employee who adopts these tactics, success requires that the entrepreneur be unable to purchase such services elsewhere for less. Thus, to be able to utilize threats of cutting back or withdrawing his services, a staff person must be valuable and, in some sense, indispensable. In view of these requirements, one key to success is long tenure, since both value and indispensability are positive functions of the specialized resources and skills that individuals accumulate through the continual performance of their jobs. The longer an individual is employed by the entrepreneur, the greater his pool of specialized resources and skills, the less easily he can be replaced (in the short run), and the better his basis for influence.

Two other bases of influence do not involve the direct participation of the bureaucrat in internal politics, but there is no reason why they cannot prove at least as intrumental for achieving desired goals. The first strategy is that of employing bureaucratic resources and skills in support of individuals who do participate in internal politics—specifically, members and subgroups whose goals are sufficiently congruent with the staff person's own goals. Such support may take a variety of forms: he may, for example, pass on important kinds of information, facilitate political contacts or access, make research and other technical services available, impart his own knowledge of the bargaining context, and so on. What he can do, in other words, is favor certain participants in group decision making by selectively conferring advantages upon them, advantages that his resources and skills place within his realm of control.

The second strategy is that the staff person can employ his central location and his control over information and expertise to shape the perceptions of actors participating in internal politics. In this manner, he might be able to alter either their goals or their strategies in such a way that his own goals are more likely to be realized. The enterpreneur, for instance, may rely upon staff to sift, interpret, and store information, and to transmit relevant data to him; he may also rely upon them for analysis or advice in matters calling for a degree of technical expertise. When this is the case, entrepreneurial perceptions of the internal and external contexts depend upon the information passed on by staff personnel, who, in turn, can vary its content and timing in an effort to shape perceptions in desired ways. A staff member in a position to do this is therefore in a position to influence the goals and strategies of the entrepreneur without actually making demands. And he may do the same thing, of course, with respect to members and subgroups, since his ability to control valuable information and expertise might be directed at their perceptions as well. By following this general course of action, then, the staff member can attempt to guide and shape the process of internal politics "from a distance" by influencing some of the premises on which participants act.

In sum, there are several different ways in which staff members can have an impact on group goals. While the different strategies are not equally available to all staff members, and while the importance of staff will vary from group to group (e.g., some may have no staff at all), the point is that there are general bases on which such individuals might have influence. They are not simply functionaries with no role to play in political decision making. The significance of this is underlined when we recognize that it is a by-product of the entrepreneur's strategies of formation and maintenance. When the entrepreneur hires staff and assigns them tasks in order to facilitate the survival and prosperity of the group, he is at the same time creating actors with opportunities for shaping processes of policymaking. Decisions about bureaucratization, therefore, have implications for internal politics as well as for the more obvious concerns of efficiency and effectiveness. For some groups, this could prove to be the most significant example of how "maintaining behaviors" condition the political goals the association will pursue.

Outsiders

It is quite natural to think of group policymaking in terms of bargaining relationships among participants inside the group, but outsiders have a role to play in this process, too, just as they do in group formation and maintenance. This occurs, first, because the basis for bargaining strength is not an actor's location inside or outside the group, but the extent to which he is able to have an effect on the entrepreneur's surplus. Since outsiders may be in a position to enhance or obstruct the realization of entrepreneurial goals, they may be able to draw upon their pivotal positions for influence purposes. Second, like certain staff members, outsiders may be able to shape the bargaining context without actually entering into it—by shaping perceptions, available options, or the costs of success.

As in the last chapter, we will single out three types of outsiders for attention—governmental officials, nongovernmental groups and organizations, and rival entrepreneurs.

Governmental officials are uniquely situated to supply valuable political benefits. While the nature of these benefits will vary depending upon the prevailing issues, the decision-making sites involved, specific entrepreneurial needs, and so on, certain kinds of resources are available to public officials in dealing with the entrepreneur. Public officials may serve as sources of privileged information—for example, about the structure of agendas, the distribution of attitudes and support among other public officials, the timing of decision making, or the most likely avenues of success. They may be able to facilitate contacts with potential allies. Moreover, they may be in a position to favor the entrepreneur over his competitors in more far-reaching respects—by recognizing him as a legitimate spokesman for a sector of society, by delegating certain public responsibilities to him, or by supporting the legal coercion of his members. And finally, of course, public officials may simply be important as formulators and ratifiers of public policy. In these and similar ways, then, governmental officials can control benefits desired by the entrepreneur. They are keys to his political success.

It is a short step to the conclusion that officials can use their positions

to wield rewards and sanctions in their relationships with the entrepreneur. As we noted earlier, their assistance may be purchased in
return for campaign contributions, information, technical assistance,
and the like. But, clearly, they might also require certain entrepreneurial policy positions as their price. In exchange for enhanced success
on one set of goals, they may demand that he abandon others, or they
may ask him to pursue or publicly support goals in which he has no
material interest. The entrepreneur will, of course, voluntarily agree to
restructure his goals as long as he expects the net result to be positive.
When this happens, group goals are not the outcome of internal processes of decision making, but of a wider bargaining process that
includes the rewards and sanctions of public officials.

Public officials may also be in a position to shape group goals without
actually making any policy demands. If they can control privileged
information, for instance, they may be able to influence perceptions
about the likely realization of certain goals, how policies would be
funded and administered, etc., and thereby affect the goals sought by
participants in internal politics. Also, in their roles as formulators and
ratifiers of legislation, they may be able to determine policy options,
the costs of success, and the like, with corresponding effects on the
goals sought by associational participants. As was true for staff members, then, public officials might employ their resources not only as
rewards and sanctions but also as means of constraining associational
relationships in which they are not actively involved.

Because the category of nongovernmental groups and organizations
is heterogeneous, we can simplify matters by suggesting basic ways in
which these outsiders might gain influence. In the first place, they may
be potential allies or coalition partners whose support—in the form of
material resources, public agreement, or whatever—enhances the
likelihood of political success in certain issue areas or decision arenas.
In return for their support, they may require that the entrepreneur
modify his goals. Second, he may engage in logrolling agreements with
actors who do not share his goals, but who are willing to trade their
support or acquiescence in one area for his support or acquiescence in
another. This amounts to a change in the goals pursued by the entrepreneur in the political system, perhaps leading him to adopt goals in
which he has no material stake. Third, if any outside actors are sub-
sidizing the group, then they are clearly in a position to make policy
claims on the entrepreneur; if the amount of the subsidy is substantial,
and especially if its withdrawal would seriously undermine the mainte-

nance of the association, the entrepreneur may have little choice (in the short run) but to shape the group's goals accordingly. Fourth, when outsiders assist the entrepreneur in supplying selective incentives to his members, they may be able to use their services as a basis for winning policy concessions. While these points can only illustrate the various roles that such outsiders can play, the general theme is clear enough: as long as outsiders can control resources, confer advantages, or inflict sanctions, they have a basis for shaping group goals.

The rival entrepreneur, if he is not actually heading an alternative group, has little basis for making political demands, since the established entrepreneur has formidable weapons for protecting his own domain against invasion. If the rival is established, however, there are several ways in which he might influence entrepreneurial goals. To begin, the above analysis of outside groups applies to the rival as well. To the extent that he controls organizational and political values, he may act as an ally or opponent, engage in coalition-building or log-rolling, and so on, with possible implications for entrepreneurial goals. Indeed, he may be in "strategic contact" with the entrepreneur more often than other groups are, since he and the entrepreneur may frequently be included in the same political issues. Thus, he may gain influence through his ability to facilitate or impede the entrepreneur's political success.

He may also gain influence through his unique relationship to their shared potential membership. He may be in a position to wage a vigorous competition for members, threatening the entrepreneur's surplus and perhaps even the maintenance of the group. He may, correspondingly, be able to propagandize the potential membership, including the entrepreneur's own members, in an effort to alter individual goals, perceptions, and calculations. Such activities could affect group goals indirectly through their effects on the goals and strategies of participants or by "forcing" the entrepreneur to coopt the rival's political goals if he is to retain his own members.

Yet these efforts can also give the rival a basis for making direct policy demands on the entrepreneur. In view of the negative consequences of competition, the entrepreneur might offer to modify his political goals to change his pattern of political support in return for certain changes on the rival's part. To take an extreme but interesting possibility: in order to minimize the insecurities inherent in their conflict relationship, the rival and the entrepreneur may agree not to make competing political appeals in recruiting members, perhaps by drawing up accepted lines of distinction between their groups.

The Entrepreneur

Until now, we have viewed the entrepreneur as the target of internal politics, and we have concentrated on how other participants might get him to respond to their preferences. Yet, clearly, the entrepreneur is not just a passive actor who simply reacts according to the forces exerted upon him by others. On the contrary, he has his own resources and skills, can develop his own strategies for internal politics, and can take steps to control the bargaining context. Thus while certain factors can contribute to the influence bases of members, staff personnel, and outsiders, the entrepreneur may be in a position to manipulate these same factors and thereby alter the strengths of the various participants. The foregoing analysis, then, must be qualified by the fact that the entrepreneur can take these considerations into account in devising his own strategies.

This suggests that we should take a look at some of the more important strategic options available to the entrepreneur. This is carried out below through a brief discussion of several considerations which, by now, are familiar aspects of the analysis.

Selective incentives can be purposely employed to modify the internal political context. An increase in the relative value of selective incentives can lead to the attraction of members with no effective basis for participation in internal politics, to a decreased likelihood that politically sensitive members will drop out or even decrease their contributions for policy reasons, and to a smaller chance that subgroups can maintain cohesion and credibly threaten to secede. These are particularly important, of course, as they relate to those members most likely to be dissatisfied with entrepreneurial policies; indeed, he might make a special effort to tie these members in with selective incentives, aiming benefits and appeals at them that are not aimed at others within the group.

Thus, to the extent that he can successfully increase the relative value of selective incentives, he gains flexibility in adopting political goals and increasingly insulates the membership and financial bases of the group from the uncertainties of internal politics. In the process, he gains protection from inevitable fluctuations in political success, his ultimate lack of control over outside actors, and his inability to satisfy conflicting political demands.

Through the manipulation of information, the entrepreneur can attempt to shape the perceptions of participants on two dimensions: their perceptions of political issues, economic conditions, and other factors that determine the nature of their political interests; and their perceptions of what political goals the entrepreneur pursues, how successfully he pursues them, and how his political activities bear upon the realization of their interests. Entrepreneurial efforts in these respects are particularly important when the political context is complex—e.g., when many issues are involved, when costs and benefits are difficult to discern—and when the individual receives a good part of his information on these matters from the entrepreneur himself. Especially in situations like this, the entrepreneur can endeavor, in effect, to generate political satisfaction among members and political support among outsiders. To the extent he is successful, he can decrease the likelihood of sanctions and increase the likelihood of rewards.

Information is also important because it gives the entrepreneur a basis for evaluating the claims of participants in internal politics. By purposely collecting information about participants—about their interests, their past behavior, their economic conditions—he is in a better position to determine who is bluffing and how much credibility he should attach to threats and promises. He is also better able to predict coalitions and conflicts among participants and to make appropriate strategic responses. All of this can give him crucial informational advantages over other participants, who commonly are not as favorably located and who, at any rate, would have difficulty obtaining corresponding information about the entrepreneur.

Staff members, to the extent that they pursue political goals at variance with his own, pose problems for the entrepreneur. He therefore has an incentive to take the political goals of staff personnel into account in deciding whether and how to employ their services. An attractive option is to hire staff who agree with his own political goals, in addition to possessing other requisites (e.g., expertise) for the jobs in question. Or, if such a balance is difficult to find, he may hire staff who are politically "neutral." Similar considerations may guide his decisions about the roles various individuals are to play—for example, "committed" staff might be best employed on the political side of the organization, whereas nonpolitical qualifications like expertise might predominate on the selective incentive side. The entrepreneur may also want to consider loyalty, attitudes toward authority, and other factors that can bear upon an individual's willingness to carry out entrepreneurial goals. By following strategies like these, he can minimize the chances that staff personnel will use their positions for bargaining purposes or for adversely shaping internal politics in other ways (e.g., by distorting information), and he will be better able to channel their resources and skills in directions consistent with his own intentions.

In many and perhaps most cases, the entrepreneur can also encourage members to perform services without becoming vulnerable. Problems could arise, however, with critically situated members on whom he is dependent for the performance of valuable services, since these individuals may use their positions for bargaining purposes. These are problems that he will want to anticipate. Ideally, he would like to gain their services without giving up anything in return; practically, he will want to "pay" as little as possible.

He has several interesting options. First, he may rely as much as possible upon staff personnel, rather than members, for the performance of valuable services. This is increasingly possible the greater the tenure, experience, and expertise of staff persons; and it is increasingly beneficial to the extent that staff members' political views determine their hiring and placement. But the entrepreneur may not want to rely totally on bureaucrats; resources may be insufficient, for example, or certain situations may call for member activity. A second option, then, is to encourage participation by members whose goals are similar to his own. Thus, if and when such members accumulate resources and skills and become critically situated, their political preferences will be consistent with his own. A third option is to rely upon members to perform services, but only on issues in which they have a substantial material stake. In such cases, members will be less able (and less willing) to threaten sanctions, since withholding valuable services will tend to have a negative impact on their own surpluses. In general, the entrepreneur need not sit idly by and allow members unconstrained opportunities for contructing influence bases; his task is to structure member participation, and perhaps to hire staff, in such a way that their services best contribute to his own ends.

In developing subgroup-related strategies, the entrepreneur would like to structure member participation in such a way that coordinated support is encouraged and coordinated opposition is discouraged. To do so, he has a number of promising options. Most obviously, perhaps, he can encourage the formation of member subgroups when they can be expected to remain nonpolitical or when their political goals are reasonably consistent with his own; he might then be able to enhance communications, services, and contributions by channeling their participation in desired directions. He can also adopt strategies of a preventive nature. He can do his best to tie members in with selective incentives, for example. He may develop a reliance upon subgroups for the performance of services, but only in those areas in which the subgroups have a direct material stake. He might be selective about the kinds of information that are channeled through the subgroup, perhaps relying upon direct communications methods that are not vulnerable to distortion and other problems. And he might offer side payments to subgroup members in return for their noncompliance in subgroup coordination—which is, in effect, a selective incentive aimed at destroying subgroup cohesion.

He can also develop strategies aimed at subgroup leaders. For example, he might deny certain leaders the role of communications middleman, attempt to shift his reliance for services to other members (even if costly in the short run), and, if the threat of material loss is substantial, he might even expel particularly effective subgroup leaders. The entrepreneur can thus seek to diminish their ability to organize and maintain cohesive subgroups by denying them resources. Perhaps more consequentially, however, he can make side payments to subgroup leaders in return for their support. Indeed, this could prove crucial, for subgroup leaders are economically self-interested, are not loyal or committed to subgroup members, and will "sell out" to the entrepreneur whenever they find it economically beneficial to do so; furthermore, if most information is channeled to members through either the entrepreneur or subgroup leaders, and if most political interactions occur at this higher level (with leaders "speaking for" their subgroups), then conditions are ripe for mutually beneficial deals to occur. In such cases, subgroup leaders can use their (partial) control over the subgroup to extract individualized benefits from the entrepreneur, while the latter can use subgroup leaders to restrain and direct the activities of subgroups—all of which is made possible by the average member's lack of information, resources, and incentives.

In sum, the entrepreneur need not allow subgroups to emerge unconstrained and make claims upon group revenues. He has strategic options that enable him to encourage certain kinds of behavior, to discourage others, and, in general, to have a hand in determining the role that subgroups are to play in group affairs.

The same is true for his relations with outsiders. His options are understandably many and varied in view of the heterogeneity of the environment, but we can single out a few of them here. In his relations with public officials, the entrepreneur can attempt to tie them in on a number of bases, making the officials dependent upon him as much as possible instead of the other way around. Technical information, information on members and potential members, campaign support, verbal support on certain policies, and so on, can be employed toward this end. The more resources and skills the entrepreneur controls and that are of value to critically situated officials, the less he will be compelled to resort to goal changes to elicit the behavior desired. A second option is for the entrepreneur to attempt to gain favored status—through being recognized as a legitimate spokesman for a sector of society, for example, or through the legal coercion of his constituents. If he achieves such status, the internal bargaining context is altered: members and subgroups have their political alternatives diminished and are increasingly tied-in, there may be an influx of members with no real basis for affecting group goals; and rivals will be of less consequence.

The first option noted above also applies for nongovernmental groups and organizations: the entrepreneur can try to collect resources and skills that are of value to these outsiders, particularly in their roles as potential allies, in an effort to make them dependent upon him, rather than vice versa. He must be especially wary of subsidies, since they breed dependency. He may also try to work through nongovernmental groups and organizations to shape internal politics. By working through media organizations, for instance, he might gain favorable news coverage, publicity and support for his views, and increased legitimacy as a spokesman.

Given the analysis of the last chapter, little needs to be said about the entrepreneur's corresponding relationships with rivals. It is clear that he has a variety of economic, organizational, and political weapons for dealing with them. The more established he is relative to a rival, the less he will be constrained to rely upon goal changes, since he has so many additional options; the less established he is, the more he may have to rely on goals as a major weapon of competition.

The courses of action discussed in this section do not exhaust the options available to the entrepreneur, but they clearly illustrate the extent to which he can be an *active* participant in internal politics—one who can respond and react to the demands of others, but who can also employ resources, skills, and strategies in purposive attempts to shape internal politics to his own best advantage. Most importantly, this serves to qualify our earlier analysis of bargaining participants and their bases for affecting group goals. For, while there is a variety of identifiable factors that afford individuals a role in group decision making, we must also recognize that the entrepreneur will be attempting, as a rational actor, to manage and structure his activities with these factors in mind. It is only by including this second side of the equation that we gain a balanced perspective on the bargaining context.

The Bargaining Process:
Two Clarifying Points

We have now considered all the major participants in internal politics, the roles they can play, and the reasons these roles are available to them. But before we conclude, it is useful to consider two additional points about the nature of the bargaining process. These help to clarify certain aspects of internal politics that, because of our method of presentation, were not easily highlighted at an earlier stage.

First, it is important to recognize that the demands of individuals are not always determined by their own immediate interests, even in the absence of cooperation. This is because there is information flowing within the bargaining context which allows participants, especially those who are very active in internal politics, to learn about the demands, rewards, and sanctions of others; and this information can lead them to adjust their own demands and strategies in important ways. If, for example, a larger member can credibly threaten to withdraw substantial contributions unless he gets his way on certain types of issues, other participants, although they may be flatly opposed to his positions on issues, may willingly drop threats of sanctions against the entrepreneur in these areas, change the nature of their demands, and perhaps concentrate upon different types of issues. They may follow this path, of course, because they are likely to lose anyway. But they may also do so because, should they win, the negative consequences unleashed by the loser(s) may far outweigh the expected benefits from political gains. For any given individual, the object is not to win every time there is a disagreement over policy, but, rather, to structure and adjust his bargaining behavior in such a way that, all things considered, he expects to be best off.

It would be a mistake, therefore, to view internal politics entirely in terms of heated competition among participants, each of whom is trying to defeat all those opposed to his own issue position. Communication and tacit coordination, short of outright cooperation, can sometimes operate to make everyone better off than he would be under unbridled competition. Such arrangements are most likely to emerge when the context contains a small number of strong participants and when bargaining relationships have continued for a long time. Indeed, it would not be unusual for there to develop a mutually recognized "balance" or "accepted distribution" of power that describes which participants should win (or be allowed to win) on which issues.

The second point of clarification is called for because individuals may lack certain kinds of information that are fundamental to internal politics. They may not realize, for instance, how internal politics "works"—and, therefore, may not even attempt to communicate what their reaction will be to alternative entrepreneurial policies. Certain policy changes may lead them to drop out of the group or to alter the amount of their contributions, without even trying to use these incentives as rewards or sanctions in bargaining with the entrepreneur. The same could clearly hold for outsiders, who may not understand the impacts they could have if only they would take appropriate action. Even the entrepreneur may be ignorant on critical scores; aside from being uninformed about the preferences of some participants, he may attribute credibility to an individual who is bluffing, and he may not understand all the factors that underly his material surplus.

In the analysis of this chapter, we simplified our approach to internal politics by focusing, in effect, on factors the entrepreneur will respond to if he is aware of them and on bargaining positions that individuals can employ if they know how to use them. Because these informational conditions will not always be satisfied, however, internal politics will not always operate "smoothly." It is not a purely mechanical process in which individuals recognize and act upon bases of influence, and the entrepreneur correspondingly weighs alternative issue positions and chooses precisely the right one. A communications middleman may unwisely fail to press political demands because he does not recognize the kind of leverage his organizational position can extend him; and the entrepreneur might unwisely adopt policies that cause an unanticipated decrease in contributions, adopting them because he lacks crucial information about member incentives.

These possibilities should also be viewed as integral components of the analysis, which, by treating information as a variable, affords us a broader understanding of internal politics than the superficial mechanical notions. On the one hand, it tells us how various types of individuals, including the entrepreneur, must structure their resources and activities in order to make themselves better off from internal politics. And, on the other hand, it allows us to understand what kinds of things can "go wrong" in internal politics and why.

Conclusion

As these final points only serve to underline, internal politics is inherently complex, involving a variety of participants, resources, incentives, and strategic options. Our framework for ordering and integrating these elements is actually quite simple, however, and it is this simple framework itself that provides us with the basis for understanding internal politics.

To recount, we view internal politics as taking place within a bargaining context, in which participants have bargaining positions from which to assert claims against the entrepreneur. The key to internal politics is that the entrepreneur will respond to these claims whenever it is materially advantageous for him to do so. For their part, participants can affect group goals by making it worth his while to respond, which they may accomplish by direct reliance upon their own bargaining strengths or, in special cases, by shaping the behavioral premises and bargaining positions of other participants, including the entrepreneur. Their ability to accomplish any of these, and, hence, their ability to affect group goals, depends upon a range of identifiable factors—some of which (information, for example) are easily manipulable by certain participants and some of which (member size, for example) are not. It is primarily with reference to these underlying factors and their interconnections that we explain an individual's basis for affecting group goals. We round out our explanation by recognizing that the entrepreneur, too, can take these same considerations into account in attempting to manage the bargaining context. Elaboration of this framework yields a variety of implications. Of these, the following are perhaps best suited for suggesting the general nature of internal politics.

1. Individual members are not permanently stratified into those who have a role to play in decision making and those who do not. Their bargaining positions are dynamic components of the bargaining context, changing as their underlying determinants change.
2. The potential for dynamism is constrained, however, and a

tendency toward solidification and stability is introduced, by the fact that the major sources of bargaining strength tend to be related and overlapping.

3. This works to the cumulative advantage of larger members, who are in the best position to contribute for political reasons and more likely than other members to be suppliers of valuable services, rival entrepreneurs, subgroup members, and subgroup leaders.

4. While smaller members are distinctly disadvantaged, certain conditions can operate to augment their bases for participation. The most important of these are perceptions of *efficacy* and the formation of *subgroups*. Despite their significance, however, such conditions cannot bestow upon smaller members the full range of advantages that larger members possess.

5. Members and the entrepreneur are not the only insiders to have a part in framing group policies. Staff personnel may also have a role to play; they cannot be viewed as functionaries who simply implement the decisions of others. Their central position and accumulated resources and skills afford them bases for affecting associational goals. This is especially true when they control information and expertise, since these might be used to shape the premises on which the entrepreneur and other participants act.

6. Governmental officials, nongovernmental groups and organizations, and rival entrepreneurs may also have bases for affecting group goals—since all are potentially able to extend or deny various kinds of economic values or to shape the parameters of the bargaining context. In many cases, these outsiders may represent the critical difference between political success and failure; and, when subsidies are extended, they may even be able to undermine associational survival if their expectations are not met.

In sum, the goal formulation process is not one in which the entrepreneur determines policies without regard for the preferences of his members, but neither is it a process in which member preferences are faithfully translated into group policy positions. In the first place, some members count more heavily than others, to the point where many or even most members may have no appreciable voice in the outcome. And in the second place, members are not the only participants of relevance; staff personnel, outsiders, and the entrepreneur have their own goals to pursue and their own bases for pursuing them. Group policies reflect the weighted preferences of these participants as well as those of members.

These and other conclusions derived throughout this chapter tell us something about the nature of internal politics. But it is important to stress once again that our conclusions rest upon a more general organizational analysis, one that is concerned with showing how internal politics "fits" into the entire system of associational behaviors. Internal politics does not occur separately from other organizational structures and processes and can only be understood by taking into account the interrelatedness of various organizational dimensions. The communications structure, structures for supplying selective incentives and collective goods, patterns of member participation, and entrepreneurial relationships with outsiders—some of which appear on the surface to be quite nonpolitical—have been shown to have significant, distinguishable effects on internal politics, to the point of determining who participates, in what ways, and with what effects. And internal politics, in turn, has been shown to condition and alter these other aspects of the organization. Although we have separated them for analytical convenience, they are all part of the same system of behavior.

Five

Departures from the Economic Ideal

To this point, we have assumed that the entrepreneur and his clients are economically self-interested. This, of course, greatly idealizes the value structures of individuals, for we know that people respond to a complex assortment of incentives in virtually every area of social life. Moreover, as regards group activities in particular, studies of small groups and larger voluntary associations have consistently suggested that values other than economic self-interest are often important determinants of individual behavior. Thus, while it seems eminently reasonable to expect that economic self-interest plays a major explanatory role in economic interest groups, there are good reasons for investigating the behavioral implications of other values as well.

In later chapters we will consider the empirical evidence in more detail. For now, we will simply drop the assumption that individuals are economically self-interested and allow for the possibility that they have heterogeneous value structures. This dramatically enlarges the scope of the analysis. The following list, while by no means exhaustive, illustrates the variety of considerations that now take on relevance as incentives for individual action—altruism, belief in a cause or ideology, loyalty, beliefs about right and wrong, camaraderie, friendship, love, acceptance, security, status, prestige, power, religious beliefs, racial prejudice.

These represent enormous complications for an analysis of individual choice.[1] Any person must be viewed as possessing a complex system of values on the basis of which he evaluates alternatives and determines the "best" available option in a specific situation. This is not an easy decisional process to depict analytically.[2] For each alternative, the individual must take into account the implications for all his values and arrive at a summary evaluation that reflects their relative importance. At least implicitly, then, he must recognize a system of trade-off relationships among values, which indicates how much of one value (e.g., status) he is willing to give up in return for varying amounts of the others (e.g., power, ideology, friendship). If we wanted to examine this process for group members generally, we would thus have to deal with contexts comprised of different individuals who may have different types of values, who may order their values differently, and who may operate according to different trade-off connections among them. And, as if this were not problem enough, we would also have to find some conceptual means for measuring, depicting, and interrelating "units" of intangible quantities (units of prestige, units of loyalty).

These difficulties, however, only derive from an analysis of individuals as isolated decision makers. When we shift to a group context and consider the dynamics of group life, problems are multiplied.[3] First, group leaders may consciously attempt to stimulate loyalty, altruism, friendships, acceptance of democratic values, etc., and may "supply" members with complicated packages of incentives that appeal to any number of underlying values. Some of the incentives, of course, may be entirely intangible, their supply essentially unobserved except by the member himself—who, for example, may contribute because he feels a responsibility to do so (out of loyalty, belief in a cause), or participate because he believes members have a duty to be active (consistent with certain democratic values). Indeed, given the different goals, situations, and perceptions of individuals, it may not even be clear what the "incentive structure" of an association is.

An additional complication associated with group contexts is that norms, beliefs, loyalties, statuses, and similar motivational elements may be generated within the group without any conscious design by leaders. Much more than for material associations, there may be a host of such incentives that are outgrowths of group dynamics and thus products of complex systems of relationships internal to the group. Moreover, socialization processes will be of much greater consequence. Along with techniques of informational control and persuasion that may be employed in material associations, factors such as group norms, social pressures, and prevailing ideologies and beliefs can function to change individual values (especially when organizational structures are designed with this in mind). These changes can be minor, but they can also be fundamental. The individual may be led to embrace a new ideology, for instance, or new perspectives on his responsibilities to others, implying marked changes in the relative importance he assigns to his original values. Note that this cannot happen in material associations, since the individual always seeks to maximize his economic surplus in such groups.

Finally, there is the thorny question of authority. Because individuals need no longer be motivated by economic self-interest, they may come to believe that the entrepreneur, by virtue of his leadership position or his personal characteristics, has a right to direct their behavior and that they are obliged (within limits) to comply. Thus, due to special qualities that may be inherent in the leader-follower relationship, at least in the eyes of some members, contributions and participation may be forthcoming simply because the entrepreneur has requested them. A thorough analysis of organizations other than material associations, then, would have to be concerned with how entrepreneurial authority develops, how it is exercised, and how it meshes with other elements of the organization's incentive structure.

This checklist of problems suggests the kind of task that characteristically faces organization theorists: while individuals do, in fact, have highly complex value structures, and while mixed motives appear to play important roles in organizations generally, it is difficult to include all these factors in a systematic analysis. So far, we have dealt with these problems by ignoring them, and this has been very helpful, for we were able to build an organizational analysis in a manageable fashion precisely *because* individuals were, by construction, one-dimensional decision makers that are relatively easy to understand. Now that this analysis has been developed, though, we can put it to use in understanding at least some of the most basic consequences of motivational deviations from the economic ideal.

The purpose of this whole procedure, of course, is to minimize the complexities that mixed motives inevitably bring with them, while at the same time fitting them into a ready-made and relatively simple framework. The analysis that follows will accordingly be very general, and will not deal in detail with the numerous types of motives, their possible combinations, and their wide-ranging effects on behavior. Instead, an effort will be made to suggest, in very broad terms, how they enter into the individual's decision to join, how they bear upon entrepreneurial strategies of formation and maintenance, and what their implications are for internal politics and group representativeness. The overarching question will be Given the past analysis, in what important respects are our expectations altered (or unaltered) when these new incentives become relevant?

The Individual's Decision to Join

How does the introduction of new motives affect the individual's decision to join? Conceptually, this is a straightforward matter that requires no essential revision in theoretical approach. Because individuals may now have values other than economic self-interest, new inducements take on relevance; these inducements can derive from selective incentives or from collective goods, and they are entered into the individual's calculations accordingly. The familiar logic of joining is left intact—the concern is still with rational behavior, and it still makes a difference in a rational individual's calculus whether the inducements appear as selective incentives or collective goods. We are led to different conclusions, however, as a result of the logical roles that these new inducements can play.[4]

When deciding how much to contribute toward the collective good, individuals will now be concerned with more than just economic gain. Workers, for example, may value political success because of feelings of solidarity with other working people, concepts of justice or equality, or adherence to a class-based ideology. Businessmen may believe strongly in free enterprise or individualism as social ideologies, not simply as rationalizations justifying their personal economic gain. And farmers may see political activity as a means of protecting rural traditions and an entire way of life, rather than merely of enhancing their personal economic positions. All, therefore, may place much higher values on group goals than their own economic situations seem to call for. Formally, this simply means that they will be acting with reference to a different set of benefit and cost curves, which will intersect at a different point (if any) in yielding optimal levels of provision and contributions. If they feel strongly enough, they could certainly find it worthwhile to contribute. Should this be so, their contributions would be quite rational—although not in their economic self-interest.

Yet an important qualification must be attached: when these

noneconomic inducements are supplied in the form of collective goods, groups will still have a difficult time soliciting funds. To have an incentive to contribute any amount toward a collective good, an individual must believe that his own contribution will enhance group success to such an extent that he will receive greater values in return, regardless of what types of values these are. His incentive to contribute is therefore mediated by the efficacy requirement, and this ever-present obstacle can only dilute the motivational impact of noneconomic inducements.

This is not a problem when they derive from selective incentives. Here, as in Olson's analysis, the nature of the decision is different than it is for collective goods. In discussing this, we can simplify matters by considering two broad types of noneconomic inducements, solidary and purposive, as distinguished by Clark and Wilson.[5] Solidary incentives are intangible values of a social nature, including such rewards as friendship, conviviality, and status. Because these generally derive from social interaction, members can generate their own solidary incentives by becoming acquainted, enjoying each other's company, and establishing social relationships that yield psychic benefits of one kind or another. All these provide selective incentives to the extent that the act of membership qualifies one for taking advantage of them. Solidary considerations can also take on a negative role in the form of social pressures. Acquaintances may make the individual feel that he "must" join if he is to avoid exclusion from social activities, withdrawal of friendship, or loss of status.

As with economic selective incentives, people who respond to solidary inducements are generally joining for reasons that have nothing to do with politics; in important respects, then, these inducements imply conclusions about interest groups that are consistent with Olson's. The major change comes with purposive incentives. These are various kinds of intangible benefits that accrue to a person by virtue of his support of causes, value systems, principles, or ends that he considers to be worthwhile. Unlike solidary incentives, these types need not derive directly from social relationships; the individual may never meet with anyone in the group or even know who the other members are. Central significance attaches to the purposes toward which its funds and activities are directed and the ends that they might indirectly affect.

Because purposive incentives may be closely tied up with group goals, it is easy to make the mistake of assuming that they must derive from the provision of the collective good, and hence that they involve the same obstacles to contributing that characterize collective goods generally. It is important to be clear about why this is incorrect. Individuals can obtain purposive benefits in two ways: when collective goods are achieved and when purposive benefits take the form of selective incentives.

We have already considered the first of these, in which the individual's collective goods calculus is altered to reflect the relevance of new values. But purposive benefits can also serve as selective incentives. An individual may, for instance, derive a sense of satisfaction *from the very act of contributing,* when he sees this as an act of support for goals in which he believes. If group policies reflect his ideological, religious, or moral principles, he may feel a responsibility to "do his part" in support of those policies, and indeed he may consider the free-rider option morally reprehensible. It is not the actual provision of the collective good that represents the source of purposive benefits in this case, but the support and pursuit of worthwhile collective goods.[6]

A worker committed to a class-based ideology, for example, might be willing to contribute to a politically oriented workers' organization, not because he expects his contribution to make a notable difference, but because this is his way of expressing support for the movement and its cause. The source of benefits is the expression of support, which is a selective incentive distinct from successful achievement of the cause. Analogously, a businessman may make contributions to a trade association because he genuinely feels a responsibility to cooperate with others for "the good of the industry"; and a farmer may pay dues to a farm organization because he feels he ought to show his support for a group that fights for "the survival of the family farm."

This leads to a crucial contrast with Olson's analysis. When economic self-interest is assumed, collective goods are evaluated by individuals only as collective goods. There are no expressive benefits to be gained from supporting them, and no selective incentives are generated in the process. Thus, contributions toward political goals are inhibited by the constraints inherent in the individual's calculus. When purposive incentives are introduced, on the other hand, group goals can affect both aspects of an individual's calculations. *Collective goods can actually generate their own selective incentives* because of the unique role that purposive incentives can play in connecting the two.

As a consequence, even the smallest of small members may join and contribute for quite political reasons.

Member Participation

Once the individual joins a group, he has various opportunities for participating within it. One way he can participate is through the performance of services of value to the entrepreneur. As we saw for material associations, these might take the form of communications or recruitment activities, facilitating access or political contacts, supplying needed information, providing organizational expertise, testifying before public agencies, signing petitions, or writing letters. And, as before, he might be motivated to engage in these activities because he expects economic gains—from being instrumental in providing the collective good, from an enhanced bargaining position, or from benefits generated by the interactions themselves (e.g., information). These motivations may now be supplemented by other considerations. When activities involve a high degree of interaction with others in the clientele, as would be the case for communications middlemen and recruiters, the individual may become an active participant for solidary reasons, placing a high value on the social relationships that can be developed and maintained through his performance of such roles. Thus, he may undertake "tasks" for the entrepreneur simply because he enjoys that kind of activity. Similar inducements could lead him to serve group goals by cultivating political contacts; or, indeed, he may be attracted to political arenas because of the power or status they promise. Aside from these incentives, which are essentially independent of group goals, the individual may also perform services for purposive reasons—because he believes in the group's policy positions, for instance, and feels a responsibility to do his part. As we noted earlier, his purposive motivations need have nothing to do with how instrumental his participation is in realizing group goals. He derives benefits from the process of participation itself, not from being pivotal to a successful outcome.

The same considerations apply for participation on what we have called the selective incentive side of the organization. In material associations, this referred to participation in committees, conferences, or meetings, in which members engaged in the mutually beneficial exchange of material values (e.g., information, problem-solving). When nonmaterial incentives take on relevance, members can be attracted by a much broader range of structured interactions. Subunits may provide forums for social and recreational activities, or they may give politically interested members a chance to express themselves in discussion or debate. Any given association may thus contain a variety of social, economic, and political subunits within which members generate their own incentives. These can then serve to tie members into the group. For some individuals, the opportunity to participate in these ways may represent their sole reason for joining.

This brings us to a special kind of subunit within which members may participate, the political subgroup. Its distinguishing characteristic is the coordination of member behavior toward ends related to the group's internal politics. Earlier we found that the critical prerequisite for effective subgroup activity, cohesion, is seriously undermined when members respond only to material incentives. Now the situation is quite different. Solidary incentives may perform an important cementing function not possible in material associations, perhaps through social enjoyment, friendship, and mutual respect, perhaps through group norms backed by social pressures to conform. These are especially likely to be important in smaller subgroups. Purposive incentives can also enhance cohesion. Members may feel a responsibility to "stick with the others" and may gain expressive satisfactions from the process of organizing and pursuing worthwhile ends; they may also recognize the authority of subgroup leaders and feel obliged to respond to their directives. Together, solidary and purposive incentives can operate to break down the centrifugal forces undermining subgroup cohesion. In the process, they supply inducements for members to participate collectively in pursuing their common interests. As a result, subgroups must be viewed as much more important actors in internal politics than was true for material associations.

Another type of political participation, apart from subgroup activities, is represented by the individual's attempt to take part in decision making. In material associations, such participation is always motivated by economic self-interest, and the kinds of rewards and sanctions that he can bring to bear are limited by his own economic position. When other incentives are important, neither of these need hold. A larger member, for example, may actually be tied-in to the group for solidary reasons, and this could affect both his incentive to press demands and his willingness to follow through on any threats to withdraw. In contrast, there may be many smaller members who are highly motivated by purposive incentives, who desire to participate actively in internal politics, and who will simply drop out if this opportunity is denied them.

Clearly, then, there are various ways in which individuals can derive benefits from participating within the association. It should be emphasized, however, that there is a two-way relationship between incentives and participation: the individual participates in order to gain certain incentives, but during the process of participation his values and perceptions may be altered, affecting the kinds of incentives to which he will respond in the future. Economically motivated participation may inadvertantly lead an individual to develop valued social relationships; activities in subunits may lead him to learn about and accept group norms; he may develop new values related to his responsibility to others, the desirability of democratic decision making, or the legitimacy of entrepreneurial directives. All of these imply changes in his future bases for joining, contributing, and participating.

In sum, an allowance for mixed motives suggests a participatory context that is significantly different from what we found for material associations. It is more open, in the sense that any individual can be highly motivated to engage in various activities, regardless of his economic position. It is also more conducive to socialization effects, in which individuals can be changed in important ways as a result of their participation. And, notably, it enhances the prospects for member involvement in decision making, especially through purposive bases for contributing and participating and through the formation of subgroups.

These points do not suggest, however, that smaller members will now become active and powerful, or that larger members will lose all of their advantages. It is still true that larger members tend to have greater economic incentives to contribute and participate, better economic positions from which to perform needed services, and more favorable economic bases on which to become subgroup members, subgroup leaders, and rival entrepreneurs. While nonmaterial incentives can undermine these, they can also enhance them, just as they can for smaller members. So, even though the nature of the internal context is definitely changed by the relevance of these new incentives, they do not erase the economic patterns of advantage and disadvantage, but rather modify them—perhaps slightly, perhaps greatly, depending upon which actors respond to what incentives and how highly they are valued.

Formation and Maintenance

The entrepreneur is viewed just as before, except that he may now possess a variety of motives. Like other individuals, he may be motivated by ideology, religion, belief in democracy, social pressures, and, perhaps especially likely in his case, such considerations as status and power. He need not be driven solely or even primarily by economic self-interest and need not make decisions designed to maximize his economic surplus.

Nevertheless, the entrepreneur remains directly concerned with the maintenance of the association, since he views the group as a vehicle for the derivation of benefits. And maintenance commonly requires at least a modicum of economic resources—for paying staff, pursuing political goals, recruiting and organizing members, communicating, supplying selective incentives, and so on, not to mention any "wages" that the entrepreneur may require for his personal needs or activities. Thus, even though nonmaterial incentives may be important motivational factors for the entrepreneur, he generally cannot avoid dependence upon economic resources. Moreover, this dependence can extend well beyond the requirements of maintenance; substantial funds may be necessary if he is to pursue his nonmaterial ends—due, for example, to the costs of lobbying campaigns to achieve ideological ends or publicity drives to cultivate public support.

For these reasons, then, the entrepreneur must generally attach importance to economic considerations even if he is not concerned with deriving any personal profits. This is a characteristic which, in a sense, binds all entrepreneurs together. On balance, in contrasting our "new" entrepreneur with the entrepreneur of material associations, the salient difference is not that he can be unconcerned with economic values, but simply that he will take economic losses (to a point) and fail to pursue economic gains (to a point) when there are compensating nonmaterial values involved.

Given this modified perspective, we can approach major aspects of organizational structure by briefly reexamining the entrepreneur's strategies of formation and maintenance, paralleling the analysis of chapter three.

Communications. His efforts at setting up an efficient communications structure can be greatly facilitated by the relevance of nonmaterial incentives. As noted earlier, an individual may willingly take on the role of communications middleman for a variety of noneconomic reasons—perhaps because of his belief in the group's goals, because he simply enjoys the social contact, or even because he believes the entrepreneur has the right to require these activities from him (as part of a perceived authority relationship). The same holds for other roles associated with the communications process, such as those of identifying nonmembers and recruiting them into the organization. When selective incentives of this type can be made to appeal to members, the entrepreneur is possessed of a pool of manpower for carrying out communications tasks, which, as a consequence, he need pay nothing to have performed. While free performance of services can also occur in material associations, there are now more incentives that might induce such behavior, and hence the opportunity for involving more individuals in the provision of more services.

Nonmaterial incentives also facilitate communications by encouraging the proliferation of subgroups. Regardless of the raison d'être of these units, they represent contexts of interaction that can be used by the entrepreneur for communications purposes: he can simplify and structure the flow of information by contacting active individuals in the various subgroups, who, in turn, can relay messages to and from people with whom they interact. Member meetings, social gatherings, and recreational outings—also stimulated by solidary and purposive incentives—can be put to similar communications purposes.

Of course, the organizational effects of these incentives are not always positive. For example, when ideologically oriented individuals or subgroups are opposed to the entrepreneur's political policies, they may derive purposive incentives from distorting information, disrupting its flow, or using their communications positions to stimulate coordinated opposition. Moreover, they may be able to employ solidary benefits, especially if a subgroup medium is available, to induce other members to do the same. Thus, solidary and purposive incentives can work against as well as for entrepreneurial efforts to set up an efficient communications structure, depending in great part on whether individuals agree with the entrepreneur's goals. This is something he must anticipate in designing his approach to communications.

Aside from their effects on members comprising the network, the new incentives will also shape the kinds of information the entrepreneur wants to transmit and receive. In part, this is because members may now belong to the group for different reasons and expect different benefits from their participation. The importance of purposive incentives, for example, could lead the entrepreneur to increase the political content of the information he supplies—in the form of facts (or apparent facts) about group goals, activities, and successes; in the form of reasoned arguments designed to cultivate support for the group's efforts; in the form of rhetoric designed to stimulate more emotional bases of support. In some groups, this kind of information and the skill with which it is packaged could prove crucial for the recruitment and maintenance of members. When solidary incentives are important, the entrepreneur is analogously induced to increase the social content of information, keeping members informed about recreational events, social activities, marriages, deaths, and similar facts concerning people with whom they are acquainted. And furthermore, of course, the operation of both solidary and purposive incentives can lead the entrepreneur to collect different kinds of information from and about members—relating to their political views, their social interests, etc. This not only helps him transmit the right kinds of information, but also puts him in a better position to supply the right selective incentives and collective goods, to facilitate bargaining relationships, and so on.

The entrepreneur may also change the content of information because of new elements now reflected in his own value structure. He may be tremendously concerned, for instance, with putting across and gaining support for a particular ideological point of view. He may be more concerned with shaping member values than with catering to them, and may persist in following such a strategy even if it results in declining membership, contributions, and profits. In contrast, he may lay great stress on democratic values and transmit and receive those kinds of information that best facilitate his efforts to stimulate member participation and interest, regardless of what their specific political goals happen to be.

In sum, it is clear that the relevance of mixed motives can have an important impact on associational communications. They affect the relative attractiveness of different entrepreneurial methods of structuring the flow of information, and they influence the content of information desired by both the entrepreneur and the membership. These changes pervade all the other aspects of organizational structure.

Selective incentives. To the extent that nonmaterial incentives are important to his clients, the entrepreneur has less need to invest in, produce, or distribute economic goods and services or to rely upon outside businesses for these things. He now has a wider range of options and can supplement or replace certain economic selective incentives with selective incentives of a purposive or solidary nature.

For instance, he can supply a member with selective incentives by "allowing" him to perform services of value to the group. Because of feelings of responsibility or the enjoyment of social relationships, an individual may derive substantial psychic returns from the process of facilitating political access, enhancing coalitional relationships with outsiders, supplying administrative expertise, or simply writing a letter or signing a petition. Through appropriate actions, then, the entrepreneur may be able to obtain valuable services, while at the same time tying members more securely into the group.

Additionally, he can supply individuals with selective incentives by allowing them to participate in decision making. They might do so through general meetings, specialized committees for the discussion of policy, or research groups; or they may even be allowed to ratify certain policy choices. Quite apart from any effects they might have on the content of group policy (and there may be none), members can gain solidary and purposive benefits from the activities themselves; and, hence, as far as the entrepreneur is concerned, the decision-making process can serve a much larger purpose than solely the formulation of group goals.

He can also use the communications structure to shape member perceptions and values and, in so doing, to increase the value of selective incentives. Whether employing direct or indirect communications, for instance, he can identify group goals, marshal facts and arguments to justify them, discuss past successes and failures, indicate the financial and participatory needs of the organization, stress the duties of membership, and underline the moral aspects of their political pursuits—all in an effort to build support for group goals, feelings of loyalty and responsibility, belief in ideological principles, and so on. These, in turn, can serve as selective incentives, motivating individuals to remain as contributing members and encouraging them to participate in certain ways.

The relevance of solidary and purposive incentives also underlines the importance of the subgroup as a source of selective incentives. Because of these inducements, the entrepreneur is in a better position to stimulate and regularize member interactions and to ensure that members generate their own incentives through subgroup activity. Moreover, with increasing communication and familiarity among members so organized, solidary and purposive incentives can take on increasing importance within the subgroup over time, regardless of the initial reasons individuals may have had for participating. The entrepreneurial task in this respect is simply to design and facilitate regularized interaction. Once this is done, diverse benefits can be generated from within the subgroup rather than supplied from without.

Two final points about selective incentives should be stressed. First, purposive and solidary inducements tend to be financially less expensive to provide than economic goods and services. They require no investment in business operations, nor the production and distribution of anything tangible. This is of crucial importance. Instead of "buying" member support through materially beneficial exchanges, the entrepreneur can "attract" it because he pursues worthwhile goals or because of the intrinsic benefits of participating in group activities. When these considerations are important to members, the entrepreneur can thus face substantially reduced material costs and risks in his efforts to put together a solvent group enterprise. This can only serve to underline the organizational implications of nonmaterial incentives and the new structural options that they entail.

Second, while members may place great value upon these incentives, and while such benefits may be quite inexpensive to supply, they do not necessarily work to the entrepreneur's advantage. This is clearly the case for purposive incentives, which can take on negative values when the entrepreneur adopts goals that members do not support; individuals may react by decreasing their contributions, dropping out of the group, or engaging in disruptive kinds of participation. In a sense, they have been supplied with selective disincentives. Solidary incentives, if they can be manipulated by policy opponents within the group, might be used to bring about similar types of responses. Thus, the entrepreneur has a wider set of incentives to draw upon and an expanded set of options in designing packages of selective incentives for his membership, but it is still problematical whether, on balance, he will be in a better or worse position than we found for material associations.

Collective goods. Earlier we saw that economic self-interest inhibits individuals from joining and participating for political reasons, and this, in turn, inhibits the entrepreneur's incentive to develop the political side of the organization; when the entrepreneur decides to move in this direction, moreover, obstacles to member participation may contribute to the attractiveness of hiring lobbyists and other staff personnel to carry out political activities. The introduction of nonmaterial incentives can change all of this. Especially when purposive inducements are important to individuals, politics becomes a more central determinant of membership, contributions, and organizational maintenance—even if all members are responding to selective incentives. In such cases, the entrepreneur has an incentive to place greater emphasis on the pursuit of political goals, and thus on encouraging appropriate kinds of political behavior.

Also, he is potentially in a better position to rely upon members themselves to fill out the group's political structure. In particular, when members believe in the group's goals or expressed ideology, feel a responsibility to support its political activities, enjoy social contacts with other members, or recognize his authority, the entrepreneur is in a good position to induce critically situated members to perform specialized services and to encourage certain types of mass participation (letter-writing, petitions). With comparatively little expenditure of material funds, then, the entrepreneur may be able to obtain valuable manpower, resources, and skills, to decrease (if desired) his reliance upon lobbyists and staff officials, and, through benefits generated internal to the participation process, tie members more firmly into the group.

In short, nonmaterial incentives encourage the development of the political structure in two ways. The entrepreneur will have a greater incentive to develop this side of the organization when individuals join and contribute to the group for political reasons. And, because members might be induced to perform a variety of political services at low material cost, the political structure can be less expensive to build and political goals less expensive to pursue. The combined effect of these can therefore leave the entrepreneur with quite different structural incentives than we found for material associations.

Bargaining. It is clear that nonmaterial incentives can, in fact, play an important role in encouraging and cementing productive bargaining relationships among individuals. The key to their importance rests with their operation as selective incentives. While in material associations the entrepreneur must rely upon recognition of mutual dependence, the development of trust, and enlightened economic self-interest to bring about coordinated action toward the collective good, the introduction of nonmaterial benefits means that these can be supplemented by social pressures, feelings of responsibility, commitment to a cause, and so on—which serve as selective incentives that can knit individuals together and prompt each to do his part. Because nonmaterial incentives can overcome the centrifugal forces intrinsic to material associations, and because they represent an addition to the fund of incentives from which he can draw, the entrepreneur is in a better position to coordinate member contributions, activities, resources, and skills toward goals that they agree with. The facilitation of bargaining thus emerges as a more important aspect of the entrepreneur's overall organizational strategy. Indeed, its importance is underlined by the fact that solidary and purposive incentives can encourage the autonomous coordination of behavior by members themselves (the proliferation of subgroups)— suggesting a further need for central design and initiation if the energies of subgroups are to be channeled in appropriate directions. Bargaining can yield opposition as well as support, and this he would like to avoid.

Environmental relationships. As we have seen, when purposive incentives are important to members, the entrepreneur may be induced to place greater emphasis on the pursuit of the group's political goals and on the development of its political structure. This naturally leads him to place greater emphasis on relationships with strategically placed outsiders, especially public officials and coalition partners. He may now initiate or enter into more of these relationships and value them more highly because of their increased bearing upon his ability to attract members and contributions. This, in turn, implies a greater concern for marshaling the resources, skills, and support that the outsiders themselves will value and to which they can be expected to respond favorably.

Nonmaterial aspects of entrepreneurial and member goal structures will also affect which outsiders the entrepreneur will deal with and what sorts of relationships he will enter into. For reasons of ideological consistency, for example, he may refuse to enter into coalitions with certain groups whose support would facilitate political success; he may doggedly maintain close ties with public officials and outside groups who are less valuable strategically than others might be, but who are preferable from an ideological standpoint; or he may forego certain "favored" relationships with government (for example, the legal coercion of potential members) because he does not believe they are proper. Similarly, he may choose his points of governmental access, coalition partners, or logrolling partners partially on the basis of social ties, loyalty, or feelings of obligation. His willingness to accept or extend subsidies could be motivated by such nonmaterial considerations as well; he may refuse a direly needed subsidy because of the unacceptable nature of its source, and he may subsidize outsiders who pursue worthwhile causes even though he expects no economic benefit in return. He thus stands in sharp contrast to the entrepreneur in material associations—who would enter into any strategic relationship with any outsider at any time if he expected to be economically better off as a result.

Finally, the new motivational elements can have a dramatic effect upon the entrepreneur's relationships with rivals. This is primarily due to the double-edged effect of nonmaterial incentives; when these incentives are important to members, the entrepreneur is potentially better able to tie members into the group at little expense by offering them solidary and purposive benefits—yet his rivals can do the same. And, indeed, the latter have an advantage of sorts, because the entrepreneur generally cannot cater to all political preferences at the same time. Any heterogeneity among his members might be exploited by rivals, who can champion the specialized causes of the disgruntled and unrepresented without necessarily making heavy economic investments. Appeals to disaffected subgroups might be especially effective, since solidary as well as purposive incentives are well suited for motivating these blocs of members to secede. More than for material associations, then, rivals can move in at low cost to take advantage of gaps in the organization's incentive structure, gaps which the entrepreneur may find impossible to fill himself. This is an important weakness that did not plague the entrepreneur in material associations, who could tie members in on economic bases that are effectively shielded from the political appeals of outsiders.

In sum, the entrepreneur's relationships with environmental actors may be considerably affected by the relevance of motives other than economic self-interest. When these motives are important to his clients or to the entrepreneur himself, he may be induced to place greater emphasis upon the development of outside political relationships, to accumulate the kinds of resources that facilitate such relationships, to choose his partners and contacts with only partial regard for economic gains and political expediency, and to show greater concern for dealing effectively with the increased threat of rival associations.

Internal Politics: Members

As before, internal politics will be viewed as a bargaining context in which bargaining positions of various participants provide bases for influencing the entrepreneur. The fundamental change is that both the entrepreneur and the members may now be motivated by more than simple economic self-interest. From this flow other changes in the bargaining context. In particular, members can have different incentives for joining and participating, which in turn affect the kinds of rewards and sanctions they can wield in internal politics; while the expanded set of entrepreneurial values can affect the sorts of resources, skills, and information to which he will respond in formulating policies, thereby determining what can be used by members, staff, and outsiders as rewards and sanctions in the first place. Thus, the altered nature of internal politics is not reflected solely in the relationships between the entrepreneur and members; although theirs are the only value structures that (by assumption) have undergone a change, the rewards and sanctions of *all* participants are subject to change as a consequence, and so are their strategies.

We can better understand this new bargaining context by separately considering these two fundamental sources of change. With regard to members, we can examine their basis for effective participation in internal politics by suggesting how nonmaterial incentives might alter their ability to occupy basic roles within the group—the individual contributor, the performer of services, the rival entrepreneur, the subgroup member, and the subgroup leader. As in material associations, these represent general ways in which members can control and utilize values in their bargaining relations with the entrepreneur—only, in this case, the values need not be economic. Once we have taken a look at these general bases of member influence, we will turn to the entrepreneur to suggest more specifically how the nature of his values shapes the bargaining context and qualifies our perspective on member influence.

The individual contributor. Purposive incentives can have a dramatic effect on the rewards and sanctions deriving from this role. When members contribute because they support the substance of group goals or the processes through which they are formulated, or because they are loyal to its general purposes, they can make their contributions contingent upon a wide range of entrepreneurial choices—the political policies he pursues, the strategies he adopts to pursue them, and the degree to which he allows for democratic participation. Member evaluation of the entrepreneur's political choices can thus give them a rational incentive to decrease or increase their contributions or, indeed, to secede from the group altogether—even if, from a purely economic standpoint, it is not to their advantage to do so. The political preferences of even the smallest members can be translated into rewards and sanctions of value in internal politics. It makes a difference whether they are offended, outraged, apathetic, satisfied, or supportive.

This need not handicap the entrepreneur. He can use his communications structure (among other resources) in an effort to enhance loyalty, generate political satisfaction, and, in general, make purposive incentives work for him in tying members into the group at low material cost. The important consequence is not that purposive incentives must work against the entrepreneur—but, rather, that the political preferences of average individuals, whatever their content and direction, can make a difference for the maintenance objectives of the entrepreneur, the policies he adopts, and how he pursues them.

Solidary incentives have a less exciting role to play, since these benefits usually operate to tie members into the group for nonpolitical reasons. Outside of their employment in subgroups, their primary effect is to shield the entrepreneur from any adverse political reactions from members, operating much like economic selective incentives. When friendships, social events, and frequent interaction are important to them, average members may willingly endure undesired group goals. And, at a higher level, larger members may moderate their demands and constrain their use of sanctions, placing greater value on harmonious social relationships, and perhaps simply enjoying the prestige that goes along with making substantial contributions.

The performer of services. There are many valuable services that members might perform for the entrepreneur, ranging from letter-writing to the facilitation of political access, and nonmaterial incentives can variously affect their willingness to engage in such activities. This naturally has implications for internal politics. Members now have different motivational bases for participating and for using their services as rewards and sanctions.

In this respect, solidary incentives are primarily important in subgroups. Outside this coordinating arena, they represent means of motivating members to perform services on nonpolitical bases that are difficult to translate into enhanced bargaining positions; because members gain values from the social process of participation, they may easily lose some of these values if they vary their level of performance in response to the entrepreneur's political choices. As with contributions, it is purposive incentives that stand to have the greatest impact on influence potential, since these incentives can make the performance of services contingent upon the entrepreneur's political policies and strategies. While it remains true that larger members are in better positions to be communications middlemen, to make political contacts, and so on, purposive incentives can supplement economic considerations to render services a more readily available basis of influence for "average" members and a more important factor in internal politics. Unlike in material associations, members need not participate because they view their activities as instrumental to the group's success (or failure), or because they are "selfishly" maneuvering for a stronger bargaining position. When purposive incentives are important, they may also participate because they gain expressive benefits from the process of participation itself—and, hence, they are more easily induced to engage in activities for or against group goals, depending upon whether they support them. Especially when purposive motivations are widespread, therefore, the entrepreneur has a greater incentive to take the political preferences of members into account in order to anticipate their participatory responses to group policies.

The rival entrepreneur. Nonmaterial incentives imply a more important internal political role for the rivals than we found in material associations. In the first place, it is potentially less expensive to form a competing association to the extent that members respond to these new incentives; secession is a more credible and serious threat as a result, particularly when the rival happens to head a subgroup. Rivals can cultivate heterogeneity among the general membership, champion the policies of the unrepresented, and take advantage of existing social bonds in an effort to create a foundation for a successful competing group. A second reason is simply that individuals may have greater incentives to become rivals. This is partially due, of course, to the fact that groups may be less expensive to form, and thus that rivals are more likely to be successful than they are in material associations. But it can also be due to such rival characteristics as commitment to an ideology, the desire for status or power, and the enjoyment of social interaction; these can lead rivals to invest considerable time, energy, and material resources in their efforts to organize members, much more than if they were only calculating on the basis of economic costs and benefits. Third, leadership abilities, devotion, drive, sincerity, or charisma may give rivals a degree of personal appeal (trust, admiration, respect, affection) and authority among members, and a basis for inducing them to become followers. Finally, rivals are not as easily bought off through entrepreneurial side payments when motivated by values other than economic self-interest; for moral, religious, or

ideological reasons, the connection between the rival and his constituents, or between the rival and his cause, may be difficult or impossible to disrupt.

For these and related reasons, rivals potentially have greater sanctions to wield in response to the nature of group goals and strategies. Accordingly, the entrepreneur has stronger incentives to take the policy
preferences of rivals into account in plotting the political directions the
association is to take.

Subgroup members and subgroup leaders. The fundamental prerequisite for subgroup participation in decision making is some degree
of cohesion. In material associations, the centrifugal forces of
economic self-interest work against cohesion, inhibiting the role of
subgroups in internal politics. But because nonmaterial incentives can
operate to overcome free-rider tendencies among members, helping to
knit them together in the pursuit of common ends, there can be a
proliferation of new political participants with various means of asserting claims against the entrepreneur.

In conjunction with their effects on cohesion, nonmaterial incentives
can enhance the subgroup's basis for influence by motivating members
to employ their contributions, services, and skills toward subgroup
goals and to cooperate in making threats of secession. Interestingly,
however, purposive and solidary incentives can operate differently in
this respect. Purposive incentives can be connected to the nature of the
subgroup's goals; when this happens, the bargaining strength of the
subgroup is a reflection of the support its goals evoke from constituents. Solidary incentives, on the other hand, derive from social
pressures, group norms, friendships, and the like, which are essentially
unrelated to the political goals being sought. Hence, certain members
may willingly pool and coordinate their contributions, services, and
skills for nonpolitical reasons and, under the guidance of subgroup
leaders, these resources might be channeled toward the political goals
pursued by the subgroup in the bargaining arena. This increment to the
subgroup's bargaining strength is not a reflection of political support at
all, but rather a by-product of the operation and manipulation of social
selective incentives.

Aside from their effects on average members, nonmaterial incentives
also have an impact on subgroup influence through their effects on
subgroup leaders. These are essentially the same as those outlined
earlier for rivals: the greater ease of forming cohesive subgroups, the
extra incentives for becoming a subgroup leader, the possibility of

cultivating leader-follower ties of a socioemotional nature, and the decreased likelihood of being bought off.

In their effects on both potential members and leaders of subgroups, then, nonmaterial incentives can help to overcome incentive barriers to cooperation and coordination. The implications are highly favorable for interested individuals to pursue political ends collectively within the bargaining context, especially when we recall the plight of the average member in material associations. To the extent that the new incentives are motivationally important, heterogeneity among the general membership is more likely to find structural expression and thus more potent vehicles for inclusion in policymaking processes.

Internal Politics: The Entrepreneur

We can round out our discussion by considering the implications that nonmaterial aspects of the entrepreneur's value structure can have for internal politics. In effect, the above analysis was carried out independent of entrepreneurial values, since we focused upon the resources, skills, and behaviors that members can make contingent upon group policies and political activities. Yet these general factors do not in themselves determine the strength of member bargaining positions, for the specific nature of entrepreneurial values will determine what kinds of rewards and sanctions he will respond to and how he will weight the resources controlled by individuals.

Altered entrepreneurial values also have effects on the bargaining positions of staff personnel and outsiders, whose rewards and sanctions are now being evaluated according to different criteria. Should the entrepreneur now find it important to stress political success and the development of political structures, for instance, staff members who control political information and expertise and perform valuable political services will find they have stronger bases for influence; and critically situated public officials and coalition partners will also tend to have enhanced bargaining positions.

The nature of entrepreneurial values not only has a direct effect on bargaining positions by supplying the criteria of evaluation; it also has an indirect impact by determining how the entrepreneur, as an active participant, will attempt to shape the bases that these individuals may possess for asserting their claims. His values will affect, for example, what kinds of member participation he encourages (if any), what qualifications he looks for in hiring staff, what responsibilities he delegates to members and staff, what types of outsiders he relies upon for political assistance, and so on. All of these ultimately help to delineate the store of rewards and sanctions that participants can employ in internal politics.

In sum, it makes quite a difference what specific kinds of values are now guiding entrepreneurial behavior. While for material associations we could characterize his approach very simply with reference to economic self-interest, we must now admit the possible relevance of a host of disparate motives which singly or in combination can lead to a variety of sharply contrasting behaviors. Furthermore, it is not as useful to generalize about these considerations, as we did with members, by employing the categories of purposive and solidary incentives. Unlike members, the entrepreneur has a pivotal organization role to play as *the* central decision maker, and variations in his personal system of values can have major impacts on internal politics and its policy outcomes.

From an analytical point of view, the problem is that we cannot possibly examine all the motives he might possess, even though we recognize that they can have important implications. The task is too immense. What we can do, however, is to single out a few nonmaterial values that are of particular interest. This is carried out below by assuming, first, that the entrepreneur is motivated by narrow ideological goals to the virtual exclusion of all other considerations; and second, that he is primarily motivated by democratic values, including, above all, a desire to reflect member interests faithfully in group policy. Their contrasting implications, along with what we found for material associations, will help to clarify the questions of why and to what extent motives other than economic self-interest can make a difference at the entrepreneurial level.

When the entrepreneur's main concern is with the pursuit of narrow ideological goals, an immediately important consequence is that group policies are no longer tools to be employed toward increasing membership, contributions, valuable services, and the like. The group's goals are not means to such ends, but are ends in themselves that take on value because of their ideological nature; they are, from the entrepreneur's standpoint, the raison d'être of the association. They are not to be compromised or moderated; and they are definitely not to be replaced, since the entrepreneur would have no incentive to maintain the association in their absence. Unlike the entrepreneur of material associations, he maintains the association in order to pursue specific political objectives, not the other way around.

This structures and rigidifies his approach to internal politics. In a sense, he has lost a degree of freedom through his unwillingness to respond to diverse member preferences and must rely upon the other mechanisms at his disposal—which, of course, become policy directed, given his priorities. Generally, he will try to make the maintenance of the group independent of political responsiveness. To build a stable financial and member base, he may endeavor (if ideologically acceptable) to tie in individuals with economic selective incentives, legal coercion, or social rewards and pressures, all of which reflect nonpolitical motivations that can be kept out of internal politics. His political appeals, on the other hand, will be quite specialized, designed to cultivate those individuals who already agree with his goals and to convince dissenters, particularly those who are politically motivated, that they should change their preferences in ideologically appropriate ways. The communications structure is crucial in this regard, supplying the channels through which facts, propaganda, personal persuasion, and other agents of influence can operate to create a larger and more homogeneous clientele of politically motivated members.

As far as member participation inside the group is concerned, it is of utmost importance that such activities be controlled and directed by the entrepreneur. Participation may be used to tie in members more securely for nonpolitical reasons and to provide services that enhance the group's political success. It may also be used as an expressive outlet and source of benefits for politically motivated members who, already in ideological agreement with the entrepreneur, can be allowed to participate in decision making; since the important decisions about goals have already been made, such participation can be meaningful to those involved without leading to any deviations of consequence from policy positions acceptable to the entrepreneur. The major danger of participation (of any kind) is that interaction among members may stimulate the formation of subgroups opposed to group goals. One of the entrepreneur's chief tasks is to prevent this from happening. Thus, he must be careful about how he structures member activities and, most notably, how he stimulates and directs the activities of those members who join (initially) for nonpolitical reasons.

The entrepreneur's perspective on relationships with nonmembers is also oriented by ideological considerations. Staff personnel, especially those performing sensitive political functions and informational activities, will need to be ideologically acceptable as well as technically qualified; indeed, ideology may be so important and restrictive a criterion that the entrepreneur may willingly settle for employees who are not very well qualified in other ways. In his relationships with outsiders, he will tend not to use goal changes as a resource in attracting access or support from those in a position to facilitate political success; instead, he will try to accumulate other kinds of resources of value to pivotal outsiders, inducing them as best he can to promote his cause, but without extending them a role in internal politics.

In short, the primacy of narrow ideological goals prohibits the entrepreneur from responding to political diversity. To compensate, he tries to cultivate existing support, to persuade and convince dissenters to adopt acceptable goals, to tie in potential dissenters on nonpolitical bases shielded from internal politics, to build an ideologically homogeneous staff, and to carry out external political activities without compromising basic goals. All of this, however, implies problems for both the group's maintenance and its political success. When constituents are politically motivated—because of purposive incentives, perceptions of efficacy, or subgroup coordination—policy disputes can lead them to reduce their contributions, to drop out, or to participate negatively. While these possibilities are present in any group, regardless of entrepreneurial goals, they are most dangerous here, since the entrepreneur is unwilling to respond to member political preferences in order to prevent them. Dissenting larger members and subgroups, for instance, may simply be allowed to secede in lieu of altering associational goals to please them. The result will tend to be a smaller, financially weaker association than could otherwise have been attained, but one that reflects an adequate degree of ideological homogeneity among its politically motivated members. Smaller membership and financial bases, in turn, affect political success, as do the nontechnical requirements placed upon staff members, the entrepreneur's strategic inflexibilities in dealing with outsiders, and the enhanced opportunities he inadvertently extends to rivals. He would rather be less successful pursuing ideologically pure goals than more successful pursuing those that are ideologically incongruous and unacceptable. Indeed, the latter is not even "success" as far as he is concerned.

The entrepreneur thus behaves quite differently here than the entrepreneur of a material association, due at base to his unwillingness to use group goals as tools for building an organization. This, it turns out, is a luxury for which he pays a price. Maintenance and political efficacy are connected in various ways to the nature of group policy, and inflexibility in formulating the latter necessarily gives rise to problems and constraints in pursuing the former. These may certainly be worth it as far as the entrepreneur is concerned, and insufficient reason for undermining ideological consistency. The point is simply that the size, composition, and behaviors of the group will be affected through his efforts to attain such consistency, and he must give up certain values and organizational advantages in the process.

We can now turn our attention to a second type of entrepreneur, who we will assume is highly motivated by a belief in democratic norms, and whose central concern is to represent faithfully the interests of individuals in his clientele. How does his organizational approach compare with those discussed above? To begin with, he does not view group goals as ends in themselves, as the ideologue does, but, rather, as means of reflecting individual interests. Value attaches to goals not because of their substantive nature, but because of their connection to the membership. Thus, the entrepreneur is not only willing to compromise; he has an incentive to bring about compromises among members, to aggregate interests, and generally to modify and shape group goals as a function of member interests.

This, in turn, has consequences for his employment of various organizational mechanisms. Like the ideologue, he may seek to tie in members for a variety of nonpolitical reasons, including economic selective incentives, in order to increase membership and contributions and to enhance the prospects for stability and political success. Yet, once individuals belong to the group, he will attempt to see that they are properly represented in its policy positions; nonpolitical incentives may be employed to recurit them into the group, but not to keep them out of internal politics. When the entrepreneur makes political appeals, they may be quite broad, formulated so as to highlight the inclusive interests that constituents have in common (say, as farmers or businessmen) and that tend to distinguish them from other social actors. More specific policy appeals may also be made, with the suggestion that various interests can expect to be fairly heard in internal politics and fairly represented in group policy. The entrepreneur is not concerned with creating homogeneity or with convincing dissenters to toe an ideological line, but with building an avenue of representation for whatever heterogeneity exists in the clientele. This is reflected, too, in his use of the communications structure, which is more a means of finding out what member interests are than of shaping those interests that exist. When it is employed as an influence device, on the other hand, information will be used to enhance belief in democratic procedures, the need for tolerance, the duty to participate, and so on. This is an altogether different use of information than we found for the ideologue or for material associations.

Member participation is an integral part of the ideal democratic association, which means that the entrepreneur is concerned with stimulating member participation in decision making as well as in the performance of services. Participation is not something to be feared and strictly controlled, but something to be encouraged and directed in such a way that democratic linkages between member interests and group policy can be better assured. Subgroups can have a positive role to play in this respect, organizing members on more homogeneous political bases and facilitating the aggregation of interests. To be sure, the entrepreneur may in some cases want to inhibit their development—e.g., if their strength might threaten group maintenance or his ability to formulate group goals democratically. But, since their emergence may be inevitable anyway, he may choose to encourage the development of political subgroups in an effort to provide structural reflections of major interests—yielding, for example, systems of functional or geographical representation. In this way, he may be able to circumvent imbalances by creating countervailing powers, ensuring that various interests have their watchdogs. As small groups, they may also be used in socializing members to democratic norms, prompting them to feel an obligation to participate, a tolerance of the views of others, a willingness to compromise, and so on.

The pursuit of internal democracy will similarly affect the entrepreneur's relationship with nonmembers. In the hiring of staff members, political criteria will remain relevant, but will stress balance and impartiality, with perhaps a general sympathy for the sector's political cause (e.g., the "plight of the farmer"). While hiring is subject to such constraints, knowledge, technical expertise, and efficiency should loom as more determining criteria here than for the ideologue; moreover, staff personnel should tend to be less detached from the membership, since participation, interest articulation, and interest aggregation are central aspects of the internal environment. In his relationship with governmental officials and other outsiders, the entrepreneur has something in common with the ideologue: he will be somewhat unwilling to alter the group's goals in efforts to attract their support, relying instead upon other types of resources and strategies. He will be less inflexible in this respect than the ideologue, and will engage in logrolling or compromise when necessary to achieve a degree of success in certain areas. But, because associational policies are formulated as reflections of member interests, there is something special about them that removes them from the realm of expediency. In contrast to the entrepreneur's perspective in material associations, moreover, outsiders are not viewed as just another set of participants in internal politics; according to democratic norms, goals are to be formulated by insiders and, as far as possible, outsiders are to be excluded.

While this may come across as a highly desirable internal context from a democratic point of view, there are potentially severe problems inherent in the entrepreneur's approach. This is primarily due to the fact that his democratic rules of political responsiveness are not designed to extract support from those with strong material bargaining positions. For instance, powerful members and subgroups, controlling major contributions and valuable services of various sorts, may have economic incentives to leave the association or to withhold contingent values when their interests are not reflected in policy. Yet there is no mechanism to ensure that policy reflects their interests, since the entrepreneur shapes policy democratically to reflect the interests of all members equally and encourages mass participation in decision making. In the extreme, he may find himself primarily representing members who are not politically motivated, while those who are politically motivated—and in the best position to supply material support—become disaffected and exercise sanctions. For the luxury of following democratic rules, then, the entrepreneur must be prepared to pay a price in the form of contributions, services, and membership that can be denied him by powerful participants.

These difficulties are endemic to an economic group that tries to be democratic. There are, however, certain conditions that can operate to lessen their severity. (a) There may be no larger members or subgroups than can undermine the size, financial base, or political effectiveness of the group; instead, economic selective incentives and widespread democratic sentiments may account for these desirable aspects. (b) Larger members and subgroup leaders may themselves believe strongly in democratic norms. (c) Heterogeneity among larger members and subgroups may reflect heterogeneity in the membership as a whole, enabling the formulation of policies that are at once democratic and acceptable to materially powerful members. (*d*) The membership may be quite homogeneous, leading to the same result.

The entrepreneur will naturally strive to bring about these kinds of conditions. The central point, however, is that—like the ideologue—he has problems that the entrepreneur of a material association does not have due to nonmaterial values that constrain his flexibility. In building an economic interest group, he may have to accept a smaller, financially weaker, and less successful organization than could have resulted if only his democratic intentions had not gotten in the way.

These illustrations are simplified, of course, and we might expect that the entrepreneur will commonly be less single-minded in his devotion to particular values. But the discussion here helps to underline the fact that, because the entrepreneur is a group participant of pivotal importance, the nature of his value system makes a great deal of difference for internal politics as well as for other aspects of associational life. Different values will lead him to different perspectives on member participation, different uses of the communications structure, and so on—all of which have a hand in determining the substance of group goals, the size and financial basis of the group, and its degree of political success.

We should take explicit note of two consequences of special interest. First, the entrepreneur's nonmaterial values help to determine the extent to which the association will be internally democratic. As we illustrated above, certain values can lead him to encourage meaningful participation by ordinary members and to construct strong links between member preferences and group goals. Other entrepreneurial values, in contrast, can lead to decisional unresponsiveness and to quite undemocratic internal settings. Indeed, as when narrow ideological goals take precedence, the parameters of internal politics may emerge as much less conducive to democracy than they are in material associations—where group goals are at least highly open to variation and susceptible to influence from a variety of points of view.

The second point is that, whatever the entrepreneur's nonmaterial values, he should expect to pay a material price for the privilege of pursuing them. This is another way of saying that he behaves differently than he would if economically self-interested, making sacrifices in the form of a lower personal income, a smaller membership, a weaker financial base, or a less effective political structure—in order to reap ideological, democratic, humanitarian, or other nonmaterial values that, from his perspective, are more important. Thus, when entrepreneurial values (and hence decision rules) are different from what we found in material associations, whether internal politics proves to be more democratic or less democratic as a result, there will be economically undesirable ramifications for various political and nonpolitical aspects of the group. Democracy cannot generally be achieved, nor other nonmaterial values elevated to top priority, without the kinds of negative economic consequences that, in material associations, the entrepreneur would consciously and single-mindedly strive to avoid.

Conclusion

In this chapter, we have attempted to deal with motives other than economic self-interest in a simple and straightforward fashion—using Clark and Wilson's classification of incentives whenever possible, using the same framework and logic that guided the earlier analysis, and emphasizing contrasts with the material association norm. This approach fails to do justice to the scope and variety of human values and is not intended to provide a comprehensive examination of their behavorial consequences. It is designed to provide a better rounded understanding of interest groups, suggesting why and in what general respects nonmaterial values can make a difference when supplementing the economic self-interest of individuals.

The analysis need not be summarized here. It is clear enough by this point that these "new" values have an impact on member decisions to join and participate, the organizational roles of subgroups, entrepreneurial mechanisms of formation and maintenance, and the nature of internal politics—and that these involve a variety of important deviations from the material association norm. Rather than review all of this, we will simply suggest some of the broader implications for two very basic aspects of interest organizations, their representativeness and their stability.

Representativeness. Both solidary and purposive incentives can directly enhance the prospects for democratic pressure upon the entrepreneur by distributing bargaining strengths among affected individuals and by providing a favorable basis for subgroup action. Should the entrepreneur deny them representation, they are more likely to secede from the group, and subgroup leaders and rivals are better able to supply alternative vehicles of representation. Thus, entrepreneurial unresponsiveness should tend to reduce political heterogeneity within his own group and encourage the development of new groups around more homogeneous political interests. This exit process in itself brings about stronger congruence between member preferences and group goals. On the other hand, nonmaterial incentives can also enhance representativeness by bringing about greater responsiveness. This can happen, first, because the increased rewards and sanctions wielded by average members may lead to a greater reflection of their interests in policy. And, second, it can result from nonmaterial aspects of the entrepreneur's own goals—which, in some cases, may lead him to strive for more equal representation and for higher levels of member participation in decision making.

In short, certain incentives enhance the entrepreneur's willingness to respond to member preferences—while, if he is not willing to respond, politically dissatisfied members are more likely and better able to secede as a result, reducing political heterogeneity. This stands in marked contrast to the material association context, where economic selective incentives function to tie in members, economic self-interest undermines the cohesion and effectiveness of subgroups, rivals can less easily attract members and establish solvent alternative vehicles, and the entrepreneur formulates policy with singular attention to economic considerations.

Stability. Largely for reasons just discussed, nonmaterial incentives sow the seeds of instability. Any political heterogeneity can stimulate overt opposition among average members and can be exploited by subgroup leaders and rivals. Moreover, heterogeneity and opposition are difficult to avoid through organizational design, since disruptive nonmaterial inducements are hard to control—political issues may rise and fall in salience, political success may be impossible to attain, member enthusiasm may wax and wane, and social interactions among members may change, all due to factors that are beyond the entrepreneur's reach. And if conditions are right, such inducements are inexpensive for opposition leaders to supply in coordinating members, asserting diverse policy positions, and wielding serious sanctions. Thus, especially when purposive values are widespread, nonmaterial incentives can operate to undermine the stability of heterogeneous associations, providing a basis for a greater number of groups that are politically distinct and more internally homogeneous. In a world of material associations, by contrast, economic selective incentives—which are relatively expensive to supply and easy to manipulate—serve to shield a group's membership and financial base from the uncertainties of politics, thereby minimizing these sources of instability. The sole relevance of economic self-interest allows a material association to become larger and more diverse, with much less danger of fragmentation, sanctions, or secession. Indeed, the larger it becomes, the more powerful the entrepreneur's material weapons for eliminating rivals and otherwise fortifying the group's maintenance. In the absence of nonmaterial incentives, both the proliferation and homogeneity of groups are undermined while the stability of existing groups is enhanced.

There is no assertion here that nonmaterial incentives always enhance group representativeness and undermine organizational stability. It is possible to imagine special contexts in which quite the opposite would occur. To emphasize these, however, would be to overlook the truly essential and distinctive role that such incentives can play. Stating this role most generally: they have the potential for producing a more dynamic group context in which politics, political preferences, and group goals are more centrally determining factors than in material associations, linking political considerations more directly to associational size, structure, and internal processes.

Part Two

Evidence on the Bases
for Membership

Six

The Traditional Background

Part 1 presents a logical analysis of interest organizations. This analysis recognizes the importance of a number of different types of participants, integrates a variety of organizational dimensions, and goes well beyond the simple logic of membership with which we began. Nevertheless, as the preceding chapter's work can only underline, it is the logic of membership itself that represents the most fundamental theoretical component. It not only outlines the nature of the decision to join, but also helps us to understand how individuals can be expected to behave as members, the nature of their exchanges with the entrepreneur, and the consequences of all this for organizational formation, maintenance, and internal politics. In shifting from a logical to an empirical analysis, then, the most basis question we can ask is Why do members join?

Definitive answers are not easy to come by. There is simply not very much research to go on, although there is probably as much on the bases of membership as on other internal dimensions of interest groups. Of what research there is, moreover, almost none has been structured by the kind of conceptual scheme we have adopted here. The simple distinction between collective goods and selective incentives is a rarity, there is only sketchy data relating membership to different types of individual values, and there is nothing of any consequence relating informational or perceptual conditions to the membership decision. In view of these problems, we will center our attentions on a crucial question that is more easily approached (but still not easily answered)—the question of whether members join for essentially political or nonpolitical reasons. The analysis of part 2, then, will be primarily concerned with determining what the empirical evidence can tell us about the relative importance of political and nonpolitical inducements.

The scope of the analysis will extend beyond a narrow evaluation of the available studies. An attempt will be made to place the most relevant empirical work within a broader evaluative framework by piecing together the background of theory and research that has conditioned what social scientist know, or think they know, about why people join interest groups. In doing so, we will be more broadly concerned with the traditional way in which interest group membership has been approached and understood, with the impact this has had on the conduct and interpretation of empirical research, and with the kinds of research that do and do not fit into the traditional scheme of things.

All of this will be carried out in the following way. In this chapter, we will outline and evaluate the major components of the traditional background. This background includes the general theoretical notions supplied by pluralism and, to a lesser extent, structural-functionalism. It also includes the essentially supportive, data-based notions derived from two substantial bodies of research—studies of small groups and studies of larger voluntary associations. Once this broad background is mapped out, we will move on in chapter 7 to consider research that has been carried out specifically on economic interest groups—labor unions, farm groups, and business associations. We will then follow up on these research efforts in chapter 8 by presenting some new data on group incentive structures, gathered from a survey of the members of five economic interest groups.

Group Membership:
The Theoretical Background

Systematic thinking about why members join interest groups has been shaped, above all, by the pluralist theoretical tradition, which has long provided a general orientation for those seeking to understand the "place" of interest groups in democratic politics.[1] Three elements of pluralism have greatly influenced conventional understanding of the act of joining. The first element is the tendency to approach social and

political systems from the standpoint of the interests they contain—
and, more specifically, the tendency to see diverse interests as the
fundamental basis of social and political pluralism, with organized
groups as secondary phenomena that arise from interest bases.

Madison, for instance, wrote about "factions," which were collec-
tions of individuals motivated by common purposes. He was not describing formal organizations and did not attribute importance to these
aggregates because of their structural qualities or capacities for endur-
ance. He was describing instead a pluralism of interests, the likelihood
that individuals would concert their resources and activities on the
basis of common interests, the dangers for liberty and stability implied
by such action, and the constitutional and social means by which the
dangers might be avoided.[2] Alexis de Tocqueville differed from Madison in singling out voluntary associations and in extolling the positive
functions they perform in maintaining a vibrant democracy. Like
Madison, however, his emphasis is not on groups as organizational
structures but, rather, on the underlying interests that give rise to and
are reflected in group activity. His pluralist democracy consists first
and foremost of a pluralism of interests, which stimulate collective
action for their promotion—for "An association consists simply in the
public assent which a number of individuals give to certain doctrines,
and in the engagement which they contract to promote the spread of
those doctrines by their exertions."[3]

For both these writers, the essence of pluralist society is that there
exist diverse interest bases which motivate individuals to combine for
their realization. The nature of their perspective is well summarized by
Lowi:

> In providing us with a basis for a pluralist view, Madison spoke of
> factions; he said nothing about groups. And a faction is not a group.
> De Tocqueville also does not use groups in his formulation . . . With
> Madison, he viewed pluralist society as composed of large num-
> bers of persons *in the process of forming groups*, rather than
> a society that is organized in groups. A fresh reading of de Tocque-
> ville on voluntary associations gives a strong sense that what
> he had in mind as the genius of American politics was a peacetime
> version of the old Minutemen, poised to act on an issue at a mo-
> ment's notice, but, until called, remaining private individuals en-
> gaged in their own selfish pursuits.[4]

This perspective on society, and on the distinctive relationship between interests and groups, is more fully embraced by some pluralists

than others. It is perhaps least characteristic of those theorists who are sometimes called "philosophical pluralists," among them Maitland, Figgis, Laski, and Cole—who sought to legitimize the existence of private associations and to promote their role as governing and representational units.[5] But even with these writers, the prevailing view was that associations are based upon, and are expressions of, certain social interests that are of fundamental importance. According to Laski, for example, "associations exist to fulfill purposes which a group of men have in common."[6]

Variations among theorists aside, a major legacy of the pluralist tradition is this notion that groups arise spontaneously from common interests. The link between a pluralism of interests and a pluralism of groups rests with the motivational role of interests. When individuals find they have interests in common that can be advanced through collective action, they are stimulated to form groups on that basis. This mode of thought left its stamp on subsequent theory and research. In particular, it helped to shift scholarly concern away from the question of why individuals join interest groups. The answer, after all, appeared so obvious that there was little need to investigate and little theoretical interest in doing so.

The second influential element of pluralism has been touted as an analytically sophisticated version of the first. It rests with the conceptual approach supplied by "group theory," which was first formulated by Bentley, then elaborated and popularized by Truman and Latham.[7] More than any other scholarly efforts, the works of these writers put interest groups on the political map—increasing knowledge about their numbers, types, and activities, stimulating widespread recognition of their political importance, and encouraging empirical research. But, in retrospect, it is clear that they also left considerable confusion in their wake. And this confusion, it seems, actually operated to enhance the influence of pluralist notions about group membership.

Some of the confusion is due to a frequent misinterpretation of group theory's basic concepts. As Bentley stressed again and again, his was "an attempt to fashion a tool"—meaning a conceptual and theoretical tool for understanding politics. More specifically, he was proposing that a conceptual framework oriented around the concepts of "group" and "interest group" be employed in moving toward a theory of politics. The ultimate purpose was not the construction of a theory of interest groups; rather, the concept of interest group was advanced as a tool for understanding political behavior generally. Truman and

Latham maintained this orientation while applying it more comprehensively to the modern American context (and correcting for some of Bentley's polemical excesses). Today, Truman's *The Governmental Process* is widely recognized as the representative text.

The reason for misinterpretation rests with the dual use of the term "interest group." On the one hand, it is used as an analytical device for approaching political activity and is defined accordingly. Truman defines an interest group as "any group that, on the basis of one or more shared attitudes, makes certain claims upon other groups in the society for the establishment, maintenance, or enhancement of forms of behavior that are implied by the shared attitudes."[8]

A collection of individuals becomes a group, according to Truman, when they interact with some frequency; and they thus become an interest group when they interact on the basis of shared attitudes and make claims consistent with them. Furthermore, "the shared attitudes . . . constitute the interests".[9] This inevitably brings us back to the conventional pluralist notion that common interests form the basis for interest groups and that the policies interest groups pursue reflect those common interests.

These conventional notions pervade his theoretical treatment of group formation and the motivations for group membership. On balance, he stresses two underlying sets of factors as explanations for the emergence of groups: (*a*) those factors—e.g., specialization, division of labor, and other aspects of modernization—that create distinctive social interests, and (*b*) those more immediate, "disequilibrating" factors—e.g., impending threats to specific interests—that serve to stimulate individuals to act on the basis of those interests. To put this another way: a pluralism of groups arises from a pluralism of interests when individuals are stimulated to pursue their common interests due to various types of "disturbances" that rouse them into action.

An interest group maintains its essence, however, regardless of its extent of organization, since the latter characteristic simply tells us something about the ways in which members interact. As Truman puts it, "The existence of neither the group nor the interest is dependent upon formal organization . . . . Organization indicates merely a stage or degree of interaction."[10] If interactions among members are highly structured, the group becomes an "organized interest group." If interactions are entirely lacking, it is called a "potential interest group," which, in effect, is simply an amorphous bunch of people who happen to share certain attitudes. But all interest groups, ranging from the highly organized to the potential, have a basic trait in common: their members possess common interests on the basis of which claims are at least potentially asserted against other groups in society.

For the group theory variant of pluralism, then, the interest group is an analytical entity which has common interests and the pursuit of common interests built right into it. This is carried out in order to provide the theorist with a conceptual tool to structure his approach to all of politics. He is directed to look at politics in terms of the various interests that are involved, whether organized or unorganized, the individuals who share those interests, the extent to which they interact on that basis, and the methods they adopt for pursuing common interests. From the perspective of group theory, all politics is interest group politics—but this is true by analytical design, and says nothing more than that politics is being interpreted through the employment of a special conceptual device.[11]

This says nothing about the nature, importance, or political roles of those actual organizations which are commonly referred to as interest groups. In the first place, whether the National Association of Manufacturers, the AFL-CIO, the Farm Bureau, and other political groups are interest groups in Truman's sense is an empirical question. Do their members interact and make claims on the basis of shared attitudes? If not, then these organizations do not qualify as interest groups. In principle, any given organization may have to be viewed as consisting of many different interest groups. In the second place, those political organizations ordinarily referred to as interest groups represent just one of a whole range of political actors which must be conceptualized through the specialized conceptual apparatus of group theory. Thus, "interest group politics" should not direct our attention exclusively or even primarily to these organizations, even if some of them do in fact prove to be interest groups in Truman's sense. The fact that they are ordinarily called interest groups has no bearing whatever on the theoretical role they should play in a group theory of politics.

This brings us to a major failing of the group theorists. They have not remained consistent with their theoretical program. After carefully setting out the interest group concept and the general logic of their approach to politics, they have proceeded in application to place almost exclusive *substantive* emphasis upon those organizations ordinarily characterized as interest groups. In doing so, they have equated, without empirical justification, the analytical construct with its concrete organizational namesake. The wider, analytical content of the group concept is not completely lost in the process—Truman is careful to call these actors "organized interest groups" to stress their high degree of structure and sometimes uses the term "interest group" to refer to various kinds of shared-attitude groupings. Nevertheless, in the substantive analysis, it is the so-called organized groups that occupy center stage, and his study of interest group politics comes across as a study of how interest organizations participate in, affect, and are affected by the larger political system.

Truman does not, however, demonstrate that these entities meet the definitional requirements that would justify calling them organized interest groups. Ironically, in one of the most detailed treatments available on internal associational life, he demonstrates just the opposite: he points out that associations tend to be run by an active minority, he embraces important aspects of Michels's explanation of oligarchy, and he argues that expressed and latent disagreement with associational policy is common. His analysis of internal politics is, in effect, nothing less than an examination of how policies emerge in the absence of shared policy attitudes among members. It is important and revealing precisely for this reason—that is to say, precisely because the objects of his attention often are not interest groups according to his own definition.

This is a paradox unintended by Truman and not generally recognized by his readers, who have largely ascribed significance to other aspects of his analysis. More specifically, *The Governmental Process* is primarily remembered both for its comprehensive analysis of what interest organizations do in politics and for its group-oriented approach to politics. Only rarely is it suggested that these aspects deal with two quite different kinds of "interest groups" and that the substantive analysis is not by any means a straightforward application of the theoretical framework.

Regarding the act of membership, in particular, the net impact of Truman's group theory has been to reinforce the traditional pluralist notion that common interests are the motivational basis for group formation. Actual interest organizations are paraded as interest groups, which, by definition, are comprised of individuals who interact on the basis of shared attitudes. Group formation, in turn, is explained in terms of how these shared attitudes come about and how individuals are stimulated to act to achieve them. Thus, by virtue of the dual employment of the interest group concept, the bridge between the analytical and the concrete has proved an all too easy one to cross, in both the development and subsequent interpretation of group theory. While "analytical pluralism," as it has been called, succeeded in introducing a degree of rigor and systematic analysis into the mainstream of pluralist thought, the most fundamental pluralist beliefs—about interests, groups, and their motivational connection—were left intact and indeed were afforded additional support.

The traditional beliefs about common interests, together with the conceptual confusions inherent in group theory, have helped to perpetuate a third characteristic of pluralism. This is the tendency for interest groups to be thought of in political terms—as political groups that engage in political activities and recruit members on the basis of their support for certain political goals. Pluralist thinkers, however, are only partially responsible for this view. Certainly Tocqueville, the philosophical pluralists, and the group theorists did take into account nonpolitical aspects of the group system, noting that there are diverse types of groups based on nonpolitical interests and that political groups have their nonpolitical aspects. The telling point is that pluralist modes of thought have been embraced by political scientists, who, of course, are distinctively concerned with thinking about, describing, and explaining political behavior, and who have naturally tended to emphasize the political aspects of pluralism.

Within the group universe, the important groups are seen as those that become political interest groups by pursuing their goals through governmentally related action. Moreover, the common interests on which these groups are based, and which their goals express, are viewed from this same political perspective—interest groups arise from shared political attitudes and maintain their membership base by pursuing goals consistent with them. Thus, even though it is well known that many associations, especially economic associations, provide numerous nonpolitical services for members, these tend to be overlooked as important aspects of the groups themselves. With the focus on politics, political goals, and political interests, and with the traditional tendency to bind common interests securely to group goals, the motivational value and potential implications of the nonpolitical received very little attention.

Before moving on to other matters, we should pause to note that, while pluralism is the theoretical tradition that seems to have had the greatest influence on prevailing beliefs about interest groups, there is another approach that deserves at least some mention: structural functionalism. This is a wholistic approach to politics that, at least in its more elaborate and sophisticated forms, does not have deep roots in political science; and, while somewhat in vogue for a period of time, it has so far failed to generate much in the way of useful theory and research on interest groups. Like pluralism, however, its language as well as the rudiments of its theoretical perspective have been prevalent in the political discourse of recent decades. It is in this subtle fashion that structural functionalism, especially as popularized by Almond, appears to have influenced scholarly views on interest groups.[12]

Briefly, structural functionalism understands politics as a system of interrelated behaviors and (distinguishing it from other systems approaches) singles out certain functions that must be performed if the system is to survive. In his best-read work, Almond outlines five input functions (recruitment, socialization, communication, interest articulation, and interest aggregation) and three output functions (rule making, rule application, and rule adjudication). These functions are performed by structures, and the major empirical questions center around which structures perform which functions, how well, in what ways, and so on. Interest groups enter into the framework as structures and are analyzed accordingly.

Almond argues that, in a "developed" polity, functional requirements will tend to be carried out by highly specialized and distinctive structures. Within the Almond scheme, interest groups perform the interest articulation function: they are the channels by means of which narrow demands are transported from the social system into the political system. There, the demands are aggregated by the parties, whose task is to combine and rationalize the demands articulated by others. Additional structures—corresponding to the legislature, the executive, and the judiciary—then take over in translating these and other inputs into policy outputs of various kinds.

This assuredly oversimplifies structural functionalism. But these are precisely the concepts and rudimentary theoretical elements that have shown the greatest staying power in political science. And this is what counts. In particular, we are frequently reminded that interest groups are primarily "interest articulators," while parties are primarily "interest aggregators." The almost unavoidable consequence is that interest groups tend to be portrayed as more or less homogeneous units whose internal processes are not of great theoretical concern; conflict, dissension, and compromise are after all characteristics of aggregation processes—and parties, not interest groups, are the proper agencies of interest aggregation. Thus, when structural-functional language is used to describe politics, there is often an implicit tendency to take a one-dimensional view of interest groups, or at least to emphasize the articulation aspect of what interest groups are, what they do, and why they are important.

Concerning the question of individual motivations, the subtle influence of structural functionalism has dovetailed nicely with the effects of prevailing pluralist modes of thought. By stressing the articulation function of groups, handing the aggregation activities over to parties, and diluting the significance of internal group processes, it has indirectly helped to perpetuate the notion that interest groups exist on the basis of narrow common interests and serve as vehicles for injecting these interests into politics. Certainly it has not encouraged an empirical investigation of what actually goes on inside these vehicles. Thus, while pluralism must be adjudged the major influence, elements of structural functionalism appear to have played supporting roles in diluting the theoretical importance of member motivation.

Group Membership:
The Data Background

In recent years especially, discussions of voluntary associations have not been carried on in the absence of empirical findings. While speculation, unsystematic observation, and traditional modes of thought have played their parts, a good deal of research has been relied upon as well. Some of this data refers explicitly to economic interest groups and will be examined in the following chapter. Here, we will offer a brief description of the sort of information that has gone into an evaluation of voluntary associations generally, suggesting the data background that has helped to color fundamental notions about interest groups.

The components of this background are two bodies of research: studies of small groups and studies of larger voluntary associations. With very few exceptions, these represent research efforts by social-psychologists and sociologists, not political scientists. It is not very surprising, then, that the vast portion of their work is not about interest groups, political issues, political interests, or political motivations and thus that most of their work is only of indirect relevance to our present theoretical concerns. Indeed, even when they have included political considerations within their purview, they have tended to structure their analysis around questions that have little bearing on the theoretical issues dwelled upon earlier. Nevertheless, these studies are quite important; they are frequently cited in political analyses, and they have helped to shape prevailing beliefs about the incentives to which interest group members respond. Because political scientists have generally avoided undertaking such studies themselves, they have had little alternative but to understand interest groups through information collected for quite other purposes.

The study of small groups derived initially from theory and research on large organizations, especially business firms.[13] Its development was spurred by the now-famous Hawthorne experiments, which suggested that what happens inside a large organization cannot be understood with reference only to its formal structure, nor with reference solely to the economic rewards by means of which it most obviously attempts to induce compliance. Substantial importance was ascribed instead to the informal groups—the small, face-to-face groups not reflected in the organizational chart—to the social relationships among members of such groups, and to the essentially noneconomic rewards and pressures that characterize group life, shape member attitudes, and influence member behavior.[14]

In at least one respect, this discovery was a fortuitous one for researchers—for small groups are much easier to study than larger organizations. The result in the years since the Hawthorne experiments has been a burgeoning literature on small groups. Many studies have taken as their subjects groups that have been artificially created in the laboratory, and whose internal and external environments have been controlled in accordance with specific research designs. Other studies have attempted to describe and explain behavior in on-going groups in the field—work groups, for example—which offer a more realistic but typically less manageable context. Whether carried out in the field or in the laboratory, however, they are employed to shed scientific light on the principles underlying organizational behavior.

We can generalize somewhat to suggest the motivational perspective that these studies promote. Most commonly, group members are viewed as possessing certain psychic needs that serve as the motivational basis for their behavior, prominent among them needs for acceptance, security, respect, status. The group is viewed as a social system in which members seek to gratify their needs through social relationships with other group members. The group is maintained when members are willing to remain within it, and thus when their needs are being met satisfactorily. Or, to put this another way, the group is maintained when members are attracted to it because of the need satisfactions they derive. The strength of this attraction is a measure of the group's cohesion. In the final analysis, then, the group is seen as a social system whose maintenance and, more generally, whose ability to endure stressful conditions, depend upon the extent of its internal cohesion—which is a reflection of the social bonds existing among its constituent members and the satisfaction that these imply for individual needs. The key benefits that members derive from group life are social and expressive, not economic. The theoretical emphasis is accordingly on "affective attachment" and "socioemotional involvement." These are the motivational elements that bind group members together.

Affective factors explaining group maintenance also play a role in determining the extent to which individual attitudes and behavior will be influenced by group life. Probably the most important vehicle of influence is group norms; once they have developed out of member interactions, individuals will tend to conform to them and to accept (internalize) them to the degree that they are attracted to the group, and hence to the degree that felt needs are met through group membership and participation. Acceptance of group norms may subsequently have a feedback effect, strengthening affective attachments. Furthermore, when the group is engaged in the pursuit of certain goals (which often occurs because they are assigned tasks by the researcher), its instrumental abilities depend upon the extent to which group norms and affective attachments allow for instrumentally appropriate influences on member behavior. They are most likely to work in this direction when group goals are embraced by members and serve as sources of expressive benefits, thus connecting the affective and the instrumental. But successful goal-pursuit does not require such a connection. Instrumental behavior may come about when the goals themselves are of no motivational value to members, as when social rewards induce individuals to complete intrinsically unrewarding tasks.

When one or more leaders emerge within the group, they must somehow deal with the fact that goal achievement is closely related to the affective basis of member involvement. This brings us to a fundamental distinction in the small groups literature, the distinction between two basic leadership tasks: the socioemotional task of group maintenance and the instrumental task of goal achievement. These tasks are often reflected, moreover, in the emergence of specialized leaders—

socioemotional leaders and instrumental leaders—who undertake their performance within given groups. The central leadership problem, which often requires at least tacit coordination among leaders, is that of attaining a proper balance between affective satisfactions and instrumental performance. Sole focus on the latter will tend to undermine the affective bonds that tie members into the group, while undue emphasis on socioemotional considerations will cause the efficiency and effectiveness of goal pursuit to suffer. What is called for is a meshing of these aspects, such that affective attachments and group norms operate to encourage the kinds of attitudes and behaviors that support the group's instrumental ends.

Admittedly, this limited outline does not do justice to the complexity of small groups theory and research. It is nevertheless adequate for our purposes, because the simplified concepts and regularities noted above are actually quite central to popular perspectives on voluntary associations generally. For the most part, writers have been willing to make the inferential leap from small groups to groups of any size, arguing, or more often assuming, that we can learn about larger associations by studying their microcosmic counterparts. Underpinning this is the related argument that larger associations, regardless of formal structure, are comprised of many informal subgroups, to which the small groups research directly applies. This is consistent with the lesson of the Hawthorne experiments and represents at least a plausible justification for the inferential leap. Another reason for making this transference, however, is simply a practical one: few detailed studies of need satisfaction, group norms, cohesion, attitudinal changes, and behavioral influences have been carried out with reference to larger voluntary associations. The small groups literature thus appears as an available store of the right kind of social-psychological information, information that is relevant to larger groups but difficult to collect in that complex a social system.

It is still another question whether or not this transference is valid. Abstract arguments can and have been made on both sides, but the answer can only be obtained through detailed studies of voluntary associations and, as we will see below, their current state is substantially inadequate as a basis for confident evaluation. The important point, at any rate, is that research on small groups has in fact colored prevailing notions about member involvement in voluntary associations and about the nature of interest group membership in particular.

It imparts a documented perspective on member motivations and imparts a more general perspective on the linkages that connect member motivations, group maintenance, and goal achievement.

In application to voluntary associations, these notions reflect more a mood than a set of strictly formulated beliefs. They do not require us to reject economic motivations as bases of individual action, for economic rewards and sanctions can clearly have a bearing upon the satisfaction of basic human needs. Nor do they require us to view the factor of group size as an insignificant consideration, since it is well known that social relationships are affected by differences in the number of participants. The importance of the perspective, rather, is in its emphasis—on the similarities across groups, on the social nature of group life, on the satisfaction of needs through social interaction, on the affective bonds that help keep the group together, and on the socioemotional prerequisites of goal achievement. Viewing voluntary associations from this standpoint, we are led to focus on the noneconomic forces at work on the individual. Even when explicitly economic goals are being pursued by the group, and when the individual is considered to be in substantial agreement, we are encouraged to underline the expressive bases of belonging, feelings of responsibility, pressures toward cooperation and conformity, and the role of social interactions with like-minded members. These are the socioemotional foundations of goal pursuit.

Such notions pervade the literature on groups. To take the most notable example: David Truman, in his substantive analysis, relies heavily on the concepts, perspectives, and findings of small groups research in a systematic treatment of groups generally. Major importance is attributed to the need for acceptance, pressures to conform, and group norms as forces that bind individuals to the group, shape and strengthen shared attitudes, and influence behavior. The inferential leap from small groups (for which data is plentiful) to large interest organizations (for which there is very little) is frequent and usually inconspicuous. Truman is quite aware of what he is doing, however, and argues that it is justified. In his analysis of leadership, for instance, he says:

> It will be obvious that the bulk of the data upon which these propositions about leadership rest are drawn from relatively small groups not fully organized. This limitation does not detract from the usefulness of these propositions, for if they are psychologically valid for that stage of group life antecedent to formal organization,

they are also likely to be appropriate to more formalized situations. Human behavior is not basically different in these two stages of group life, which, as has been noted before, blend imperceptibly one into the other.[15]

His analysis of internal politics, we should note, often cites small groups research when motivational questions are being discussed—and, not coincidentally, sees the primary leadership task as that of maintaining cohesion, especially through the cultivation of shared attitudes.

Even more importantly, perhaps, this stress on the affective bases of member involvement is well illustrated in Sidney Verba's *Small Groups and Political Behavior,* which is probably the one book on small groups that has been most widely read in political science. Verba believes that socioemotional bonds are of central importance for the maintenance of groups of all sizes:

Insofar as the group can achieve some satisfactory balance between the instrumental and the affective aspects of its interaction and a stable leadership structure is developed, the group will be effective and contribute to the satisfactions of its members. Insofar as such a balance cannot be reached and such a structure is not developed, groups will either fall apart or continue operating at high levels of tension. This problem, we can assume, is faced not only by small groups, but by larger organizations and political systems as well . . . The question must then be asked: how do social systems—whether small experimental groups, on-going groups, organizations or political systems—maintain a satisfactory level of affective integration at the same time that they carry on instrumental activities whose tendency may be to lower the degree of affective satisfaction of the participants?[16]

In all essential respects, this same motivational perspective on associational membership can be found in the second component of the data background, research on voluntary associations.[17] This component is underdeveloped by comparison, at least with regard to the kinds of motivational questions that concern us here. The vast majority of studies has been carried out by sociologists, who have tended to investigate the social characteristics of individuals—class, education, occupation, race, sex, religion, and so on—and to correlate these characteristics with participation (often just membership) in voluntary associations. Social-psychological questions about attitudes, personality, and socialization have received relatively little attention.

Not only is there a discernible imbalance in the literature; but, of those studies that are oriented around social-psychological considerations, most do not deal specifically with motivations to join or participate. They tend to focus instead upon the general psychological or attitudinal distinctions between members and nonmembers, between active and inactive members, or among all three. Rose, for instance, suggests that associational activists are less anomic and more tolerant than average citizens;[18] Tannenbaum and Backman argue that active members are more likely to hold uniform attitudes than inactive members;[19] Almond and Verba demonstrate that feelings of political competence are higher for active members than for inactive members, and higher for inactive members than for nonmembers.[20] A number of other studies suggest that associational membership is correlated with such personality traits as extraversion, sociability, friendliness, self-confidence, optimism, assertiveness, aggressiveness, dependability, and creativity.[21]

To be sure, those types of social-psychological research are at least indirectly related to the reasons individuals join groups. The natural compulsion to account for documented differences across classes of individuals inevitably gives rise to the question of whether (a) the psychological and attitudinal characteristics play a motivational role, disposing some people to participate in groups more than others, or (b) the process of participation has socializing effects on participants, thus bringing about the observed characteristics. Some writers have seen fit to consider this problem, while others have not, but any conclusions are mainly speculative, since there is very little data of direct relevance on which to base an evaluation. Studies simply are not designed to provide an answer; data on socialization, in particular, are largely lacking.

What, then, does the literature on associations have to say directly about why individuals join interest groups? With some exceptions to be reviewed in the next chapter, not very much. Generally speaking, when studies have been carried out to investigate motivations, political groups have not been singled out as distinctive associations worthy of special attention, nor have economic incentives played a prominent, interesting, or distinctive role in their motivational schema. Additionally, again with a few exceptions, there is no attempt to distinguish between collective goods and selective incentives; rarely is there even a hint in this direction.

What we find instead is that the motivational studies as a whole appear to have come out of the small groups tradition. In the first place, they tend to have adopted the same concepts in structuring their approach to member involvement and group life; attitudes and behavior tend to be approached in terms of fundamental needs, social pressures, group norms, feelings of duty or responsibility, and so on. Second, there is often an implicit theoretical perspective that places emphasis upon the socioemotional bases of involvement and that effectively directs attention away from economic and political factors. This is true even when the groups under study happen to be economic interest groups. Indeed, it is much easier to find research on social interactions, group norms, and avenues for need satisfaction within such groups than it is to find even the simplest information on whether or not members support the political positions taken by the group.

A third element of commonality with the small-groups literature is manifest in a tendency to study associations as instances of a more universal phenomenon, "group life." Thus, when motivational studies are (infrequently) carried out, they tend to bear upon the need satisfactions and attitudes of members, active and inactive members, and nonmembers—placing only secondary importance, if any at all, on how these may vary across different types of groups. They are first and foremost "groups," whose members are variously involved in "group life." And finally, a fourth bond between the two areas of research rests with the fact that theoretical and empirical works on voluntary associations, plagued by inadequate information relating to microlevel considerations, often rely upon small groups research to fill in the evidence gaps in the literature. The latter studies are referred to, quoted, footnoted, in an effort to document the existence of certain characteristics of associations and their members. This only serves to reinforce the other similarities noted above.

In brief, while most studies of voluntary associations deemphasize or avoid social-psychological considerations, focusing instead on social-background characteristics, those that deal directly with motivational variables tend to reflect a close correspondence to small groups research. Member involvement tends to be understood in terms of needs, need gratification, group norms, and related concepts; and theoretical emphasis commonly falls on the socioemotional bases of individual attraction to the group. The distinctive importance of economic groups, economic incentives, and political goals thus tends to be lost in a more general, all-inclusive approach to associational behavior. Indeed, some writers have gone so far as to present romantic, even whimsical views of what voluntary action "means" to the individual participant. The following characterization comes from one of the leading students of voluntary associations.

> Thus, when we speak of voluntary action at the level of individual behavior we are not talking about human behavior that is primarily motivated by physiological needs or personal-social necessity, nor about what one does because of coercion or sociopolitical necessity, nor again about what one does mainly to earn his living or to gain direct, immediate economic benefits. What we are talking about is human behavior that is essentially *motivated by the desire for other kinds of psychic benefits of one kind or another.*
>
> . . . The essential notion is that *individual voluntary action, as defined here, is what we do not because we have to but because we want to in view of the higher level psychic benefits it may give us and in view of some commitment to a larger goal.*[22]

These summary comments on the data background are sufficient to convey its general thrust. There is, however, one aspect of the associational literature that we have yet to consider, but that deserves mention as a potential source of productive research. This is the typology that divides associations into two classes, expressive and instrumental. These types have been recognized for some time in sociological analyses, but have been popularized and most seriously explicated in the research efforts of Jacoby and Babchuk, Gordon and Babchuk, and a few others.[23] Expressive groups are defined as those in which activities are internally oriented, provide immediate gratifications to participants, and are ends in themselves. Instrumental groups have the opposite properties—activities are externally oriented toward some goal, gratifications are deferred until goals are realized, and activities are means to an end rather than intrinsically beneficial. This is a promising typology because it singles out for special attention those groups that pursue goals in an external context, highlights the motivational role that goals can play, and gets away from the tendency to underline the socioemotional bases of member involvement. While it has yet to produce any useful research, it might eventually help to encourage an examination of why individuals join instrumental groups.[24]

Analytically, however, it is largely inadequate. It is obviously grounded on the favorite small groups distinction between the socioemotional and the instrumental aspects of group life, which are simply transformed into associational types. There is no good reason for this, other than the everyday observation that some groups pursue externally directed goals and others do not. Moreover, it completely overlooks important motivational factors. Where, for instance, do economic selective incentives fit in? The answer is that they do not fit in at all; they are certainly not expressive, nor are they goal-related (instrumental). By continuing the unwarranted emphasis on the socioemotional and the instrumental, the typology almost guarantees that the far-reaching significance of economic factors will be missed.

There are additional problems with the expressive-instrumental distinction as well, some of them due to its incorporation (via definition) of the unfounded belief that individuals join groups out of agreement with group goals. But a discussion of these matters would take us too far afield. Instead, we should simply stress that this typology, which appears to be popular among students of associations, is inappropriate for the study of interest groups. At best, it may eventually generate some information on why members join associations; but even then it is not likely to be the kind of information we are looking for.

Conclusion

In sum, the data background on member motivations is largely the product of work carried out by sociologists and social psychologists, who tend to view groups as systems of social relationships. Commonly, they are not directly concerned with political or economic activities, goals, attitudes, and issues, but, rather, with the more general social and psychological aspects of group life, as manifested in both small groups and larger voluntary associations. Most of the data background on why members join interest groups, then, derives from studies that have not specifically taken interest group members themselves as subjects of analysis.

As we have suggested, the two components of the data background are closely connected; in particular, the literature on voluntary associations, or at least that part of it dealing with motivations, substantially reflects the social-psychological concepts, theoretical perspectives, and empirical findings of the small groups literature. By virtue of these linkages, they are able to supply a fairly coherent view of member involvement in groups.

This data background has operated in combination with the theoretical background, particularly the pluralist tradition, to influence conventional perspectives on member motivations. To be sure, they do not provide an explicit, clearly defined set of ideas and relationships. Indeed, in some ways, they even appear inconsistent with one another. For instance, pluralist thought asserts that members join in pursuit of common interests, while empirical works have suggested that group maintenance might occur without member support for group goals, via affective attachment. But apparent inconsistencies of this sort are not of primary importance here. We are less concerned with contrasting specific elements than we are with portraying the popular view of interest groups that both the theoretical and data backgrounds have helped to bring about and support. And popular views are not always logically precise.

At the heart of this eclectic perspective is the simple notion that both common interests and socioemotional attachments have roles to play in understanding member involvement. Interest groups are organized for the "purpose" of pursuing certain goals in an external environment, and individuals tend to become members because they generally support the group's efforts. In Truman's language, they join because they have certain shared attitudes that are reflected in the group's goals. Or, as Jacoby and Babchuk phrase it, "people will affiliate with instrumental associations to advance the goals which such associations seek." [25] But each interest group is potentially more than an instrumental vehicle for the pursuit of common interests; it is to some extent a context of social interaction within which members seek socioemotional satisfaction. Some of these benefits may derive from sources (friendship, recreation) that are quite independent of group goals. Yet, because interest groups exist for the purpose of pursuing goals, social relationships and group norms are largely oriented around those goals and help to influence individual attitudes and behavior in appropriate ways; moreover, the goals themselves can serve as bases of affective attachment whether or not members interact frequently.

Thus the satisfactions of members tend to be connected to the nature and pursuit of associational policy. This is most easily seen when groups are large and member interactions infrequent, since here group goals are the only real object of affective attachment. But even in small interest groups with high levels of interaction and participation, it is the goals that are of predominant importance; they provide the motivational basis for the existence and direction of group life. The most significant thing to know about an interest group, then, is the nature of its goals. Socioemotional satisfactions are made possible mainly because of shared member attitudes about associational policy, and help to support the organizational vehicle.

In terms of our own theoretical framework, then, this clearly leads to a distinctive perspective on the nature of interest groups as organizations. It claims, in essence, that economic self-interest and economic selective incentives are not major motivational factors, that the crucial roles are played instead by the kinds of nonmaterial values and incentives introduced in chapter 5, and that our organizational expectations—about communications, administration, internal politics, stability, and the like—should be shaped accordingly. If we are to believe the traditional theoretical and data background, actual interest groups do not even closely resemble the material associations of our earlier analysis. To the extent that the logical analysis of part 1 helps to explain individual and organizational behavior, the explanatory key rests with the departures from the economic ideal examined in chapter 5.

Seven

Studies of Economic
Interest Groups

While the theoretical and data backgrounds have combined to dominate popular modes of thinking about member motivation, the empirical question remains: Why do individuals join interest groups? As we have argued, the bulk of the group literature provides little information of direct relevance, although it does supply broad theoretical notions that are, in some sense, documented by research. There is, however, a comparatively small number of studies, carried out specifically on economic interest groups, that helps to shed more detailed light on the kinds of motivational questions that concern us. Most of these studies deal with labor unions, but there are at least some data available as well for farm and business groups. The nature of existing information for each type of group is briefly outlined below, allowing for conclusions which, while tentative, take us several important steps beyond the traditional perspective on membership.

Labor Unions

In investigating why workers join unions, we will make one major departure from generality by considering American workers separately from European workers. Although only sparsely documented by research on union members, there is a virtual consensus among educated observers that workers in these two contexts tend to reflect sharply different motivations in their organizational behavior. The European worker is said to place substantial emphasis upon class consciousness and feelings of solidarity, while the American worker is primarily motivated by economic self-interest. Because these incentive bases have important theoretical consequences, it is useful to maintain the separation in our own discussion.

Turning first to American unions, we can begin by distinguishing between their economic and political aspects, suggesting the kinds of benefits that each can generate for members.[1] On the economic side, the salient component is, of course, the collective bargaining structure—responsible for higher wages, valuable fringe benefits, better working conditions, and other changes resulting from negotiation with management. But there are many other economic benefits that unions often provide as well: seniority rules and procedures protect member jobs and opportunities; unions pursue member grievances, help solve problems in the workplace, and sometimes supply legal assistance; they may provide employment information, job training, and educational opportunities; they may offer discounts on commercial products and other economic benefits unrelated to the workplace. There are thus any number of supplementary ways that unions might operate to make an individual member better off economically, especially with respect to job security. Higher wages and better working conditions are only part of a much broader package of benefits.

Unions often have a political side to them as well, on which public policy positions are formulated, resources are allocated for their pursuit, and members are supplied with certain benefits. The policies can be found to embody a range of interests; sometimes they are narrowly economic, reflecting specialized worker interests in technical issues, and sometimes they take the form of broad social policies concerned with such issues as civil rights and foreign affairs. Similarly, their pursuit also takes various forms: lobbying at local, state, and national levels, efforts to influence public opinion, supporting candidates in elections, participation in party nomination processes, etc. All unions are not identical in these respects, of course; broad social policies and active political participation, for instance, are more characteristic of national unions and the AFL-CIO than of the individual locals comprising them. But the locals, too, often have their political sides, especially if they are large and well financed.

The economic and political components of the union each supply members with collective goods and selective incentives. The collective goods derive from those functions that unions are most widely recognized for performing. Collective bargaining leads to higher wages and better working conditions, which are collective goods to the extent that they are available to all workers in a given jurisdiction, regardless of membership in the union. (If they are only available to union members, however, these benefits can operate as selective incentives.) The pursuit of political goals, on the other hand, often leads to pro-labor candidates, legislation, and administrative rulings that represent benefits for union members and nonmembers alike. These are supplemented by various selective incentives. On the economic side, probably the major selective incentive is job security; but, as noted above, there may be quite a number of additional selective incentives that also enhance the value of union membership—pensions, educational opportunities, job training, discounts, and so on. On the political side, by contrast, the selective incentives are likely to be purposive as well as economic: members who agree with group goals, especially if motivated by class consciousness and feelings of solidarity, may join and participate because of expressive benefits gained from doing so.

Two further considerations help to round out our characterization of union benefits. First, the union is also a social context, and the social relations among members may have some motivational bearing on their behavior. Union membership may extend solidary rewards due to friendship, status, recreational activities, clubs, and the like, and interactions may at the same time generate social pressure to join and conform. The second consideration, which is of special consequence in the American context, is the legal environment—which encourages and protects union security agreements and thus legitimizes "compulsory membership." The vast majority of American union members, approximately 75 percent, are covered by such agreements and *must* belong to the union if they are to keep their jobs.[2] This, in effect, is another type of economic selective incentive that operates in conjunction with the others. Security agreements do not force individuals to join, but instead give them a particularly compelling economic reason for joining.

The widespread existence of security agreements does not in itself imply that most union members join because they must. There is a varied set of incentives—economic and noneconomic, collective and selective—to which members might respond; and, regardless of security arrangements, these may clearly play motivational roles in workers' decisions to join. Even if an individual is required to belong in order to keep his job, we may find that his major motivation rests with a purposive support of working-class ideals or with a personal concern for seniority advantages, and that he would have joined in the absence of security arrangements. The question of member motivation therefore remains an open one, despite the prevalence of compulsory unionism, and it is the task of empirical inquiry to sort out the relative importance of the various incentives involved.

This task is addressed squarely by Olson, whose analysis of unions is one of the few studies carried out within a collective goods/selective incentives framework.[3] He singles out a number of potential inducements for union membership, including such noneconomic considerations as social pressure and violence. He concludes that, while a variety of incentives—especially social incentives—seem to have played motivational roles in the emergence of the first craft unions (which were small), and while these probably continue to play a role in the smaller locals of today, the major explanatory element in most unions is compulsion. This is the effect primarily of union security agreements, and secondarily of threats of physical force. As Olson puts it, "Most unions can no longer draw a great deal of strength from small groups, and a union's noncollective benefits cannot usually be sufficient to bring in very many members. Smallness and noncollective benefits can probably now explain only the exceptional union. In most cases it is compulsory membership and coercive picket lines that are the source of the union's membership."[4]

Olson does not substantiate this conclusion with reference to survey research because there is really nothing there to draw upon; thus, he is not able to point to large numbers of workers who actually say that their union membership is due to compulsion. Instead, he relies upon aggregate figures for the growth of union membership over time—showing, among other things, that dramatic increases in membership occurred subsequent to legal changes, particularly the Wagner Act of 1935, which allowed for compulsory unionism. Indeed, total union membership jumped 55 percent in 1937 alone.[5] Given the data constraints that Olson had to deal with, his argument is quite convincing. His aggregate figures give us good reason for believing that compulsion does in fact play an important motivational role.

Just how much importance we should ascribe to the compulsion factor, however, remains unclear. When member motivations have been empirically investigated, attention has commonly been focused on the different benefits associated with membership and on their importance to individual workers; there has been no systematic attempt to take the separate motivational impact of compulsion into account. As a result, we are somewhat able to determine the relative motivational roles of noncompulsory elements, but we have little basis for determining their individual or combined importance vis-à-vis compulsion.

In reviewing some of the more basic empirical findings, then, we must keep the limitations of these studies in mind. We will usually be dealing with what individuals value most about union membership and not with the precise reasons they may have for retaining membership. Thus, the values involved may not be pivotal. To take only one example: a worker may say he places greatest value on the union's political activities—but, if he had been asked, he might have added that he would nevertheless drop out if membership were not compulsory. In this instance, the individual's membership will appear to be politically motivated when this is not the motivation that explains his decision to join. Our discussion of empirical findings will be unable to make these more subtle distinctions. The best we can do is to suggest the kinds of incentives that members seem to value most, while being careful in offering deeper interpretations.

The most general conclusion to be drawn is that the conventional stereotype of the American worker appears to be fairly accurate.[6] The average union member places primary value upon his own economic interests, views his union instrumentally as a means for achieving economic benefits, and ascribes little salience to the political goals and activities of the group. This is not true for all members, of course, and it is less characteristic of activists than the rank and file. Activists tend to be more interested in political issues, more supportive of union political activities, and more willing to involve the union in broad social policies.

One illustration of this distinction can be found in the work of Seidman and associates, who construct a sevenfold classification of union members on the basis of their research.[7] The nature of union incentive structures is best suggested in their discussion of three of these types: the ideological unionist, the good union man, and the crisis activist.

The ideological unionist. Workers in this category are ideologically motivated, joining and participating in union affairs because of their devotion to an overriding cause. They find politics of key value. "The number of union members of this type is very small, probably not exceeding two per cent at the highest, but where they exist they tend to participate actively in union affairs and frequently become candidates for office.''[8]

The good union man. Workers of this type are distinguished by their dedication to the union itself rather than to an overriding cause per se; ideology may, however, play a secondary role. ''Most active unionists . . . are good union men, as is a proportion of the inactive rank-and-file. The number of good union men is unlikely to exceed ten percent of the membership, and in most locals will probably be under this figure. Good union men, with a sprinkling of ideological unionists, make up the leaders and the active groups.''[9]

The crisis activist. These workers are normally inactive and rarely take part in the union's internal affairs, becoming active only during a crisis, such as a strike. Their involvement in the union is instrumental, not expressive or social. ''They see the union as an agency to which one regularly makes payments and from which,˙in turn, one obtains substantial benefits from time to time. . . . They rarely discuss their duties to the union spontaneously, as good union men do, but rather the potential benefits and rights they think should flow almost automatically in return for payment of dues. . . . [They] are very numerous among rank-and-file unionists, probably outnumbering any other type in many locals.''[10]

The picture that emerges from this and other studies, then, is one of a union context in which only a distinct minority of members places predominant emphasis upon political matters; most are concerned first and foremost with deriving direct economic benefits for themselves. We can elaborate the general picture by sketching in a few additional details about average members. First, it appears not only that they are economically motivated, but also that they ascribe greatest salience to the selective incentives generated by the economic side of the organization, most prominent among them job security. Tannenbaum and Kahn, for instance, found job security to be the one most important motive for union activity.[11] Roberts, upon asking union members what benefits they received through their membership, found that most of them emphasized job security.[12] These and other studies seem to suggest that, while workers certainly value higher wages and better working conditions, and while they would much prefer that their union focus on collective bargaining functions at the expense of political functions, their membership decisions are influenced to a greater extent by economic benefits that are more directly personal: protection, assistance, support.

A second characteristic rests with the nature of member participation. The typical member is only infrequently involved in union affairs; attendance at regular meetings, for example, tends to be around five to ten percent for most locals.[13] Apathy and indifference are the rule rather than the exception. Moreover, when average members choose to become active, their activities are usually stimulated by nonpolitical issues and circumstances, rather than political ones.[14] These characteristics are, of course, understandable if we agree that members tend to be motivated by economic self-interest.

A final characteristic, obviously implicit in the points above, is that expressive and social incentives do not seem to have much motivational value for most American workers, at least in terms of their membership decision. Purposive incentives, particularly those deriving from class consciousness and other elements of class-based ideologies, may have been quite important in the early stages of union formation. This goes without saying for the most radical unions, such as the Industrial Workers of the World; but it is certainly plausible as well for many industrial unions comprising the early CIO. Whatever the case may have been years ago, however, purposive incentives no longer seem to be a major impetus for worker involvement.[15] As Tannenbaum has suggested, "the missionary spirit, the emotions, the disaffection and hostility toward management, the old 'Solidarity Forever' no longer have great meaning and force."[16] There is little basis for believing that social benefits are any more important than expressive incentives. It is true that solidary incentives seem to have been very important in the early days of union development, especially in the craft unions of the American Federation of Labor. And even today it is clear that social relationships, friendships, and acquaintances are particularly likely among union members—who, in contrast to members of many other groups, work together as well as belong to the same association. But social incentives do not appear to have a great deal of bearing on the membership decision.[17] It appears, moreover, that unions commonly have not been very successful in structuring activities so as to generate valuable social benefits. As Lipset notes, union "attempts to impose extra-vocational activities artificially usually fail."[18]

In sum, most union members seem to be tied in to their organizations for nonpolitical reasons. In essential ways, they are paradigmatic Small Members—they stress economic benefits, they place high value on selective incentives, their membership is not contingent upon political considerations, and their individual contributions have little political impact. This appears true, moreover, even without our systematically taking into account the motivational role of legal and physical coercion, on which there is no real research. These can only operate in conjunction with other economic incentives to tie in members more firmly still on nonpolitical bases, reinforcing our tentative conclusions.

Before moving beyond the American context, we should pause to add a few qualifying comments about union activists; for in focusing on average members, we have stressed basic differences between the two types of workers without at the same time suggesting their similarities. In particular, it would be a mistake to view union activists as driven by ideology, class consciousness, and democratic norms—as purposively motivated "vanguards" of working-class organizations. While these motivational traits are more characteristic of activists than the rank and file, their intensity should not be exaggerated. Indeed, the evidence seems to indicate that the primary incentives for union activists in America are the economic and status rewards that activity and especially organizational office can promise. Tannenbaum and Kahn found "little if any indication of class consciousness" among union activists[19] and, in comparing them to the rank and file, suggest that they are only somewhat more politically oriented: "[Actives] give greater priority to goals of a broad and general nature, although the differences are typically small. . . . Highest priority is given by both actives and inactives to goals involving bread-and-butter issues; increasing the local's political action or its say in the running of the plant ranks relatively low. These data are consistent with the view of 'simple pragmatism' as characterizing the American labor movement."[20]

Along with these attitudinal characteristics, certain objective, job-related characteristics have often been empirically associated with activism. Activists tend to be higher than rank-and-file members in pay, skill, seniority, job status, and job satisfaction—which clearly suggests that activists do in fact have more to protect in terms of economic and status values.[21] These economic and status incentives seem to operate even more strongly when the object is the gaining and holding of official union positions. Especially in the United States, there is usually much more money and status attached to a union position than to any job that an ordinary member might hold, and a better chance as well to rise out of the working class both economically and socially. Thus, the union is not only a means of protecting one's job, but it is also an organizational repository of new, better jobs and an accessible vehicle for upward mobility. In Lipset's words, the union office tends to be viewed more as a "career" than a "calling."[22]

In short, the motivational differences between active and average union members are noticeable but undramatic. Activists have a greater tendency to be ideological and concerned with political matters, and the label "economically self-interested" is probably less applicable to them than the rank and file. Nevertheless, it seems clear that the average activist is not primarily motivated by these distinguishing purposive values. The American stereotype appears to hold more or less accurately for both types of members, with immediate, personal rewards generally taking precedence over suprapersonal bases of involvement.

It has been conventional wisdom for some time that European workers are possessed of quite different motivating values, the essence of which can be found in class consciousness and feelings of working-class solidarity. As for the question of why these should prove important in Europe but not the United States, reference is commonly made to contrasting historical traditions—especially to Europe's feudal past, the continuation of rigid class distinctions throughout modernization, serious limitations on upward social mobility, relatively late extension of the suffrage, and other social conditions that operated to insulate and oppress the working class. Out of this historical matrix of politics, society, and culture, it appears, came a tendency for citizens to perceive politicoeconomic problems in terms of class interests rather then individual self-interest, and a tendency to approach their solution through collective action rather than individual action. Even though the overriding goals are economic, then, the "typically European" forces for cohesion emerge as noneconomic: a purposive sense of weness, the social rewards and pressures deriving from solidarity, a responsibility to do one's part in supporting the class and its cause.[23]

Empirically, there is no denying that European workers are in fact more ideological and class-conscious than their American counterparts. This shows up in various ways. In the past few decades, for example, studies have consistently uncovered strong class bases for voting behavior, party identification, and attitudes on issues, as well as for general perceptions on the nature of salient political divisions in society; similar research has documented the considerably weaker role of social class in American politics.[24] Historical studies of the development of trade unions (and political parties) are fraught with the same kinds of motivational contrasts—and, significantly, receive strong support from the fact that European unions have generally been able to enroll a greater proportion of the working class, while relying to a much lesser extent on union security agreements.[25] This suggests that European unions may have that "something extra" that American unions lack, the expressive involvement of workers.

Recent surveys of union members, however, indicate that the European stereotype was more accurate for the earlier, formative stages of the workers' movement than it is for the modern period. Specifically, it appears that workers are steadily becoming less ideological and class conscious in their bases for union involvement and more economically self-interested—a process that has been called the "privatization" or "Americanization" of the European worker. Various factors have contributed to this process. Rising incomes, along with the electoral and policy success of unions and labor parties, have perhaps diluted earlier feelings of disaffection, hostility, and urgency. Trade unions have become increasingly centralized and bureaucratized, and less conducive to expressive individual involvement. Moreover, the unions are increasingly viewed as part of government, since they often participate as insiders in the formation and administration of public policy; and they have perhaps lost their distinctive claim upon the emotions and loyalties of members as a result. Whatever the valid explanation, the process of privatization appears to be a reality. From a motivational standpoint, European workers are increasingly coming to look like American workers.

Studies of workers in various European nations—Britain, Germany, France, Austria, Holland—support this notion that the conventional stereotype no longer even approximates the calculus of most union members.[26] We can illustrate their conclusions with reference to two recent research efforts. One is by van de Vall, on a sample of workers belonging to the Dutch Federation of Trade Unions. The other is by Goldthorpe and associates, on a sample of workers belonging to several different unions in the environs of Luton, England.[27]

Van de Vall's data is presented in a particularly instructive fashion: first, he shows that most members actually perceive the federation as a political organization—as an integral component of the welfare state whose primary functions are performed at this higher level—while, second, he shows that most members join the federation for decidedly nonpolitical reasons. The major bases of membership are economic selective incentives, most prominent among them "conflict insurance, i.e., the provision of legal and material assistance in the case of individual grievances."[28] This union benefit, which obviously corresponds to our earlier notion of job security, is the single most important motivation for joining. "Although some influence of the union's role at the national level cannot be denied, the major causes of the gain or loss of members must be sought in the on the job situation of the individual worker and in the ways in which the union increases his security."[29]

Operating in combination with economic benefits to tie members into the union are social pressures: fully one-third of the members gave this as their main reason for joining, with parents and fellow workers representing the major influences. These workers join the union "mainly on account of the convictions of others. In the light of what has gone before, it is clear that for these workers joining is merely an adjustment of outward behavior, which influences neither their image of the union nor their assessment of its value."[30]

About one-fourth of the members do join for reasons that bear upon the nature of the union's political goals. But, significantly, this motivation is almost exclusively restricted to the older workers. "In the welfare state, it is not the young who come to the union with high ideals. On the contrary, sociocentric motives are extremely rare among members of the younger generation: among the older blue collar workers they are over five times as common, and among the older white collar workers nearly four times as common. This may well be how the trend toward individualization manifests itself in the established trade union."[31]

Whether or not the data indicate a time trend, however, depends upon the extent to which they capture an age-cohort phenomenon, as van de Vall contends, or a life-cycle phenomenon, in which the younger workers will become more ideological as they continue membership in the union. Whatever the answer, it is interesting to know, nevertheless, that not only do most workers belong to the union for nonpolitical reasons—but, in addition, the union is recruiting new members who are even less political than the average.

The study of British workers by Goldthorpe et al., while it does not investigate the age question, comes to precisely the same conclusion about the diluted significance of broad social and political goals.

> Unionism has often represented more to workers than simply a
> means of economic betterment; it has been seen also as a form of
> collective action in which solidarity was an end as well as a means

and as a socio-political movement aiming at radical changes in industrial institutions and in the structure of society generally. In our view, the most distinctive feature of the unionism of the workers we studied is the *extent* to which these wider ideals have ceased to be of significance . . . .

. . . Insofar as we have been able to make use of comparative data, it is, we suggest, fairly clear that the unionism of the workers we studied is distinctive in its instrumental and "self-interested" emphases.[32]

Like van de Vall, the authors take steps to highlight the fact that such nonpolitical motivations are found within organizations that carry on extensive political activities. They note, for instance, the degree to which voluntary worker payments of the political levy (which goes to the Labor Party through the union's political fund) are often made, if at all, for reasons that have nothing to do with support for political goals. In their sample, about 30 percent of the members contracted out; and, of those who did contribute, many (from a third to half, roughly) did not know they were making a contribution. "That is to say, either they do not think they pay the levy but have not contracted out or they admit to having no knowledge of the levy at all. This means, then, that, in addition to the relatively high proportion of those who do contract out, we must recognize also a further sizable category of men who have no awareness of the main way in which, as union members, they are implicated in political affairs."[33]

It is reasonable to speculate further that, of those workers who knowingly made political contributions, some proportion doubtless did so out of social pressure from their fellow workers, especially if these forces are as strong as van de Vall suggests. (The authors do not test for this.) For this sample of workers, therefore, it seems likely that at least half of the funds collected through the political levy are derived from members who make their contributions for nonpolitical reasons. While this may or may not hold true for British workers generally, it remains a striking comment on the underpinnings of "voluntary political contributions."

As these two studies illustrate, then, the evidence seems to signal a shift away from the conventional European stereotype of class-consciousness and ideology toward the American stereotype of economic self-interest. To be sure, European workers appear to be more politically oriented than their American counterparts, and there remains an appreciable gap separating them on our evaluative scale. But all indications are that this is not the qualitative disjunction it was once thought to be, that there may be a time trend toward convergence, and that it is motivational change among the Europeans alone that is probably responsible for any convergence in the recent past.

For neither the American nor European contexts are we able to arrive at a very detailed picture of union incentive structures. But the outlines now seem reasonably clear. The most important conclusion by far is that most members join unions for reasons that are primarily nonpolitical. This appears to be true in both Europe and the United States, conventional stereotypes notwithstanding. Moreover, the explanation seems to lie not with the collective goods generated by the economic side of union organization but, rather, with certain identifiable selective incentives: job security, legal compulsion, supplementary economic benefits, and social pressures.

The relative salience of the different selective incentives is less clear. As far as the noncompulsory aspects of unionism are concerned, job security is the one benefit (really a constellation of benefits) that stands out from the others in both Europe and the United States. Beyond this, however, the two contexts are probably rather different. In the United States, legal compulsion is a nearly universal fact of union life and may play a major motivational role; it may even be more important than job security. In Europe, on the other hand, ideology seems to be salient for at least a larger minority of members. Furthermore, social pressure probably plays a major role in the retention of members. It may be, in fact, that social pressure is the European version of compulsory unionism, representing a kind of "coercion" that is social rather than legal in nature, but that functions equally efficiently as a nonpolitical mechanism for tying members into the union. To take this speculation one step further: it may be that class-consciousness and feelings of solidarity, while strongly held by only a minority, are sufficient in Europe to generate social pressures upon many in the less ideological majority—who might join, then, not out of their own ideological convictions, but because of social pressures generated by the ideological convictions of others. Once inside the union, they may then stress direct economic and solidary benefits over against broad-social and political goals. If this relationship between ideology and social pressure is true, it suggests a distinctive way in which the declining European tradition continues to leave its mark upon workers and their organizations.

Farm Groups

With labor unions, the problem is not so much that studies of union members are lacking but, rather, that so few of them deal with the motivational bases of membership. With farm and business groups, however, the problem is more serious—for their members have only rarely been the subjects of any kind of analysis. When researchers have turned their attention to these economic sectors, their focus has been almost exclusively upon the organizations as corporate entities. As a result, there is not much direct evidence on who belongs to these groups, who the activists are, how the organizations are run, and what kinds of incentives attract member support. Union membership is an open book by comparison.

In this section, we will inquire as best we can into group membership in the farm sector, dividing the analysis into two parts. In the first, we will approach motivational questions indirectly by taking a look at certain characteristics of general farm organizations; in the second, we will consider several studies that directly investigate the motivations of farmer members. The analysis will be confined to the American context in both, since there is little evidence of a comparative nature and what there is does not stress the motivational stereotypes so prominent in the union studies. The same will apply in the following section on business groups.

The American farm sector sports many different types of groups. There are, for instance, several major farm organizations claiming to represent farmers generally—the Farm Bureau, the Farmers Union, the National Grange, and the National Farmers Organization. There are also a number of specialized commodity groups—based on cotton, milk, livestock, etc.—and various kinds of cooperatives. This organizational diversity has not been reflected in the interest group literature. Virtually all attention has been directed at the major farm organizations, since these appear to be the most politically active and influential. The result is that very general information about the emergence, development, and basic traits of these major groups is easily available; and quite a bit of detailed information is available on the Farm Bureau. The historical presentation of this material is commonplace in interest group texts.[34]

Tentative conclusions about member motivations can be inferred from these organizational studies. This is the approach that Olson adopts, much the same as he did with trade unions, applying his conceptual framework to evidence collected for other purposes. He channels most of his efforts into an analysis of the Farm Bureau, with brief attention to the other groups, emphasizing the critical recruitment role played by insurance, cooperatives, and (for the Farm Bureau only) government subsidies and hegemony over governmentally administered benefits. These and other mechanisms enable farm groups to generate an array of economic benefits available only to members, which serve as inducements supplementing any that may derive from political goals and activities. By tracing organizational development in the farm sector, Olson argues convincingly that it is the former incentives that explain why most farmers join their respective groups.[35] This is buttressed by the fact that the Farm Bureau is the largest, richest, and most stable of all farm organizations and, not coincidentally, also has the most impressive package of selective incentives.

There is good reason for accepting Olson's claim. It is clear that farm groups do supply economic selective incentives, and the group supplying them "best" also happens to be more successful than any of its rivals. At this point, we could do what Olson and others have done by embarking upon a review of the organizational evolution of these groups. But this ground has been covered again and again in the literature and little would be gained by covering it yet another time here. It seems more useful to take a brief "inside" look at two major groups, the Farm Bureau and the Farmers Union, with special reference to two studies that appeared after Olson's book was first published: Samuel R. Berger's analysis of the Farm Bureau, *Dollar Harvest*,[36] and John A. Crampton's *The National Farmers Union*.[37] While neither employs the collective goods–selective incentives distinction, they provide detailed descriptions of both the business and political sides of organizational structure, and they are acutely aware of the nonpolitical as well as the political bases of member involvement. Their organizational analyses are highly revealing as a result.

We can begin by stressing the well-known fact that the Farm Bureau had the deck stacked in its favor from the start, due to its special relationship with government. Its emergence was encouraged and its maintenance subsequently fortified by legislation designed to distribute educational and technical advantages to farmers: the Morrill Act of 1862 established land-grant colleges in the states; the Hatch Act of 1887 authorized extension services (educational programs, experimental stations) at these colleges; and the Smith-Lever Act of 1914 authorized federal grants to states willing to set up county farm bureaus to cooperate with extension workers (county agents). The states then developed the pattern of giving funds only to those counties, and thus only to those county agents, organizing a specified number or proportion of farmers—and the result was a proliferation of farm bureaus. These quasi-public local organizations, established for the distribution of nonpolitical benefits to farmers, joined together in 1919 to found the American Farm Bureau Federation, which quickly became an important political organization.[38]

In its formative years, then, the Farm Bureau had a favored status that entailed several major organizational advantages: it was subsidized by the government, county agents had an incentive to recruit new members and ensure group maintenance, and the farm bureaus had an effective monopoly over the distribution of educational and technical benefits within the farming sector. None of this has anything to do with the political preferences of individual farmers.

These advantages helped the Farm Bureau get off the ground, but they are only the beginning of its success story. Over the years, the American Farm Bureau and its constituent state organizations developed what can only be described as an incredible array of business operations. Most, but not all, of these are related in some way to farming and initially benefited from the fact that many such services were not being adequately provided at the time in rural areas. The best known of the Farm Bureau's services is insurance—life, auto, fire, etc. This is a tremendous moneymaker for the organization, which in 1968 had a nationwide network of 55 insurance companies with more than $1.5 billion in assets and more than $7 billion of life insurance in force. Moreover, it has a special relationship (via overlapping personnel, agreements, financial transfers, and other organizational connections) with another huge insurance network, Nationwide Insurance, which operates in 45 states.[39]

In addition to insurance, the Farm Bureau sells a great variety of products—which, again, are usually but not always related to farming. Chemicals, fertilizer, grain, oil, twine, and tires are just some of the commodities involved. Some of the state organizations also act as marketing agents for their members, buying and selling what the latter produce. In addition to these services, the Farm Bureau structure contains a range of other activities that are further removed from the needs of farmers. It owns property and real estate, derives substantial advertising revenues from its news publications, and even operates a travel agency.

To classify the Farm Bureau simply as a political association, then, would be a serious mistake. It is also an immense agribusiness whose assets run into the billions. Furthermore, the coterminous development of distinct political and business sides of the organization is by no means an accident. They coexist in a hugely beneficial symbiotic relationship. The precise nature of this relationship is quite a complex matter from both a legal and an organizational standpoint, and its various elements would be difficult to disentangle even if the Farm Bureau were willing to make the necessary information available, which it is not. Some of the general interconnections between the business and political sides are nevertheless plain, due largely to Berger's thorough research efforts.

The business operations are crucial to the political association in several ways. First, because many of the services and commodities are sold only to members—that is, because they are selective incentives—the association is much better able to recruit and retain members, many of whom are not farmers at all. This is the aspect of Farm Bureau business operations that Olson places greatest emphasis upon in his own analysis. Second, while the business operations are legally separate from the Farm Bureau, they are nonetheless controlled by the parent organization, which is able to channel money into its coffers in a variety of different ways—e.g., through rent for office space, dividends, and fees for staff services. Moreover, a good portion of this money is derived from business operations that sell goods and services to nonmembers as well as members. In other words, some Farm Bureau businesses sell to anyone; in such cases, the businesses are not means for gaining members, but are simply sources of revenue. Finally, the Farm Bureau is able to derive still greater benefits from its business operations because of the fact that the association itself, as a legally separate "nonprofit" entity, receives favored tax treatment. Because of its legal tax status, money funneled into the association is either not taxed at all or is taxed at a lower rate than would apply to an ordinary business.[40] In this way, the Farm Bureau is able to use its business operations in generating additional revenues over and above what could otherwise be expected.

The business operations, on the other hand, derive considerable benefit from their special relationship to the association. In the first place, they have direct access to membership lists—which, in the sale of farm-related goods and services, gives them a degree of competitive advantage over outsiders. Relatedly, they have an effective monopoly over advertising in Farm Bureau publications, which, in reaching vast numbers of potential clients, extol the virtues of Farm Bureau goods and services without supplying objective information on alternatives. Furthermore, because the association's property, rents, staff fees, dividends, etc., receive favorable tax treatment, it can "charge" its constituent organizations less on these counts if it likes, thus cutting their costs of operation. Thus, if Farm Bureau leaders desire they can use their favored tax status to pass on still other competitive advantages to their business appendages.

In addition to all of this, many Farm Bureau businesses are organized as cooperatives, which are nominally controlled by members but actually controlled by Farm Bureau leaders. And these cooperatives qualify for special tax treatment too. As business operations, therefore, they have a competitive advantage all their own—an advantage derived in no small part from their special connection to the association, since the latter supplies the cooperatives with "members" (customers).

In sum, then, the Farm Bureau is partly a political association and partly a giant business network, two organizational sides that have been fitted together through mutually supportive relationships that guarantee the well-being of each. This kind of analysis does not provide us with any direct evidence on why members join, but it is highly suggestive, to say the least. Most prominently, the Farm Bureau has a full-blown system of selective incentives that benefit from major competitive advantages. In all probability, these valuable incentives serve to tie many individuals into the group for nonpolitical reasons.

The impact of nonpolitical benefits is also apparent from the large numbers of nonfarmers that belong to the group. As of 1971, for example, there were 7000 Farm Bureau members in Cook County, Illinois, but only 1000 farms; and in Indiana, there were 50 percent more Farm Bureau members than there were farms of all types.[41] Moreover, the association can also claim "nonpeople" as members—businesses, towns, counties, school boards, and other entities finding associational services attractive. The exact proportion of nonfarmers comprising the group's membership is unknown, and the Farm Bureau has consistently refused to give an occupational breakdown. Berger believes the actual proportion to be greater than 20 percent of the total.

It is, of course, possible that, despite the Farm Bureau's impressive supermarket of services, many members join wholly or partially for political reasons. They may frequently value both the nonpolitical and political inducements the group has to offer; and, especially if purposive incentives have strong appeal, even members who value economic services may make contributions that are contingent to some extent on politics. We simply cannot know for sure what incentives are pivotal in the minds of members. From an organizational analysis of the group, however, it is clearly the nonpolitical aspects that consistently stand out.

The formative years of the Farmers Union were markedly different from those of the Farm Bureau in two important respects. The first is that the Farmers Union was not a governmentally favored organization; it was neither subsidized nor an integral component of policy administration. Rather, it was on its own recruiting members—and it had to compete with a rival group whose development was officially supported. The second contrast is that the Farmers Union was from the beginning a political organization. It was organized in 1902 by founders whose beliefs were firmly rooted in the Populist tradition. Many were former members of the Farmers Alliance, which had earlier been a major organizational force behind the Populist movement. It was, above all, a vehicle of protest—against the agencies of capitalism, concentrated wealth, political bossism, and those forces that generally undermined the well being of the average family farmer.[42]

At this time, the Farmers Union was also engaged in the development of cooperatives. Because these are business organization capable of supplying individuals with direct economic benefits, their development stood to have highly positive consequences for the size and stability of the group, consequences of which the rival Farm Bureau was ultimately to take great advantage. Yet Farmers Union leaders seem to have emphasized cooperativism not just because of its organizational implications, but also because of its congruence with their ideological aims. Recruitment appeals to farmers were made partially on the basis of economic self-interest and partially on the basis of ideology, with stress upon their integral connection.

For decades, however, the Farmers Union experienced serious organizational problems. Ideological appeals, even during the depression years, were not successful in recruiting masses of farmers into the group. Many of its cooperatives failed. And, to make matters worse, some of its thriving cooperatives split off from the group to take an independent course. While it had made some headway in political arenas, particularly during the New Deal, the Farmers Union remained weak in terms of membership and financial resources.

This state of affairs did not continue unabated into the modern era. The Farmers Union eventually was able to institutionalize itself as a prosperous, established interest organization—smaller and more regionally localized than the Farm Bureau, but an organization to be reckoned with. The obvious question is How did this happen? How was the Farmers Union able to surmount its initial difficulties, broaden its member base, and achieve a substantial degree of financial security?

The answer seems to rest with the fact that, over time, the Farmers Union developed a system of business organizations that facilitated group maintenance in much the same fashion as in the Farm Bureau— chiefly by supplying a range of nonpolitical incentives for membership and by serving as a source of revenue independent of member dues. The group's main business appendages are insurance companies and cooperatives, but it provides other goods and services as well. These have been put to use over the years as organizing mechanisms, and their successful adoption suggests an evolved leader perspective on what it takes to secure a firm organizational base. Indeed, in 1941 an NFU official was moved to write in the group's newsletter: "We believe in the value of a legislative program, but we do not believe they are worth much as a means of building an organization."[43]

From this more pragmatic perspective, business operations are officially viewed as means of achieving ideological ends. This is vividly apparent in Crampton's account of how James G. Patton, president of the Farmers Union for over two decades, explains the organizational role of insurance.

> Sensing a conflict with their ideology, the Union's officials justify the venture entirely in terms of what it can do for membership building. Patton habitually reminds conventions that the organizations' insurance companies are not businesses but "engines of democracy—engines for building the Farmers Union . . . " They meet the needs of effective organizing: "you need money, you need manpower, and you need something that will render a service to farmers and make it worthwhile for them to stay in the Union."[44]

The cooperatives too are major "engines of democracy." While they are separate entities, they often contribute substantial amounts to group coffers and also help recruit and retain members.

> Four of the six states where the Union is the majority farm organization today have been heavily sustained by "education funds" set

aside for them by the Union's cooperatives. These state unions are able to spend more on organizing and services than states receiving no such help. The Farmers Union Grain Terminal Association alone contributed over $1,500,000 to the state organizations in the Dakotas, Montana, Minnesota, and Wisconsin from 1943 to 1950. Some Union cooperatives also check off the Union's dues out of patronage dividends, which helps the state union maintain its membership. North Dakota is so blanketed with cooperatives that some members' dues are checked off several times, requiring refunds by the Union.[45]

In short, the development of a system of business organizations not only corresponds temporally to the successful institutionalization of the Farmers Union, but their development is also candidly recognized by group leaders as a crucial foundation for their political association. The reasonable implication is that a group which grew initially out of a social movement and was organized by ideologically motivated activists was able to become relatively large, effective, and secure over time only by relying upon nonideological appeals and inducements. Thus, for the Farmers Union—just as for the Farm Bureau—there is every reason to believe that many members join and "support" the group for reasons that have no necessary relationship to its political goals.

This is especially interesting because the Farmers Union, even while becoming an agribusiness of sorts, has maintained its distinctively antibusiness ideological posture in politics. Today the Farmers Union is, as it has always been, the liberal force in the farm sector, the spokesman for the little guy, and a frequent ally of labor and the Democratic party. The analysis above, however, suggests that the group's ideology is probably not a straightforward reflection of member preferences. And furthermore, not only does it appear that many members join for nonpolitical reasons, but there is no evidence to suggest that the average Farmers Union member is either small or liberal. In view of group policies, the membership appears heterogeneous.

It is reasonable to expect a badly off farmer to affiliate with the organization most articulate about his situation. It is reasonable to expect a liberal farmer to vote Democratic. But the evidence is that the Union's members are not badly off by farm standards and that most of them are Republicans. . . .

Is there a constituency of liberal farmers who, consistently with their perception of the economic and political world, join the most liberal farm organization and make up a majority of its members? Neither national officials nor the rapporteur for the Minnesota study local say so. Neither suggests that the ideological drive comes from the rank and file. Neither claims more than a consensus on the farm sections of the Union's program.[46]

As for where the ideological drive originates, Crampton's analysis points to a governing minority—a committed core of ideologically motivated members who are internally active, self-perpetuating, and occupy the official positions of leadership. It is not the group's members, but its leaders who are "the best evidence that there exists a liberally inclined constitutency of farmers. . . . They go far toward explaining the existence of the Union as a liberal movement."[47]

What all of this suggests is that the liberal Farmers Union and the conservative Farm Bureau, while often engaged in conflict in the larger political system, are not nearly as different as they may at first appear. In each case, business organizations emerge as central determinants of successful institutionalization, generating selective incentives that tie in members and generating revenue that can be used for a range of political and organizational purposes. The result is a political association that is comprised to some extent, and perhaps to a very great extent, of individuals whose membership is explained by nonpolitical inducements and that receives a substantial proportion of its financial support from sources independent of member dues.[48]

These points are significant in view of the fact that the Farm Bureau and the Farmers Union are the two major political forces in the American farm sector. The literature on farm organizations does not really tell us anything about the other groups in the sector, however; and, while we cannot know, it is always possible that in some groups virtually all members join out of an interest in politics and collective action. There is one group in particular that stands out as a likely candidate—the National Farmers Organization. It is the most militant of all major farm groups, apparently has not developed a network of business organizations, and seems to have a relatively high level of member involvement. Yet there is too little evidence on the NFO to support a conclusion one way or the other.

We can now turn from analyses of specific associations to consider those surveys that have been carried out on farmer members generally. There are not many, and only a few deal with questions of why they join their organizations. But such studies at least provide us with a kind of direct evidence that is noticeably lacking in organizational analyses.

What evidence there is, it turns out, supports the notions we already have about why farmers become group members. Interestingly, two of the better studies are concerned with members of farm co-operatives—which have traditionally been viewed and written about with great stress upon cooperative principles, moral values, and protection of the agrarian way of life. Indeed, early research on these organizations tended to center on the belief that these purposive inducements are the salient motivational factors, and often concerned themselves with ways these bonds could be strengthened to fortify the maintenance of cooperative enterprises. The importance of "favorable attitudes" and loyalty were stressed as a consequence, and efforts were made to probe for their determinants with little attention to purely economic costs and benefits.

The more recent studies suggest that, even if these purposive inducements were at one time of primary motivational importance, they are no longer of great prominence. Brown and Bealer, reporting on interviews with 322 members of cooperatives in a Pennsylvania county, found that the dominant incentives were economic.[49] They were surprised by this at the time (1957), in view of what they call the "theory of the cooperative," which emphasizes the traditional moral and ideological aspects of doing business the cooperative way. Moreover, upon dividing members into motivational types, they found that the ideologically motivated were much more likely than the economically motivated to feel a personal responsibility to be active, informed, etc., and to feel that they had a say in how the cooperative was run. This can only strengthen suspicions that, for many members, economic benefits are all they expect out of "group life."

A second article by Copp, based on interviews with 800 members, also suggests the dominant motivational role of direct economic incentives.[50] When asked their reason for joining, only 85 cited a belief in cooperative principles, while 174 pointed to market considerations, 474 stressed that they had no other economic alternatives, and 31 said they did not know. Thus, the vast majority of individuals do not place major importance on traditional cooperative values. Copp sees this as characteristic of cooperative members generally. "Contemporary studies show that farmers see cooperatives primarily as vehicles for individual goal satisfaction rather than as organizations which are good in themselves. Ideology appears to play a small role in American farmer cooperatives. American farmers see cooperatives as tools for securing economic satisfaction, not as tools for effecting social change."[51]

There is less motivational information for general farm associations than for cooperatives, and what there is does not take us very far. But the evidence is suggestive. The authors of *The American Voter,* for instance, included organizational membership in their analysis of the political attitudes and behavior of farmers. They inquired into the extent to which members were "interested" in their farm organizations, seeking an indicator of their political involvement, and found that "of those who do belong, the proportion willing to indicate 'a great deal of interest' in the organization is small. In fact, members of farm organizations show almost exactly the same distribution of interest in those organizations as is reported by union members for their local union organization. Given the fact that union membership is notoriously involuntary, this similarity is in itself striking."[52] The probable explanation for this "striking" finding, of course, is that many farmers join groups to receive economic goods and services and, although legally uncoerced, are like workers in joining primarily for nonpolitical reasons.

That economic selective incentives play the major motivational role in general farm groups is again supported in a study by Warner and Heffernan, who, in a rare departure from the norm, oriented their research around the collective goods–selective incentives distinction.[53] In a sample of Wisconsin farmers, they found that proportionately few members stressed political or social benefits, while economic selective incentives, especially in the form of insurance, were far and away the major benefits to be gained from joining.

Although the direct motivational evidence for farmers is highly sketchy, then, it consistently points to the salience of direct economic benefits and supports our organizational analyses of the Farm Bureau and the Farmers Union. Considering the evidence as a whole, we are therefore led to virtually the same conclusion for the farm sector as we were earlier for the labor sector. It is possible that politics plays a major role for some members and a secondary role for many, but the average member probably places primary value on nonpolitical inducements.

Business Groups

The business sector is an interesting contrast to the labor and farm sectors. In the first place, as several published listings of voluntary associations and lobbying organizations can attest, "the business community is by a wide margin the most highly organized segment of society."[54] Indeed, it appears that there are as many business groups as there are groups of all other types combined. It is also a very complex sector, with its associations—ranging from the National Coal Association to the National Retail Dry Goods Association to the Pin Manufacturer's Institute—reflecting even the most minute functional distinctions among business enterprises; they are so specialized, in fact, that firms often find it necessary to belong to many different associations. Another distinguishing trait is that many business groups, especially the the more narrowly based trade associations, are small in membership; they frequently contain fewer than 50 members.[55] And finally, the business sector is noteworthy because it is here that the phenomenon of Olson's Large Member is most likely to have major implications for the maintenance and internal politics of interest groups. In the labor sector, there are no such Large Members; and in the farm sector, the typical organizational pattern is one of low dues and mass membership, which effectively rules out direct reliance upon only a few farmer contributors.[56] But with business associations, and especially with the smaller ones, this sort of reliance is fairly common. According to Key, "in almost half of them, nearly 50 per cent of the cost is borne by a handful of members."[57]

These characteristics make the business sector an intriguing subject for study, particularly in view of the extensive power that business firms and associations are reputed to have in politics. Despite these considerations, however, the fact of the matter is that business groups have rarely been systematically studied. Organizational analyses are few and far between. Beyond them, there are a few surveys of group members that ask for their evaluation of group services; but because of the way in which questions are worded, these studies are usually not very revealing.[58]

The size and complexity of the group universe, combined with the underdeveloped state of research, make it difficult to generalize about why businessmen (as individuals or as spokesmen for firms) join business associations. What evidence there is, however, suggests that business members are more likely than worker or farmer members to have joined for political reasons. This is not to say that all, or even most of them, are politically motivated, but simply that politics seems to have a greater role to play vis-à-vis economic services in explaining membership in business groups. This difference deserves to be recognized, although there are reasons why it should not be exaggerated.

We can turn first to the general business associations, those that organize broad categories of business interests. Some of these, like the National Association of Manufacturers and the Chamber of Commerce, claim to "speak for business" on a vast range of political issues; while others, such as the various associations of small businesses, claim to speak for some nonspecialized subset of the sector. Organizational analyses of these groups suggest that purposive appeals are often relied upon in inducing nonmembers to join and that the groups' political goals, activities, and distinctive ideologies are attractions of real importance to continuing members.

The National Association of Manufacturers, for instance, was from the beginning a political interest group—emerging in 1895 to represent manufacturers on a variety of economic matters, exclusive of labor relations, and becoming several years later a militant organizational opponent of the developing labor movement.[59] Through the decades it has continued to rely upon ideological appeals. While these have enlisted the support of only a small proportion of manufacturers (presently about 7 percent), the NAM has succeeded in attracting a number of very large firms—which, while a distinct minority, provide most of the association's finances, occupy most of its official positions, and dominate its policymaking. They are the stable core of the association. There are many smaller firms as well, but their high turnover rate indicates that the NAM has a difficult time retaining these members with purposive appeals, despite the ongoing efforts of numerous recruiters in the field.

There are alternative explanations for the NAM's differential success rate with large and small firms. We might suggest, with Olson, that the largest firms constitute a small group whose members contribute because of their expected impact on political outcomes;[60] the smaller members, less likely to perceive such an impact, are accordingly harder to hold onto. But it also is reasonable to speculate, as Wilson does, that members of both sizes tend to be motivated by a sense of duty or responsibility and that the large members are simply better able to afford the economic costs (dues) of following through. The argument, essentially, is that firms of different sizes tend to have different trade-offs between economic and noneconomic values, the smaller firms tending to be more "careful" with their money. As Wilson points out,

> The NAM exists, not because it is small or oligarchical, but because it has discovered that out of the several hundred thousand manufacturing enterprises in the United States, it can attract as

members between 13,000 and 15,000 by purposive appeals aimed at
the ideological belief of certain firms in the importance of a militant
defense of the "free competitive enterprise system." To the very
largest corporations, the cost of NAM membership, even at the
highest dues quota of $65,000 a year, is trivial; they constitute,
therefore, a stable core of the membership. . . . For the smaller
firms, the dues even at the lowest rate of $200 per year, are not
trivial, great efforts must be made by association salesmen to recruit and hold them, and the turnover is high, especially when
business profits are pinched or perceived political threats are few.[61]

Much the same can be said for the Chamber of Commerce, which,
while not so militant as the NAM, has utilized purposive appeals in
recruiting member firms. "The appeal of the Chamber to prospective
business members is essentially the same as that of the NAM—the
'duty' of firms to support the activities of an organization that seeks to
defend 'the American philosophy of enterprise favoring limited government and the motivation of production by incentives within the
framework of a free competitive market economy.' "[62]

Like the NAM, the Chamber has failed to recruit even 10 percent of
its potential members, experiences high rates of turnover, employs
organizers to replenish membership ranks, and is fortified by a committed core of dependable and economically well-off supporters, including many trade associations.[63]

Political incentives also appear to be quite prominent within those
associations claiming to speak for small business—e.g., the National
Federation of Independent Business, the National Small
Businessmen's Association, the Conference of American Small Business Organizations.[64] Associations of this type are highly ideological in
their appeals, vociferously assert their political distinctiveness from
one another, and aggressively compete as rivals in recruiting firms on
this basis. Over the years, a great many groups have emerged, com-
peted unsuccessfully, and died out. But some have been able to endure, apparently through political appeals alone. According to Zeigler,
"The national small business organizations which have survived—a
tiny fraction of the original fifty—have done so on the strength of
emotional inducements."[65] Not surprisingly, Zeigler's analysis shows
that these groups experience high rates of turnover (sometimes as high
as 90 percent annually) and rely upon paid organizers for member
replenishment. Their similarities to the NAM and the Chamber are thus

clear, although they are at a disadvantage because they are not able to count upon large firms for a more assured financial base.

In sum, then, analyses of general business associations suggest that many of these groups have certain traits in common: greatest stress is placed upon political appeals to members, and these may explain why the average member joins; these appeals are able to attract only a small percentage of potential members; of those who are actually induced to join, many subsequently drop out, indicating that they are not securely tied in by group incentives; paid organizers are necessary to ensure that membership losses are offset by new recruits. Thus, in contrast to the Farm Bureau, the Farmers Union, and established labor unions, the general business associations appear to stand out as "politicized" organizations—and as organizations that experience certain problems as a result.

This seems a reasonable portrayal in light of what evidence we have. It is also reasonable when we recognize that not only do these groups apparently fail to offer impressive packages of selective incentives, but they are also at a distinct disadvantage should they try to do so. The general interest organizations possess heterogeneous memberships with heterogeneous economic needs, needs that are effectively catered to by specialized trade associations. Hundreds upon hundreds of the latter groups, organized on narrower and more homogeneous bases, supply varied packages of goods and services that are designed to appeal to unique clienteles. Because these major mechanisms for tying in members are substantially preempted by trade associations, the general business groups are left to rely to a much greater extent upon ideological appeals.

Even in view of these points, we should nevertheless be wary of holding too firmly to the conclusion that most members join for political reasons. Analyses of the general business groups tend to focus on their political goals and appeals, with little or no attention to whatever nonpolitical incentives they do offer. This is partially due, it seems, to traditional pluralist perspectives on group life and to the tendency to look at leaders and active members rather than the rank and file. It is also due to the fact that these groups simply do not offer impressive packages of selective incentives. But even unimpressive packages may be important to an explanation of membership. In the Chamber, for example, many members are affiliated with local chambers, which can supply individuals with opportunities for social interaction, the exchange of information, business contacts, and the like. Moreover, for virtually every business group of any size, there will be news publications whose informational content is of some value—and member surveys, as well as our own data in the next chapter, suggest that businessmen consistently rate information as one of the most valuable services a group can provide.[66] Thus, we should balance the above characterization of general business groups with a recognition that the role of nonpolitical services has been relatively unexplored and could actually explain the decisions of many members.

This possibility is underlined by Marsh's recent study of the British Confederation of Industry. A sample survey of its member firms suggested that "collective goods would seem to be a major incentive for membership, particularly, although not exclusively, among the larger firms. Olson's analysis seems to have limited utility as far as this particular interest group is concerned."[67] But it also found that economic services—especially information—are highly valued, and that fully 77 percent of the smaller (less than 200 employees) firms claimed that this was their main reason for joining.[68]

For the American context, the organizational importance of services is well illustrated by Wike's detailed account of the Pennsylvania Manufacturers Association. Like a small-scale NAM, it was formed for political reasons and claims to speak for Pennsylvania manufacturers generally; but, unlike the NAM, it has aggressively and successfully constructed nonpolitical mechanisms for attracting members.[69] Most notably, it almost immediately went into the insurance business and established local associational subunits partially for the purpose of selling insurance and (simultaneously) recruiting members. "The formation of the insurance companies, especially the Casualty Insurance Company . . ., served as an excellent means of expanding and strengthening the Association. Similarly, the organizational structure of the Association, i.e. the local associations and the branch offices in the state, served not only to strengthen the Association by promoting its influence, but also as a potential means of promoting the development of the insurance companies."[70]

Its two insurance companies (casualty and fire) sell assorted types of insurance—but only workmen's compensation is restricted to the association's members. Other types are sold to nonmembers, enhancing corporate profits—which, as with the Farm Bureau, are "available" in various ways to association leaders. While the budget of the association itself is not large, the budgets of its business appendages "run into the millions of dollars annually".[71] Another major feature of the PMA is its Employer's Advisory Council, whose technical information, research, and advice on labor-management relations provide major benefits for member firms.

Thus, the PMA has been able to overcome the disadvantages of generality and heterogeneity, putting together business operations that both attract members and generate revenue. It is a short step to the inference that many, perhaps most, of its members join for nonpolitical reasons. This suggests, in turn, that a number of other general business groups may have followed a similar developmental course. While we cannot know for certain, we must admit the possibility that those groups that have captured the spotlight—namely, the NAM and the Chamber—may not be very representative.

At bottom, however, it is not the general organizations that give the business sector its distinctive markings, but the more narrowly constituted trade associations—and probably the most heralded characteristic of these groups is their (frequently) small size. In looking beyond the major business organizations, then, we are confronted with a new factor conducive to politically based membership. Some writers have suggested that the size factor is crucially important in this regard. Schattschneider, for example, contends that small size extends business groups substantial organizational and political advantages over other types of groups, and that this, in turn, biases the interest group system as a whole. "Special-interest organizations are most easily formed when they deal with small numbers of individuals who are acutely aware of their exclusive interests. To describe the conditions of pressure-group organization in this way is, however, to say that it is primarily a business phenomenon."[72]

Olson also emphasizes the advantages of small size. While he recognizes that many trade associations supply selective incentives, he believes that "smallness must be the reason that so many of them exist."[73] This is offered as the major distinguishing characteristic of the business sector. "The laboring, professional, and agricultural interests of the country make up large, latent groups that can organize and act effectively only when their latent power is crystallized by some organization which can provide political power as a by-product; and by contrast the business interests generally can voluntarily and directly organize and act to further their common interests without any such adventitious assistance."[74]

Arguments of this sort suggest that, for those trade associations acting as interest groups, members tend to join in response to political considerations. But this is only speculation. It is important to realize that political motivations are not necessarily implied by small size and that such a motivational conclusion may be inaccurate. To begin with, many trade associations are not small, so for them the presumed advantages do not apply. Secondly, even when the group is fairly small, only one or several members may contribute because their contributions make a political difference. Indeed, the larger members should have a difficult time getting the smaller members to cooperate on economic grounds alone—for the latter will always get the benefits of political action, while the former will lose considerably if they fail to initiate it. Hence, other things being equal, smaller members will often have little economic reason for cooperating. Moreover, trade associations provide extensive packages of economic selective incentives for their members. This is documented in studies carried out by the Temporary National Economic Committee and the Chamber of Commerce.[75] Both provide long lists of services that these groups often perform, and the Chamber study includes fairly recent data on member evaluations of services. While these surveys suggest that governmental relations is the one most frequently offered, economic selective incentives are nevertheless so common, there are so many of them, and they are so frequently used and valued by members, that it would be inappropriate to think of trade associations primarily as political structures. Politics is just one of a great many group activiites.

All things considered, trade associations do not emerge as small groups of politicized businessmen, and there is good reason for rejecting the notion that political motivations play the primary role in trade associations. It seems much more reasonable to suggest, although we cannot prove it, that the average member joins mainly for economic services, with the primacy of political inducements restricted to a minority. This is essentially the same conclusion reached by Wilson, whose own analysis (more comprehensive than either Olson's or Schattschneider's) led him to the following summary statement. "Though trade associations often were created in response to a commercial or governmental threat, and though many have at one time or another sought to nullify that threat by various efforts at reducing competition or obtaining new legislation, most trade associations today, to judge from the scanty literature about them, exist primarily to provide services to member firms for which the latter are willing to pay."[76]

In respect to the relative salience of political and nonpolitical motivations, then, the business sector is perhaps not markedly different from the farm and labor sectors. It is true that some of its most visible groups—the NAM, the Chamber, the national associations of small business—appear to be based largely upon political inducements; and it is also true that the small size of many trade associations yields a propitious context for political action. But once we get beyond the literature's tendency to highlight the political and inquire more deeply into the range of benefits that business groups supply to their members, we find a profusion of nonpolitical incentives. It appears that, in both general and specialized organizations, and in groups of virtually any size, these often represent a particularly attractive basis for membership. While we cannot be sure why businessmen become group members, the nature of their organizations suggests that, with a few notable exceptions, the role of political motivations has been overly stressed.

Conclusion

Limited though it is, this analysis of the business, farm, and labor sectors gives us a degree of insight into why individuals join groups. Evidence of various kinds, bearing both directly and indirectly upon member motives, points beyond the confines of the prevailing theoretical and data backgrounds and suggests summary conclusions that contradict conventional notions about group membership.

Above all, it seems clear that the pluralists are incorrect in asserting that common interests play the major motivational role in these kinds of groups. Some individuals do join groups primarily in support of political goals; in some groups, like the NAM and the Chamber of Commerce, politics may even be of primary importance to the average member; and it is very possible that political inducements often play secondary roles that are hidden by the literature's focus on primary reasons for joining. But, despite these qualifying considerations, group goals are generally not the keys to member support.

The data background does not fare much better. The socioemotional bases of member involvement, which have received so much attention and support in the traditional literature, are not the major explanations of group membership either. Although they are very important in some groups (for example, the European unions and the general business associations) and of great salience to some individuals, they seem to take a definite back seat to economic self-interest for the average member of the average group. Moreover, the popular small groups distinction between the instrumental and the expressive tends to be quite misleading in application to economic interest organizations. By focusing on instrumental tasks and socioemotional satisfactions, and by stressing the need for balance or connection between the two, the literature has consistently downplayed those incentives that are related to neither—economic selective incentives. The social-psychological studies are least revealing, and extension of their findings is most dangerous, for groups in which these inducements play a major role.

All of this adds up to support for basic aspects of Olson's original critique—that selective incentives play crucial motivational roles, that political activities are largely by-products of the sale of selective incentives, and that there is no necessary congruence between member goals and group goals. These are far-reaching theoretical concessions that underline the contribution of Olson's analysis. Nonetheless, the weaknesses of the traditional background should not be exaggerated. The overall impression conveyed by the interest group studies is simply that the average member ascribes more importance to nonpolitical than to political inducements and that he primarily seeks economic gain rather than purposive or solidary incentives. It does not suggest that politics is unimportant, nor that purposive and solidary incentives can be safely ignored. Indeed, what evidence there is implies that an exclusive theoretical focus on nonpolitical benefits and economic self-interest would lead to an incomplete and inadequate explanation of group membership. And, in view of the analysis of part 1, we should expect it to lead as well to a seriously biased perspective on interest groups as organizations, one which overlooks the range of interesting consequences these deviations from the norm can have.

Eight

Some New Data

This review of the interest group studies tells us something important about the broad outlines of group membership. Within these outlines, however, many questions remain to be answered and a good deal of research obviously remains to be done. At the least, tentative conclusions about group membership need to be more fully documented, the more subtle aspects of incentive structures need to be investigated, and more systematic attention must be directed to variations in incentive structures across groups and sectors.

In this chapter, we will take a few steps in this direction, presenting some additional data from a survey of the members of five economic interest groups. As in the past two chapters, the focus will be on the relative salience of political and nonpolitical inducements. But we will also be in a better position to look beyond the primary reason for joining and, in so doing, to arrive at a more detailed account of the bases for membership.

The Member Survey

The question of which groups to single out for study was guided by a simple set of criteria. First, groups were required to have at least fifty members; this was an attempt to eliminate the complications intrinsic to small, face-to-face groups, and to allow for a focus on those large groups so central to Olson's original analysis. Second, they had to have organizational goals that were pursued through political activity. Third, they had to be economic groups other than labor unions, which were eliminated because of the additional research problems presented by legal coercion. And fourth, their leaders had to agree to the study.

Aside from these conditions, the specific type of group was not a factor in the selection process. Groups of various sorts were contacted, and five interest organizations were ultimately enlisted to take part in the research.

The Minnesota Farm Bureau. This is the Minnesota affiliate of the American Farm Bureau Federation. The MFB claims a membership of approximately 35,000 and is an active lobbyist at the state level.

The Minnesota Farmers Union. The MFU is a state affiliate of the National Farmers Union, claims to have about 23,000 members, and participates actively in Minnesota politics.

The Minnesota Retail Federation. This group is an active lobbying force in state politics and is comprised of about 1400 retail enterprises. Because of chain stores and multiple ownerships, however, only about 600 are dues-paying members, and these were the subjects of the survey.

The Minnesota-Dakotas Hardware Association. While hardware stores are retailers and, thus, potential members of the Retail Federation, they nevertheless have their own group, which is older, organizes its clientele in three states, and carries out lobbying activities in all three. About 900 hardware stores belong.

The Printing Industries of the Twin Cities. This is the smallest of the five groups, organizing 89 printing companies, and does not actually lobby at the state level. However, it is the Minnesota affiliate of Printing Industries of America, a national lobbying federation to which it makes very substantial contributions annually out of member dues. Lobbying questions on the survey were worded with reference to the activities of the national organization.

The survey instrument was a mail questionnaire sent out (during 1975 in two waves) to all dues-paying members of the Printers, the Retail Federation, and the Hardware Association,[1] and to a sample of dues-paying members in the Farm Bureau and the Farmers Union.[2] The final response rates varied from group to group: Printers, 74%; Retail, 62%; Hardware, 46%; Farm Bureau, 34%; and Farmers Union, 34%. Overall, these rates are not so high as we might like, but they are nevertheless satisfactory in comparison with the much lower rates often obtained from mass mailings of this sort.

The nature of the questionnaire is discussed in some detail elsewhere.[3] Here, a general indication of the order and content of those questions relevant to this analysis is sufficient.

After some preliminary queries, members were asked the extent to which they thought their own dues and contributions had an impact on the group's political success. This singled out the group's political activities for special attention and also served as a rough measure of a member's sense of efficacy.

Members were then presented with a list of their group's economic selective incentives, which were called "direct member services" and explicitly set off from lobbying activities. They were asked to evaluate each service.

Members were subsequently asked whether they would remain in the association (a) if it stopped supplying direct member services, and only lobbied; and (b) if it stopped lobbying, and only supplied direct member services. Dues were held constant. (A cross-tabulation of these questions will later provide a measure of the pivotal roles of both types of inducements.)

Members were then presented with several questions which maintained the political/nonpolitical distinction, introduced purposive and solidary incentives, and inquired into their reasons for remaining in the group.

Caveats

Before presenting the data, we should first give brief attention to two kinds of problems, both of which reflect the drawbacks of the mail survey instrument: the ambiguity of conceptual measures and the potential for sample bias. The ambiguity problem is largely due to the fact that, given our model of the individual's calculus, theoretically precise questions are difficult to state in a form that would be clear, simple, and easily understood by the average member. Accordingly, we have had to rely upon broader questions that are more easily conveyed via a mail questionnaire, and whose relationship to the model is less exact. As a substitute for precisely measuring a member's perceived marginal impact on political success, for example, we simply ask him how much difference he thinks his contributions make.

Your association "lobbies" with the legislature and executive agencies to try to achieve its goals. What effect do *your own* dues and contributions (and *only* your own) have on the association's *success or failure* in achieving its lobbying goals?
———a big effect
———a noticeable effect; my dues and contributions *do* actually make a difference for the group's success or failure in lobbying
———my own dues and contributions do not "really" make a difference for the group's success or failure in lobbying

And, as a substitute for probing the psychological dimensions of his expressive involvement, we simply ask whether he "feels a responsibility or an obligation" to join.

Do you remain in the association at least partly because you feel a sense of responsibility or an obligation to do so?
———this is a very important reason
———this is a reason of some importance
———this is one reason, but it is not a very important one
———this has nothing to do with why I remain in the association

It is reasonable to expect that virtually all members will understand what these and other questions are getting at and that our measures will generally provide meaningful indicators of underlying theoretical components. Nevertheless, these sorts of measures are obviously not going to be extremely reliable, and we can only qualify our conclusions as a result.

The second reason for qualification derives from the uncertain nature of the sample. Because a mail survey was employed, responding members are not a random sample of the general membership in any of the five groups. Each member decides on his own whether or not he will complete the questionnaire, and this nonrandom self-selection process underlines the possibility of sample bias. There are two possible causes of bias, moreover, both of which point in the same direction. The first is due to the fact that, in the eyes of potential respondents, the survey is obviously "political." It asks questions that often bring politics to center stage—and inquiries of this sort may be irrelevant, uninteresting, and subjectively inapplicable to members who are neither politically concerned nor active. Accordingly, they may be less disposed to respond.

The other factor is what we might call the "Olson paradox of research." The paradox arises because (*a*) if Olson were entirely correct in his assumptions about group members, no one would answer the mail questionnaire, and (*b*) if his assumptions were met by a certain subset of members, responses would be received only from members outside this subset, leaving the "economic men" entirely unrepresented in the final tabulations. Logical arguments can only be taken as suggestive. But it seems reasonable to propose that the self-selection process could underrepresent the more economically self-interested members.

Thus, if there is a bias in member responses—and there may not be—respondents should be somewhat more politically and non-economically oriented than the general membership.[4] While keeping this in mind, however, we will assume that our samples are representative enough to suggest the nature of the incentive structures in each group and to allow for meaningful evaluations along basic dimensions.

The Data

We can begin to see the nature of organizational incentive structures by taking a look at the direct member services (economic selective incentives) they offer, and how these are evaluated by members. From table 1, it is clear that all five groups offer members extensive packages of services in return for their contributions and that members put organizational services to a good deal of use. Member appeal is especially widespread on services of a general nature—notably information and insurance, which are offered with apparently great success in all groups. But a non-negligible portion of the membership also values virtually every one of even the most specialized services (farm records program, freight bill auditing, etc.), which were doubtless designed, at any rate, to appeal to special subsets of constituents.

These figures clearly suggest that economic selective incentives are important member inducements and that we are on firm ground in attacking the traditional tendency to overlook the nonpolitical aspects of "political" organizations. On the other hand, data on the perceptual and value characteristics of members suggest that there also exists a rational basis for politically motivated membership. To begin with, most members believe that their individual contributions *do* make a

Table 1.   Member evaluations of group services (% rating services as valuable)

Printers (N = 65)		*Retail* (N = 353)		*Hardware* (N = 390)	
Service	%	Service	%	Service	%
Information	89	Information	93	Information, local	84
Labor relations	83	Insurance	58	Information, national	78
Health-welfare programs		Transportation pooling	18	Insurance	62
for employees	52	Freight bill auditing	22	Accounting services	25
Profit-ratio studies	68	Collections service	13	Store fixtures, accesso-	
Credit and collections	29	Computer billing	9	ries, planning services	45
Screening of employees	25	Seminars, conferences,		Sales training, employee	
Cost surveys	60	etc.	54	aids	31
Training of supervisors	48	Individual assistance		Co-op advertising	
Committee on vocational		with complaints, etc.	55	program	23
training	23			Promotions	40
Discussion of common				Cost of doing business	
problems	66			survey	49
Individual assistance				Individual assistance	
with complaints, etc.	82			with complaints, etc.	53

Farm Bureau (N = 565)		*Farmers Union* (N = 550)	
Service	%	Service	%
Information, general		Information	87
farm	72	Field staff services	42
Information, legislative		$1000 accidental death	
newsletter	57	insurance	76
Casualty insurance	68	Other insurance	54
Prepaid health insurance	61	Conferences, seminars	43
Group purchasing	43	Protection program	64
Marketing services	26	Educational bus tours	47
Citrus fruit program	33	Youth program	49
$1000 accidental death		Marketing, purchasing	
insurance	49	services	53
Farm records program	14	Individual assistance	45
Seminars, conferences	33		
Individual assistance	39		

difference for their group's political success or failure. As shown in table 2, the figures are in fact highly similar for all groups: between 60 and 70 percent of the members perceive their contributions as having an effect on political outcomes. Many individuals, even if acting purely on the basis of economic self-interest, may therefore find that

Table 2.   Effect of contributions on group's success or failure (%)

Effect	Printers	Retail	Hardware	Farm Bureau	Farmers Union
Big effect	3	4	9	6	12
Some effect	62	59	59	56	59
No effect	35	37	32	39	30
Total	100	100	100	101	101
(*N*)	(63)	(336)	(375)	(559)	(537)

they have an incentive to join at least partially for politically reasons. The uniformity across groups is intriguing because it suggests that perceptions of efficacy may be widespread among group members generally, throughout the group system, and that the average member does not view his contributions as a drop in the bucket. It is also interesting to note that, in conjunction with high levels of efficacy, information is the organizational service most widely valued by members. It could well be that member perceptions of efficacy are frequently stimulated or reinforced by leaders, who, in structuring information, can shape member estimates of their contributions' political impact. Certainly leaders have the opportunity to do so, given the value members ascribe to information.

In addition to widespread perceptions of efficacy, there appears to be a purposive dimension of member involvement: many individuals indicate that a feeling of responsibility or obligation is an important consideration in their decision to maintain membership. As shown in table 3, the portion of respondents rating this reason as "very important" or "of some importance" is 50 percent or more for four of the groups. The Farm Bureau stands apart from the others, with 35 percent ascribing importance to this dimension; but even this figure is respectable, translating into large numbers of individuals who claim purposive reasons for joining. Thus, group differences aside, the data suggest that members of economic interest groups often consider purposive inducements as well as purely economic gains to be of direct relevance to their calculations. And, although feelings of responsibility need not always be politically rooted, their relevance serves to underline the potential for politically based membership and to enhance the likelihood that collective goods can generate their own selective incentives.

Table 3.   Importance of feelings of responsibility as a reason for joining the group (%)

Importance	Printers	Retail	Hardware	Farm Bureau	Farmers Union
Very important	16	21	18	11	23
Some importance	38	36	35	24	27
Little importance	33	25	27	26	20
No importance	14	18	20	39	30
Total	101	100	100	100	100
(N)	(64)	(348)	(398)	(584)	(572)

By these rough measures, then, it appears that many members do possess perceptual and value characteristics conducive to political action. Thus, while economic selective incentives seem to be important member inducements, there is a rational basis for the inducement value of group goals as well. The task at this point is to inquire into the incentives for membership. One way of doing this is to ask members their primary reason for joining. We can see from table 4 that, when members are given five basic reasons from which to choose, very few indicate that social rewards or social (or economic) pressures are their main reasons for belonging. Apparently, solidary incentives are not very important organizational means of attracting and retaining members. Only three reasons are singled out with any frequency: direct services, lobbying, and feelings of responsibility. Of these, individuals

Table 4.   Main reason for joining (%)

Reason	Printers	Retail	Hardware	Farm Bureau	Farmers Union
Services	86	44	56	54	34
Lobbying	0	27	14	25	37
Social	2	1	0	4	5
Responsibility	9	27	26	12	20
Expected to join by others	2	1	3	4	4
Total	99	100	99	99	100
(N)	(64)	(326)	(391)	(571)	(564)

often indicate that either lobbying or feelings of responsibility represents the chief reason they join. But services is the modal response in
all groups except the Farmers Union; and, when members are forced to
choose between services and lobbying, as shown in table 5, it is only in
the Farmers Union that economic services takes second place.[5]

Table 5.   Major reason for joining, if choosing between services and
            lobbying (%)

Reason	Printers	Retail	Hardware	Farm Bureau	Farmers Union
Services	94	NA	76	66	44
Lobbying	6	NA	24	34	56
Total	100	NA	100	100	100
(N)	(65)	(NA)	(398)	(570)	(561)

These figures suggest a few simple conclusions. First, and not surprisingly, the relative importance of these incentives varies from group
to group. The Farmers Union appears to be the "most political" of all;
and, interestingly, while the analysis in chapter 7 suggests that both the
Farmers Union and the Farm Bureau owe much of their organizational
success to their agribusiness appendages, it seems clear that the salience of politics as a member inducement varies markedly across these
two farm groups (in Minnesota). Among the business interest groups, it
is in the most generally based organization—the Retail Federation—
that politics seems to have the greatest salience. The Hardware and
Printer groups are functionally specialized trade associations, and both
rely heavily on economic services to attract member support. This is
especially true in the Printers, which comes very close to Olson's
idealized notion of organizational incentive structures.

In terms of an overall evaluation, these data support the contention
of other studies of economic interest groups: that economic services
have greater inducement value than politics. It is once again the nonpolitical bases of group membership that stand out. At the same time,
the motivational roles of lobbying and feelings of responsibility are not
at all insignificant; while they are hardly the crucial factors the
pluralists make them out to be, they are certainly more prevalent than
Olson's original analysis would lead us to expect. Moreover, questions

about the major reason for joining are unsuited for answering the really central theoretical question—the extent to which member decisions are contingent upon political considerations—for the fact that a member joins "mainly" for services can easily hide the possibility that his decision also pivots on politics. To classify such individuals as non-political in their bases for membership would be to overlook an important component of their membership decision and thus an important determinant of their organizational behavior in connection with group goals.

We can inquire into the pivotal role of politics with the help of tables 6 and 7. Table 6 indicates what members say they would do if the group

Table 6. How members would react if their group stopped providing services, but still lobbied (%)

Reaction	Printers	Retail	Hardware	Farm Bureau	Farmers Union
Stay in	20	43	40	44	58
Drop out	80	57	60	56	42
Total	100	100	100	100	100
(N)	(65)	(354)	(401)	(587)	(577)

stopped providing economic services and only lobbied, while table 7 indicates what members say they would do if the group stopped lobbying and only provided economic services. We can see that, in all groups but the Farmers Union, most members would drop out if their economic services were taken away; and, in all five groups, most

Table 7. How members would react if their group stopped lobbying, but still provided services (%)

Reaction	Printers	Retail	Hardware	Farm Bureau	Farmers Union
Stay in	94	57	70	77	63
Drop out	6	43	30	23	37
Total	100	100	100	100	100
(N)	(65)	(352)	(400)	(583)	(580)

members would maintain their membership if the group stopped lobbying. This testifies, again, to the relative attractiveness of services, but it also is apparent from these figures that politics is of widespread relevance. In all groups but the Printers, for example, 40 percent or more would maintain their membership if the group stopped supplying services altogether and only lobbied.

When responses to these questions are cross-tabulated, members can be classified according to the incentives that appear to be pivotal to their membership decision. This is illustrated in figure 3. Members in category 1 would remain in the group if it only lobbied, but also if it only supplied direct services. Either one is sufficient to justify membership, while neither is necessary. For those in category 2, on the other hand, lobbying is both necessary and sufficient—these individuals will stay in if lobbying is offered, but drop out if it is not. Members in category 3 give the opposite responses; for them, membership pivots entirely on whether or not direct member services are supplied. And, for members in category 4, the combination of lobbying and direct member services must be provided if membership is to be maintained.

Stay in if group only supplies economic services?

		yes	no
Stay in if group only lobbies?	yes	each sufficient (I)	lobbying only (II)
	no	services only (III)	both necessary (IV)

Figure 3

Olson's theory implies that virtually all group members should fall into category 3, "services only." For each of the other categories, politics plays a pivotal role in member decisions to stay in the group. Table 8 sets out the actual percentages of respondents falling into the various classes. From the figures, it is once again clear that services are quite important. In all groups but the Farmers Union, "services only" is the modal category; and, in every group, more members join for

Table 8.   A classification of members according to which incentives are pivotal to their membership (%)

Incentives	Printers	Retail	Hardware	Farm Bureau	Farmers Union
Either services or lobbying	19	23	28	32	38
Lobbying only	2	21	12	12	20
Services only	75	34	43	45	24
Both services and lobbying	5	22	17	10	17
Total	101	100	100	99	99
SUM:					
Services only	75	34	43	45	24
Politics somehow pivotal	25	66	57	55	76
Total	100	100	100	100	100
(N)	(64)	(351)	(398)	(580)	(571)

"services only" than for "lobbying only." The dominance of services is most extensive in the Printers, where fully 75 percent of the respondents indicate that their membership pivots only on the provision of these selective incentives. But it is also quite high in the Farm Bureau and Hardware Association, where almost half of the members are tied-in on this basis. The inducement value of services is underlined by the data in table 9, which suggest that services are also more salient than politics as a secondary incentive for membership. When lobbying is the member's main reason for joining, he usually ascribes a pivotal role to services as well; but when services represent his main reason for joining, he is less likely to ascribe a pivotal role to lobbying. In the Retail Federation, for example, services play a secondary role for 60 percent of those members who join primarily for politics, while politics plays a secondary role for just 47 percent of those members who join primarily for services. This inequality holds for every relevant group. Thus, economic selective incentives are not only more likely to play the major role in the decision of members, but they are also particularly important as secondary bases for membership.

On the other hand, these figures also tell us that politics is usually a factor of consequence in member decisions to join. Looking at the summary data at the bottom of table 8, we can see that, for all groups but the Printers, a majority of members ascribes a pivotal role to politics—76 percent in the Farmers Union, 66 percent in the Retail Federation, 57 percent in the Hardware association, and 55 percent in the Farm Bureau. And we can see from table 9 that, even when members say they join primarily for services, this often hides the fact that their membership is also contingent on politics. In the Hardware group, for example, 39 percent of those joining primarily for services also ascribe a pivotal role to politics—and in the Farmers Union most such members do. All of this is quite out of line with Olson's expectations and can only serve to qualify the nonpolitical thrust of those interest group studies that focus on the primary reason for membership. The figures here strongly indicate that political incentives are in fact very common and that they are integral to an explanation of why members join.

Table 9.   Main reason for joining by the pivotal role of incentives (%)

	Incentive	Printers	Retail	Hardware	Farm Bureau	Farmers Union
Members joining mainly for services	Services only	80	53	61	69	41
	Politics somehow pivotal	20	47	39	31	59
Total		100	100	100	100	100
(N)		(56)	(141)	(217)	(312)	(183)
Members joining mainly for lobbying	Lobbying only	--	40	46	36	37
	Services somehow pivotal	--	60	54	64	63
Total		˙--	100	100	100	100
(N)		--	(88)	(54)	(142)	(206)

On balance, then, it remains true that economic selective incentives seem to be "more important" than political incentives, generally speaking, in terms of relative inducement value. But we have also found that the potential for political participation is present in group constituencies in the form of purposive motivations and perceptions of efficacy, and that, for most members, politics plays a pivotal role in their decision to join. The major remaining question at this point is Do the data indicate that purposive motivations and perceptions of efficacy are related to political involvement, as we have theoretical reasons to expect?[6]

In fact, these relationships are reflected in the data. Looking first at the figures on feelings of responsibility, we can see from table 10 that this variable is consistently related to the pivotal role of politics in all four groups.[7] In the Hardware Association, for example, the portion of members joining partially for politics stands at 40 percent for the low-responsibility members and increases steadily to 68 percent as the level of responsibility increases. A similar pattern obtains for each of the other groups. When we turn from the pivotal role of politics to the second measure of political involvement, the major reason for joining, precisely the same pattern emerges—the higher the level of responsibility, the greater the proportion of members who join mainly for lobbying reasons (see table 11).

Our expectations about perceptions of efficacy are borne out in tables 12 and 13, which show that efficacy is also consistently related to the pivotal role of politics and the major reason for joining in all groups. Referring to the Hardware Association, once again, we can see that the portion joining at least partially for political reasons increases steadily with increases in efficacy, rising from 47 percent to 72 percent; and that, with respect to the major reason for joining, the portion joining for lobbying increases from 18 percent to 34 percent. Comparable figures obtain for the other groups.

By using probit analysis, we can check to see whether each of these two-way relationships is maintained when controlling for the other independent variable, and whether the partial relationships are statistically significant.[8] The equation employed is:

$$P = b_0 + b_1 E + b_2 R + \epsilon$$
$$\text{where } E = \text{efficacy (1 = low to 3 = high)}$$
$$R = \text{responsibility (1 = low to 4 = high)}$$
$$P = \text{pivotal role of politics (0 = services only, 1 =}$$
$$\text{politics pivotal) or major reason for joining (0 =}$$
$$\text{services, 1 = politics)}$$

The results are present in table 14. For all groups and for both measures of the dependent variable, efficacy and responsibility maintain their positive impact on political involvement. All coefficients are significant at the .05 level or better, with the exception of one that is significant at .06.

Table 10. Feelings of responsibility, by the pivotal roles of incentives (%)*

Incentives	Retail				Hardware				Farm Bureau				Farmers Union			
	1	2	3	4	1	2	3	4	1	2	3	4	1	2	3	4
Services only	42	37	31	26	60	44	39	32	58	45	35	25	27	33	25	13
Politics some-how pivotal	58	63	69	74	40	56	61	68	42	55	65	75	73	67	75	87
Total	100	100	100	100	100	100	100	100	100	100	100	100	100	100	100	100
(N)	(62)	(84)	(124)	(73)	(78)	(104)	(135)	(72)	(229)	(151)	(142)	(62)	(169)	(112)	(149)	(126)

*1 = no importance, 2 = little importance, 3 = some importance, 4 = very important

Table 11. Feelings of responsibility, by the major reason for joining (%)*

Incentives	Retail				Hardware				Farm Bureau				Farmers Union			
	1	2	3	4	1	2	3	4	1	2	3	4	1	2	3	4
Services		(NA)			87	75	77	64	78	70	56	34	52	50	38	37
Lobbying					13	25	24	36	22	30	44	66	48	50	62	63
Total		(NA)			100	100	100	100	100	100	100	100	100	100	100	100
(N)		(NA)			(77)	(104)	(136)	(69)	(218)	(140)	(140)	(59)	(167)	(109)	(150)	(125)

*1 = no importance, 2 = little importance, 3 = some importance, 4 = very important

Table 12.   Effect of contributions, by the pivotal roles of incentives (%)*

Incentives	Retail			Hardware			Farm Bureau			Farmers Union		
	1	2	3	1	2	3	1	2	3	1	2	3
Services only	40	30	21	53	40	28	57	37	30	29	22	20
Politics some- how pivotal	60	70	79	47	60	72	43	63	70	71	78	80
Total	100	100	100	100	100	100	100	100	100	100	100	100
(N)	(122)	(195)	(14)	(115)	(217)	(32)	(215)	(311)	(33)	(153)	(305)	(64)

*1 = none, 2 = some, 3 = big

Regarding the political impact of efficacy and feelings of responsibility, then, our findings are consistently in the right direction, and the relationships are significant. For these reasons, they are highly suggestive. It is reasonable to expect that, had we been able to arrive at more reliable measures and carry out more exacting tests, these influences would have proved even more strongly connected to political reasons for joining. We cannot be certain about this, of course, and it is appropriate to stress the tentative nature of such conclusions; but the evidence we have is very encouraging. (For a discussion of economic size and its relationship to political involvement, see appendix C.)

Conclusion

These data were collected on precisely the type of group—large economic interest groups—most likely to conform to the original Olson

Table 13.   Effect of contributions, by the major reason for joining (%)*

Incentives	Retail			Hardware			Farm Bureau			Farmers Union		
	1	2	3	1	2	3	1	2	3	1	2	3
Services		(NA)		82	72	66	78	59	50	57	38	37
Lobbying		(NA)		18	28	34	22	41	50	43	62	63
Total				100	100	100	100	100	100	100	100	100
(N)				(116)	(220)	(32)	(210)	(300)	(33)	(151)	(300)	(63)

*1 = none, 2 = some, 3 = big

Table 14.   Probit results: political involvement against efficacy
and responsibility

			Retail (N=309)	Hardware (N=332)	Farm Bureau (N=511)	Farmers Union (N=497)
Pivotal role of politics	Responsibility:	coefficient	.14	.18	.23	.16
		(significance)	(.03)	(.00)	(.00)	(.00)
	Efficacy:	coefficient	.22	.32	.46	.19
		(significance)	(.06)	(.00)	(.00)	(.03)
Major reason	Responsibility:	coefficient	NA	.18	.30	.11
		(significance)	NA	(.01)	(.00)	(.02)
	Efficacy:	coefficient	NA	.25	.36	.30
		(significance)	NA	(.02)	(.00)	(.00)

model. And, in important respects, the evidence is broadly supportive
of that model's expectations. Each of the five groups offers extensive
packages of economic services, the services are widely used and valued by members, and they typically have greater inducement value
than politics. In one of the groups, the Printers Association, organizational incentives come very close to approximating the nonpolitical
ideal. Thus, overall, Olson appears to be correct in stressing the nonpolitical foundations of economic interest groups and in attacking the
pluralist focus on group goals and political support. These conclusions
are all the more impressive when we reflect on the possibility that there
may be a political bias to the survey responses; for if the respondents
are to any degree an unrepresentative sample, the data probably under-
state the true motivational role of economic services.

But while these findings provide strong support for the general thrust
of Olson's argument, they also suggest that his theory does not supply
an adequate explanation of the bases of group membership. In the first
place, the informational and value characteristics that Olson assumes
away prove to be empirically important—from 60 to 70 percent of the
members think their contributions make a difference for the group's
political success; feelings of responsibility are relevant considerations
for a great many members; and both efficacy and feelings of responsibility are correlated with political reasons for joining.

In the second place, political motivations are quite common. Although services are definitely the salient incentives, on the average, it is still true that a good many members join for political reasons—and, in fact, except in the Printers, most of the respondents in each group indicate that politics plays a pivotal role in their decision to maintain membership. Even allowing for a degree of bias, then, there is clear evidence that politics does have an integral part to play in organizational incentive structures—its salience varying from group to group, along with its potential for affecting associational structures and processes.[9]

This has a bearing, of course, on our broader understanding of interest groups as organizations. While incentive structures are hardly the only determinants of organizational characteristics, for example, the logical analysis of part 1 indicates that these five groups are probably very different organizationally. Because members of the Farmers Union are much more sensitive to politics than members of the Farm Bureau, we should expect corresponding differences in the content and structure of communications, administrative mechanisms for supplying selective incentives and collective goods, the distribution of influence, and the nature of environmental relationships—even though, in some respects, these two farm organizations might appear quite similar. Given their contrasting bases for membership, we can only expect the Retail Federation, the Hardware Association, and the Printers to reflect organizational differences along these same basic dimensions.

For a balanced perspective on interest groups, then, an exclusive emphasis on their nonpolitical foundations will not do—nor, obviously, will the traditional emphasis on politics. Both the nonpolitical and political bases for membership need to be taken into account and their organizational implications mapped out. Both have their own special roles to play.

Nine

Conclusion

The empirical analysis of part 2 sheds light on a very important organizational dimension, and it allows us to arrive at tentative conclusions bearing on the logical analysis of part 1. But, although not really its intention, the discussion throughout these last few chapters also illustrates a basic point with which this book began: that very little is actually known about the nature of interest groups as organizations. This is so even when it comes to such an apparently simple consideration as why their members join.

A great deal is known, by comparison, about what groups do in politics. The group literature is full to brimming with studies of how interest groups, as independent actors, pursue their goals through participation in various political arenas. Much attention has been paid to group resources and strategies, group influence, the operation of groups in legislative, executive, and judicial arenas, and their activities in elections. Largely because of these studies, there is no longer any real argument over the importance of groups as political participants. But a recognition of their importance has not given rise to much work that inquires into the organizational nature of the groups themselves. As a result, an understanding of what groups do in politics has not been grounded upon, and has not benefited from, a deeper understanding of the structures, processes, and bases of support that explain *why* groups do what they do.

The early pioneers in group research did not see fit to overlook these internal aspects. Odegard and Garceau, for instance, were concerned with exploring member interests, the bases of member involvement, and elements of internal structure in their classic studies of the Anti-Saloon League and the American Medical Association, respectively.[1] Schattschneider, in his *Politics, Pressures, and the Tariff,* explored the nature and extent of member heterogeneity in various business assocations participating in the Smoot-Hawley tariff issue.[2] David Truman, whose tremendously successful *The Governmental Process* was essentially the nexus between the early and modern periods, gave careful consideration to internal structures and processes before undertaking his extensive analysis of groups in politics, and conducted the latter by frequently relating groups' political behavior to their internal characteristics.[3]

It is the post-Truman work in political science, and this means the bulk of the group research, that reflects a decided shift away from internal matters. Indeed, since the mid-1950s, scholarly interest in theory and research on the topic has been steadily declining, and it continues to reach new lows with each passing year. During this time, with a few notable exceptions—among them Lipset, Trow, and Coleman's *Union Democracy,* Wilson's *Political Organizations,* and Olson's *The Logic of Collective Action*—little of significance has been done.[4]

Olson's contribution, however, was a truly path-breaking development, one whose theoretical shock waves were felt throughout the discipline of political science in a variety of substantive areas. Its potential for the study of groups was substantial. In distinguishing between collective goods and selective incentives and suggesting how the group context could be modeled, he seemed to have captured essential elements of the foundation for group activity; and, in doing so, he was led to startling conclusions that contradicted the prevailing wisdom. This helped to change the way political scientists think about group membership, and, even more importantly, it signaled a new beginning for interest group theory and research—a resurgence of scholarly interest, an exciting new analytical framework, and progress toward a broader understanding of political groups. Unfortunately, this new beginning never materialized. While empirical work along these lines has been minimal, theoretical developments have been more concerned with elegance and the traditional questions of economists (e.g., optimality, equilibrium) than with explaining even the most basic substantive aspects of interest organizations. Ironically, the promise of Olson's work has probably been better realized in other areas of study—leadership, public policy, urban politics, bureaucracy, international relations.[5]

The Organization of Interests

This book is an effort to move toward a broader understanding of interest groups as organizations. As such, it reflects in distinctive ways both the early and modern periods of interest group studies. Its theoretical orientation, of course, derives from the modern period, with Olson's concepts and insights serving as an initial foundation for the development of a more elaborate analytical framework. But substantively, it is essentially a return to the broader concerns of the early works, which sought to explain what groups do with reference to the nature of their membership, organization, and political environment.

This final chapter provides an opportunity to underline some of the analysis' most general implications for the understanding of groups. We can begin with the crucial question of group membership and with the two paradigms that have dominated scholarly discussion: pluralist theory and Olson's model of rational action.

It has become fashionable in recent years to reject the tenets of "orthodox" pluralist theory. The reasons are primarily logical, deriving from Olson's analysis of rational behavior, but also empirical; for it is now widely noted that groups do often supply economic selective incentives. The analysis of this book adds some fuel to the fire. For both logical and empirical reasons, it appears that pluralist thought is indeed remiss in pointing to common interests as the keys to membership, overlooking the distinction between collective goods and selective incentives, and promoting an overly benign view of interest groups as organizations.

These criticisms must not be carried too far, however. Above all, it seems clear that the pluralists are not wildly off target in asserting the motivational significance of common interests, even for large economic interest groups. Common interests can be important incentives for members of such groups and, evidence suggests, actually are in many cases. Furthermore, there is nothing irrational about this. It is not a mysterious aberration that cannot be explained. Once certain perceptual and value considerations are allowed into the analysis, it can be entirely rational for individuals to contribute toward the realization of collective goods that they commonly value.

The problem with pluralism, more than anything else, is an almost exclusive focus on the political and a consistent tendency to overlook the motivational and organizational roles of the nonpolitical. The problem with Olson's model, on the other hand, is that it leads to an almost exclusive focus on the nonpolitical and to a consistent tendency to overlook the motivational and organizational roles of the political. His strikingly unconventional conclusions are derived from, and are directly dependent upon, restrictive assumptions of perfect information and economic self-interest. While it is possible that these assumptions are approximated in group constituencies, there is no reason *a priori* to believe that they are—and there are empirical reasons, given the data presented here, for believing that they are not. To the extent that these assumptions break down and member decisions are shaped by perceptions of efficacy and nonmaterial incentives, Olson's dramatic conclusions no longer follow. Rational individuals will often behave differently than he expects, with politics taking on a significantly greater theoretical role.

In a sense, pluralist theory and Olson's theory represent two extremes, neither of which can provide an adequate understanding in and of itself. The solution rests with the realization that both political and nonpolitical considerations are frequently integral components of organizational incentive structures and must be systematically taken into account if interest groups are to be understood. This is what our revised approach to membership attempts to do—by building upon Olson's initial work, relaxing his assumptions, and outlining a broader set of consequences for individual behavior.

Perspectives on the nature of membership play a major role in shaping our understanding of organizations. And, in particular, the relative importance we ascribe to determinants of membership—economic selective incentives, efficacy, purposive incentives, social pressures, and others—has far-reaching implications for the characteristics we expect organizational structures and processes to take on. The dispute about the relative merits of the Olson and pluralist perspectives, therefore, is much more than just a dispute over group membership. It is by extension a dispute over a whole range of organizational characteristics and over the way in which we understand what interest groups are. That this is so, however, is not immediately apparent from the logic of membership alone. We have been able to demonstrate as much only by moving beyond the calculus of joining and constructing a larger analytical framework that contains it as an integral component. In the process, the theoretical purview was broadened to include distinctively organizational components: new types of participants, various member roles, and a set of basic organizational dimensions. It is the inter-relationship among all these that shapes the organizational nature of interest groups, and it is the way the logic of joining fits with the other components that indicates its wider theoretical importance.

In the organizational analysis of part 1, some of the most important implications have to do with how changes in the bases for membership induce changes throughout the organization. When purposive and sol-idary incentives take on increased motivational significance, for exam-ple, the organizational activity of members tends to be different than in material assocations; they have increased incentives to participate and to perform various sorts of services (positively and negatively), they are more sensitive to political changes, and subgroups are more likely to emerge as cohesive structural vehicles for the pursuit of common interests. In the maintenance efforts of group leaders, greater emphasis is likely to be placed upon the nature of the group's political goals, the allocation of resources to the political side of the organization, the political impact of communications, and political relations with outsid-ers. Furthermore, because nonmaterial incentives are typically less expensive to supply than economic benefits, rivals are better able to attract members away, especially if there exists much political heterogeneity; and this, in turn, affects the size, stability, and financial base of the group.

Internal politics is altered as well. In material associations, major sources of influence work to the cumulative advantage of larger mem-bers, with smaller members suffering from distinct, serious disadvan-tages in their efforts to affect group goals—largely due to the binding effects of economic selective incentives and to their inferior incentives and resources for performing valuable services. When nonmaterial in-centives are motivationally important, however, any individual may be able to make his contribution contingent upon politics. Cohesive politi-cal subgroups are also more likely to emerge, to wield rewards and sanctions, and to become important participants in policymaking. These and related considerations (e.g., greater threats from rivals) suggest a bargaining context that is potentially more volatile and fragmented than we found for material associations. Nonmaterial incentives thus tend to break down prevailing patterns of economic advantage and disadvantage, loosening the hold of nonpolitical inducements and distributing bargaining strengths among members.

The more comprehensive analysis that this framework enables, then, uses the logic of membership to tell us much more about organizations than simply why their members join. In so doing, it demonstrates that the debate over group membership, which has received so much attention from political scientists, has far greater organizational significance than is commonly assumed. It also has much to tell us, however, about the other organizational components—which are less often the focus of theory, research, or debate, but play distinctive theoretical roles in conjunction with the logic of membership in shaping the organizational nature of groups.

Group leaders provide the most obvious example. While everyone can agree that leaders are crucial determinants of group formation, internal structures and processes, and external political strategies and influence, the general logic of interest group leadership has rarely been the subject of systematic inquiry. Instead, what few studies there are tend to focus simply on what leaders do in various political arenas. The analysis of part 1, by contrast, centers on the more fundamental relationships between leader information and values, leader behavior, and the organizational and environmental contexts in which leader behavior arises. The focus is not on leaders per se, but on how they fit into the larger system of behavior and incentives. What leaders do in politics, for example, depends largely on the distribution of influence among participants in internal politics, which, in turn, depends on the basic dimensions of organizational maintenance and the underlying incentives for group membership. Thus, we explain the political behavior of leaders with reference to the system of which they are a part. The system, moreover, is clearly shaped by what leaders do. By evaluating and choosing among the strategic options attached to a variety of organizational dimensions, ranging from communications to environmental relationships, leaders inevitably play major roles in creating the context that conditions their own behavior.

This integrative approach allows us to understand, for instance, why something so "simple" as changing leader values can have widespread ramifications. As we have shown for three ideal types of entrepreneurial values—ideology, democracy, and economic self-interest—shifts among values translate into different uses of the communications structure, attitudes toward member participation and subgroups, recruitment strategies, criteria for hiring staff, evaluations of bargaining positions, and responsiveness to member policy preferences. All of these ultimately have their consequences for the association's size, homogeneity, financial resources, degree of internal democracy, and extent of political success. It is clear, then, that leaders with different values can be expected to adopt importantly different organizational approaches and behaviors. But it is also clear that, in so doing, they create very different organizational and environmental contexts, and these contexts will in turn have contrasting influences of their own on what leaders do, over and above the direct impact of leader values. An understanding of leader behavior is thus inevitably tied up with a more general understanding of organizations.

By almost any account, leaders and members are the most central types of participants. In focusing on them, however, and in exploring the logic of their behavior, we were led to recognize the integral importance of other types of participants—among them staff members, governmental officials, coalition partners, business enterprises, and rivals. By manipulating information, expertise, official favoritism, public policy, coalitional support, and other resources, these participants, too, can have a variety of effects on organizational structures and processes and on the very survival of the group. By virtue of the same sorts of resources, moreover, they can have influence positions for bringing their preferences to bear in internal politics; and, in some cases, they may be more consequential in shaping organizational policy than even the general membership. While the behavior of these "peripheral" actors has received little attention in the interest group literature, then, it is evident that some of the most crucial questions we can ask about interest groups can only be answered by recognizing that they are not at all peripheral to organizational outcomes, but an important part of the system of behavior that shapes what leaders and members do and what characteristics organizations take on.

If there is one summary point that most deserves to be emphasized, it is the general theme that runs throughout these paragraphs: that the analyses of basic organizational components, from the logic of membership to the roles of various participants, contribute to our understanding to the extent that they are integrated into a broader perspective on the organization as a whole. The perspective that we have constructed in this book is highly simplified in a number of respects, and it does not capture everything that might possibly prove relevant. But it does provide a fairly comprehensive framework that maps out the main organizational dimensions, their interconnections, and the ways that basic types of actors come into play. As a result, we gain a reasonably coherent picture of the whole and of characteristics that are truly "organizational" in nature.

One of the most basic conclusions that we have stressed about interest groups, for example, is that their policymaking processes can only be understood by taking into account the close interconnection of internal politics and the structural determinants of formation and maintenance. Mechanisms of communication, the administration of member benefits, the ecology of member subgroups, and patterns of relationships with outsiders—which might appear on the surface to be dimensions of behavior quite removed from politics—have significant effects on decision making, goals, and the prospects for group democracy. Conclusions of this sort are derived from analyses of specific types of participants, incentives, and resources; but they are higher-order conclusions of a general nature—about *organizational* dimensions, their properties, and their relationship to one another—and they are of major importance in telling us how the specific, "isolated" aspects of interest groups fit together into an integrated whole.

Theory and Data

It is important to be clear on methodological grounds about the kind of theoretical structure this analysis has yielded. We began with Olson's model, which makes specific assumptions about individuals and leads to specific conclusions about how individuals will behave. These conclusions are testable, although they are too often inaccurate. By allowing for imperfect information and values other than economic self-interest, we are left with a broader model in which decisions are contingent upon the informational and value premises that individuals bring to bear. If we know what their premises are, we are in a position to predict precisely what they will do. If we do not know, however, and if we are unwilling to make specific assumptions on these scores, then the best we can do is to suggest how individuals would behave under a variety of theoretically interesting informational and value conditions.

This is essentially what we have done in part 1. By setting out models of member and entrepreneurial decision making, and by "placing" these participants in fairly realistic organizational contexts, we were able to outline the nature of their organizational behavior and gain a general perspective on the way in which the various elements of the organization fit together. We were not able to generate precise predictions about why members join, whether an organization will survive, or how representative or democratic the organization will be. Our organizational analysis, then, is better regarded not as a predictive theory in any strict sense, but as a theoretical framework that links expectations with a range of informational, value, and contextual conditions—conditions that may vary empirically and are not posited in the framework itself.[6]

These conditions need to be filled in if the organizational perspective is to take on more detailed content and direction. The empirical analysis of part 2 was an effort to make an initial contribution toward this end by inquiring into the most fundamental theoretical component, the bases for membership. This was carried out in three steps: a review of the traditional background of theory and research, an evaluation of studies specifically focusing on business, farm, and labor groups, and a report of survey evidence from five Minnesota interest groups. The analysis suggests that we are on firm ground in assuming the central explanatory significance of economic self-interest, in viewing the material association as a useful standard of comparison, and in introducing complex motivational considerations in a simplified and supplementary role. The nonpolitical bases for membership prove to be of major salience, and the logical roles of economic selective incentives appear to deserve special emphasis in a more detailed organizational perspective. The analysis also suggests, however, that the informational (perceptions of efficacy) and value (purposive incentives) conditions conducive to politically based membership are prevalent among group members and that political reasons for joining are actually very common, although usually of secondary importance.

Preliminary work of this sort thus tells us something about the utility of our general theoretical approach, and it helps to fill in the logical framework by indicating the relative importance of several of the most basic organizational components.But a great deal more obviously remains to be done. Empirical considerations aside, the analysis of part 1 is amenable to more extensive theoretical development and perhaps to a more formal mode of presentation in some of its aspects. The logic of membership is a likely candidate. So are various entrepreneurial topics, e.g., the entrepreneur's trade-off between member contributions and business profits, his bargaining strategy in internal politics, or his use of market power in restricting the entry of rival organizations. There are a variety of ways, moreover, in which the general analyses of maintenance and internal politics might be extended. Subtheories could be developed and contrasted, for example, by simply positing alternative sets of informational, value, and contextual conditions— conditions which roughly obtain for interesting types of interest groups—and working out concrete sets of organizational expectations on these bases. The possibilities for theoretical elaboration are many and varied.

Yet the most acute need at this point is for more empirical research. The area of interest groups is simply data-poor, to the point where even the most basic information about organizations and their members is lacking. Needless to say, many different kinds of research are called for, and a long list of specific topics easily comes to mind. More important than specifics, however, is the general orientation that guides and constrains empirical research. The concluding discussion below centers on this question of orientation and underlines several basic points about the direction of future work.

First, given the pervasive organizational implications of the logic of joining, there are good reasons for extending high and perhaps highest priority to research on constituency characteristics. A great deal of work remains to be done, in methodological precision as well as data collection and analysis, before we can be confident about the fundamentals—the extent of efficacy, the relevance of purposive incentives, the inducement value of politics, the role of economic selective incentives—but advances in our knowledge on these counts promise, as by-products, substantial payoffs for a broader organizational understanding. Constituency research must be concerned, moreover, not simply with the incentives for membership but also with the underlying social conditions that shape the attractiveness of incentives. To take just one example: it is likely that efficacious group membership is partly a cultural phenomenon and that an individual's belief that his contribution makes a difference is influenced by a variety of socializing agents extrinsic and historically prior to his actual membership decision. Thus, we may find that individuals in some nations, regions, sectors, or social classes are significantly more disposed toward efficacy than individuals in others; and this in turn could provide a basis for explaining differences in the number of groups that form, the maintenance tasks of leaders, the role of members in internal politics, and so on. It is important, therefore, that research cast a wide net in its approach to constituency characteristics. The logic of membership is an interesting research topic in its own right, but it can also be put to use in more ambitious efforts to link social conditions to organizational characteristics.

Second, research that is explicitly organizational in focus must make an effort to avoid the pitfalls of conventional approaches. There are two that deserve special mention. One is the tendency to focus on the political aspects of interest groups. Olson's contribution notwithstanding, this tendency is a natural for political scientists and it threatens to produce a body of knowledge that is seriously limited in the kinds of information and relationships it can convey. Research on the apparently nonpolitical aspects of organizations, even if intrinsically "less interesting," is every bit as important as research on the political aspects, and the latter can neither be explained nor their organizational roles appreciated in the absence of a more balanced approach to empirical investigation. The other pitfall is that those who undertake group research might take their cues from conventional organizational theory. The problem here is that voluntary associations have been given short shrift in the organizational literature. Studies of voluntary associations are few and far between, theoretical interest in them is slight, and it is too often assumed that they can be understood largely by reference to research carried out on other kinds of organizations (usually business enterprises). The result is a general orientation toward voluntary associations that fails to underline their distinctive characteristics and can only fail to encourage the kind of specialized organizational research that needs to be carried out. While empirical work on interest groups can profitably take advantage of whatever findings and methodological techniques the organizational literature can contribute, it must be careful to do so without indiscriminately coopting the theoretical orientations in which they are embedded.

Third, it is important that research adopt a new approach to the environment. In the study of interest groups, unlike in the study of most organizations, the environment has never simply been ignored. On the contrary, because primary interest has centered around the ways in which groups operate in the political system, research efforts have often been concerned with relating system characteristics and group behavior. The focus, however, has been on how interest groups affect their political environment, and particularly on questions of political influence. When the direction of causality has been reversed, analyses of environmental impacts on the organization have rarely looked beyond group strategies, tactics, and other externally directed behaviors. What interest group research needs is a twofold reorientation. More emphasis needs to be placed on how groups are affected by their environments—and not just the political environment, but the cultural, social, economic, and legal environments that also help explain the organizational nature of groups. There also needs to be a new recognition of the truly pervasive impacts that enviromental actors and conditions can have internal to the organization, and a corresponding concern for investigating the environmental determinants of group-formation, maintenance, and internal politics. Thus, whereas past research would automatically view governmental officials as targets of influence, future research must turn the tables and explore the influence of governmental officials on the internal policymaking processes of groups, or their various roles in determining whether groups will emerge, the extent to which they will prosper, and how they will be structured. Similarly, whereas past research would tend to overlook certain elements of the environment entirely—business suppliers of selective incentives, for instance—future work must extend them a new and deserved significance.

Fourth, major additions to our knowledge can be gained from research that, either by design or cumulative effect, provides a comparative perspective on groups. Cross-national studies are likely to show that, quite apart from the obvious differences in governmental structure, legal environment, and economic development, nations also differ along a variety of dimensions that are most directly group-related. In some nations, purposive incentives and efficacy may be motivationally salient in group constituencies; group leaders may tend to be ideological or narrowly principled; outside businesses may usually be unavailable for the production of economic selective incentives; governmental officials may be hostile to the formation and political participation of interest groups. In other nations, the inducement value of politics may be weak; leaders may be pragmatic and flexible; many types of outside businesses may be willing and able to supply economic selective incentives; governmental officials may take an active hand in forming groups, discouraging rivals, and regularizing the participation of favored groups in governmental decision making. It is reasonable to believe that differences on these and other fundamental counts do indeed obtain across nations. To the extent they can be documented through empirical research, therefore, they provide a basis for deriving a variety of contrasting conclusions about national interest group systems—concerning, for instance, the kinds of interests that tend to be represented, the maintenance requirements of organizations, and the prospects for organizational democracy. Clearly, much the same sort of comparative research needs to be undertaken at lower societal levels. Just as theoretical quantities take on different values across nations, so they also vary across regions, governmental subunits (states, municipalities), interest sectors, and types of groups. Such work is necessary if we are to gain an adequately comprehensive picture of interest organization within any given nation; and, of course, it is often through intranational comparative research that we are able to make meaningful comparisons across nations in the first place.

One final point. It is common to end books with calls for empirical research and suggestions about the kinds of work that need to be done. Inevitably, the discussion tends to acquire a tone of optimism, progress, and new vistas. Even cross-national research projects begin to seem plausible expectations for the future. But, in the chemistry that gives rise to progress in theory and research, there is obviously an important element missing, for, as things stand today, there is very little interest in the systematic study of political groups. While everyone can agree that much remains to be done, volunteers are rare. If significant progress is ever to be realized, the most important first step is not the recognition that there are problems to be solved, nor even the initiation of new projects, but rather a resurgence of scholarly interest. How this might be accomplished is unclear; in some sense, it is not a step that is taken, but one that simply happens—perhaps in response to new theoretical developments, perhaps due to a variety of intangibles that bring currency to a topic. Until it does come about, however, promising avenues for research will go unexploited, and the prospects for a better understanding of interest organizations will be less bright than we might wish.

Appendix A

Selective Incentives and Dues

In order to keep things simple, the more formal aspects of the analysis in chapter 2 were constructed around considerations directly associated with the collective good. The question was: Given certain estimates of its costs, benefits, and level of supply, how much should the individual contribute? Empirically, however, the average individual usually faces a more complicated decision than this. The typical interest group not only pursues collective goods, but it also charges dues as a condition for membership and supplies selective incentives—and these, too, must be taken into account if he is to make a rational decision about contributing.

Olson did not explicitly include dues and selective incentives in the formal section of his work and, given the limited purposes of chapter 2, it was not necessary for us to do so in the text. In the first place, the increase in the number of variables produces a complex set of considerations that is better dealt with mathematically than diagrammatically. Because the mathematics becomes fairly complicated, this sort of analysis probably would not be very helpful for many readers and would threaten to distract attention from the basic points that need to be made. Furthermore, such an analysis would yield no major surprises. Estimates of the costs, benefits, and supply of the good would continue to play essentially the same roles as before, with individuals purchasing selective incentives whenever they are "worth it" in view of dues requirements.[1]

Despite these considerations, dues and selective incentives are too important simply to omit from any formal consideration. Without shifting to a mathematical analysis, we can at least take steps to illustrate how these factors might usefully be entered into a more formal analysis; and, in the process, we can suggest more clearly how they function in combination with collective goods to shape the individual's decision to join. This will be carried out below by extending the familiar diagrammatical analysis.

There are various ways of doing this. Here, we will first make several assumptions about how the individual perceives the new choice situation. Next, we will classify his entire set of choice alternatives into four general options and associate a distinct set of costs and benefits with each option. Finally, we will conduct the analysis by showing that these costs and benefits determine which general option the individual will choose and precisely how much he will contribute.

The assumptions about individual perceptions are necessary if we are to assign unambiguous roles to the new variables. Specifically, we will assume each individual perceives that

1. he is allowed to take advantage of selective incentives only when his contribution equals or exceeds his allotted level of dues;
2. when he does take advantage of selective incentives, some portion of his contribution may be "taken out" by the organization as "payment" for selective incentives and related administrative costs, while the remaining portion is applied toward the organizational costs involved in supplying the collective good;
3. when he does not take advantage of selective incentives, all of his contributions go toward the organizational costs involved in supplying the collective good;
4. other individuals will supply an amount x_o of the collective good, with $x_o > 0$.[2]

The next step is to recognize that, in deciding to join an interest group, an individual is no longer concerned with the simple question of how much to contribute solely toward the collective good. He must also consider (a) whether to contribute an amount less than, equal to, or greater than dues, and (b) whether to utilize selective incentives. When these are taken into account, the individual can be viewed as having four basic options:

Option 1: contribute nothing
Option 2: contribute some (any) amount, without obtaining selective
incentives
Option 3: contribute dues and obtain selective incentives
Option 4: contribute more than dues and obtain selective incentives

Each individual must ultimately choose one of these options. Below,
the costs and benefits of each option are outlined and a number of
symbols are introduced to represent the different values involved. By
comparing the net benefits of each option with those of the others, we
will be able to show which one is most preferred for any given individual, as well as how much he will be willing to contribute under that
option.

Option 1: The individual pays nothing and gains nothing.   .
Option 2: He contributes some amount A, in return for which he expects to receive political benefits of amount B_A.
Option 3: He contributes an amount D, equal to the cost of dues.
(The organization in turn takes out an amount C, such that
$O \leq C \leq D$, with the remainder $D - C$ then applied toward the collective good.) He then expects to receive an
amount S, equal to the value of selective incentives, plus
an amount B_D, which represents the political benefits he
expects as a return on the political expenditure of $D - C$.
Option 4: He contributes an amount D, equal to dues, plus an extra
amount E. (The organization takes out C, then applies
$D - C$ plus E toward the collective good.) He expects to
receive an amount S from selective incentives, an amount
B_D from the expenditure of $D - C$, and an amount B_E from
the expenditure of E.

We can now develop the analysis. For reasons that will become
apparent, it is useful to begin by dividing individuals into two sets. (*a*)
Individuals who, in the absence of dues and selective incentives, have
no incentive to contribute toward the collective good. These are individuals for whom the marginal cost and benefit curves intersect to the
left of x_o (the level of X others are expected to supply) or do not
intersect at all. (*b*) Individuals who, in the absence of dues and selective incentives, find it worthwhile to contribute toward the collective
good. For these individuals, the marginal cost and benefit curves intersect to the right of x_o.

Consider the first set of individuals. For each person of this type, there are obviously net costs associated with Option 2, making a purely political contribution. As figure 4 illustrates, the marginal costs of contributing directly toward the collective good are always greater than the marginal benefits. Thus, any contribution A will always exceed the benefits B_A (by an amount d). As a result, Option 1, which involves *no* costs or benefits, is preferred to Option 2, and the latter can be eliminated from further consideration.

By comparing Options 3 and 4, we can see that Option 4 must also be eliminated. Suppose the individual decides to pay dues and obtain selective incentives, and suppose that, in figure 4, A represents the amount $D - C$, which is the portion of dues applied toward the collective good by the organization. Would the individual want to contribute an *extra* amount E toward the collective good as a supplement to the amount $D - C$ already expended? The answer, clearly, is no. At the point x_A (just as for all points $x > x_o$), the marginal costs outweigh the marginal benefits; and thus any extra political contribution E must exceed the expected political return B_E. As a result, Option 3 is always preferred to Option 4.

For all persons in this set, then, the only viable choices are Option 1 (do nothing) and Option 3 (pay dues and use selective incentives). We are now interested in determining the conditions under which one will be preferred to the other. This can be carried out with the assistance of table 15, which indicates that the net benefits of Option 1 are zero and the net benefits of Option 3 are $S + B_D - D$. It follows that any given individual will prefer Option 3 to Option 1, and thus join the group, whenever

$$S + B_D - D > 0$$
$$S + B_D > D$$

Table 15

Option	Description	Costs	Benefits	Net benefits
Option 1	Contribute nothing	0	0	0
Option 2	Contribute without using selective incentives	A	B_A	$B_A - A$
Option 3	Pay dues, use selective incentives	D	$S + B_D$	$S + B_D - D$
Option 4	Pay more than dues, use selective incentives	D+E	$S + B_D + B_E$	$S + B_D + B_E - D - E$

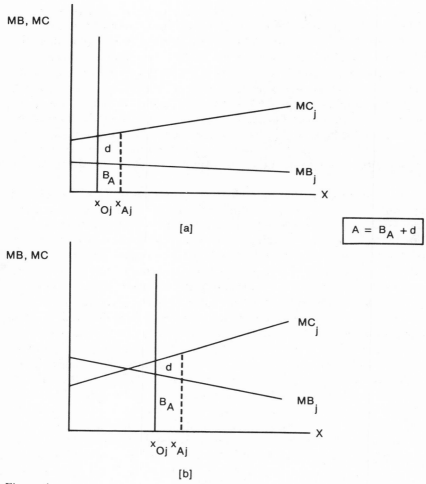

Figure 4

This decision rule is quite simple. It tells us that these individuals will join the group only if their dues costs are exceeded by the expected total value of (*a*) selective incentives and (*b*) the benefits accruing from the organization's political expenditure of $D - C$. The decision rule thus points out that individuals have two sources of benefits, one nonpolitical and one political. Moreover, it is easy to see that these components have somewhat different roles to play in the individual's calculus. One reason is that S can take on any value, and thus can be valuable enough in and of itself to justify membership. On the other hand, the political term B_D is bounded—it must be *less* than dues for this type of individual. It is, in a sense, a "small" amount. Since dues costs outweigh political benefits, B_D can only play a pivotal role in the individual's decision when selective incentives are not valuable enough to justify membership *and* when political benefits are large enough to make up the difference between S and D. In sum, selective incentives are required if he is to join, selective incentives alone can justify joining, and political benefits can only make a difference when operating in conjunction with selective incentives and when the latter do not cover dues costs.

The conclusion is that individuals may join entirely for nonpolitical reasons, but they will never join entirely for political reasons, even though there is in fact a political component present in their calculations. Under special conditions, however, they will join partially for political reasons, and the likelihood that these conditons will be met varies with member size and dues. The larger an individual is, the greater the relative value of the political component B_D and the more likely he will join partially for political reasons. The greater dues costs are, the more likely that S will be less than D, and thus that B_D will make a difference. Other things being equal, then, very large members paying high dues are the most likely to join partially for political reasons, while very small members paying low dues are the least likely.

Finally, we should note that all individuals in this set, if they decide to join the group, pay a flat amount equal to their allotted dues. It is rational for them to contribute just this amount—no more, no less— regardless of changes in political circumstances, as long as $S + B_D > D$. Thus, even though politics may play a pivotal decisional role for some members, the level of an individual's contributions does not adjust in any smooth, continuous fashion in response to political fluctuations. Because of this, dues and selective incentives can play major roles in stabilizing the membership and financial bases of interest groups.

In order to make the above decision rule more easily comparable to those for other individuals, it is useful to reexpress it in a somewhat different form. This is done with the help of figure 4 (substituting $D - C$ for A again, and B_D for B_A).

As the figure suggests: when $D - C$ is applied toward the collective good, the individual receives B_D in return. In the process, an amount d is *wasted* as far as he is concerned, where $B_D + d = D - C$. Using this equality, we can transform the decision rule to yield an equivalent expression.

$$S + B_D > D$$
$$S + B_D > B_D + C + d$$
$$S > C + d$$

Interpreting from this perspective, we see that the individual will join only if the value of selective incentives is greater than the sum of two distinct costs: the amount that is kept by the organization as payment for selective incentives, and the amount that is wasted on undesired political expenditures that the organization "forces" him to make.

We can now consider the second set of individuals—those who, in the absence of selective incentives and dues, do have an incentive to contribute toward the collective good. This incentive derives from the fact that the marginal cost and benefit curves intersect to the right of x_0, as illustrated in figure 5. For this type of individual, there are obviously net benefits associated with Option 2, making a purely political contribution. When he contributes any amount up to A_1, marginal benefits are always at least as great as marginal costs and he therefore profits from the expenditure. Were he to contribute A_1, which is optimal in the absence of selective incentives, he would receive a greater amount B_A in return. As far as this type of individual is concerned, then, Option 2 is always preferred to Option 1 (doing nothing), since the latter involves no net benefits. Accordingly, Option 1 can be eliminated from the analysis.

The nature of this choice can be simplified further by taking a closer look at Options 3 and 4. In these situations, the organization keeps a portion of his dues in order to pay for selective incentives and applies the remainder, $D - C$, toward the collective good. The question is Should he contribute just dues or should he contribute dues plus an extra amount? The answer depends upon the relation between $D - C$ and A_1—that is, the relation between how much of his dues the organization will apply toward the collective good and how much he would be willing to apply on his own.

If $D - C$ is greater than or equal to A_1, as illustrated in figure 6, the individual has no incentive to contribute anything extra toward the collective good. At the point x_D (and each point $x > x_A$), the marginal costs of doing so must exceed the marginal benefits. Thus, whenever $D - C \geqslant A_1$, the individual will always prefer Option 3 (paying only dues) to Option 4 (paying an extra amount).

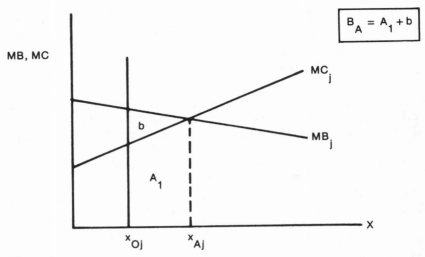

Figure 5

The result is just the contrary when $D - C$ is less than A_1. As figure 7 suggests, he will profit by contributing more than dues toward the collective good. Specifically, he will contribute an extra amount E, such that the sum $D - C + E$ is equal to A_1, at which point the marginal costs begin to outweigh the marginal benefits. In this situation, then, he will always prefer Option 4 to Option 3.

For any given individual, it must be true that $D - C \geq A_1$ or $D - C < A_1$. By considering these perceptual situations separately, we can derive decision rules for each. First, assume that $D - C \geq A_1$. Here, the individual's choice is between Option 3 and Option 2, and he will choose the former when

$$S + B_D - D > B_A - A_1$$

From figure 6, however, we can see that $A_1 = D - C - (B_D - B_A) - d$. Substitution into the above equation yields

$$S + B_D - D > B_A - D + C + (B_D - B_A) + d$$
$$S > C + d$$

The individual will thus choose Option 3 over Option 2 when the value of selective incentives exceeds the sum of (a) the amount kept by the organization and (b) the amount wasted on undesired political expenditures. This, of course, is the same decision rule employed by the first set of members. What all of these individuals share is the fact that

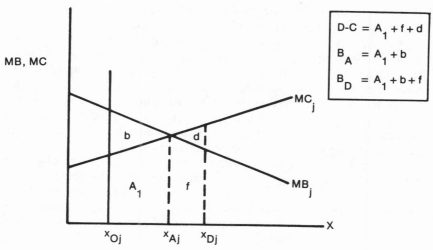

Figure 6

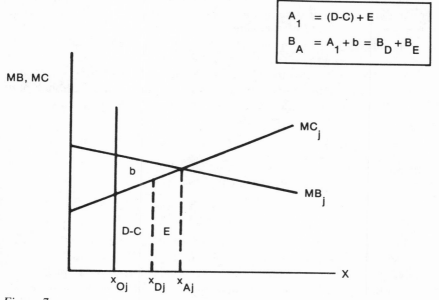

Figure 7

they are constrained by the organization to make political expenditures that they do *not* have an incentive to make on their own.

It is especially interesting that this can happen to the type of individual being analyzed here, though, since he initially had an incentive to contribute toward the collective good anyway. The question was never whether he was going to contribute, but simply how much. Because of selective incentives, however, his behavior is changed in two significant respects (assuming $S > C + d$). First, his total contribution is greater than it would otherwise have been ($D > A_1$) and, in the process, he supplies more of the collective good ($x_D > x_A$). Second, his level of contributions is no longer completely sensitive to changing political considerations. This is because, under a wide range of circumstances making $S > C + d$ true, he will pay a flat amount—dues. He will continue to make this unvarying contribution as long as the inequality holds, even if changes in political factors imply somewhat different costs and benefits.

We have another example, then, of how selective incentives can shield contributions from political considerations. In this case, even though individuals may be initially willing to make entirely political contributions to an organization, the employment of selective incentives can turn some of them into dues payers—whose contributions, while largely underpinned by political benefits, can remain constant despite some degree of variation in political factors.

Now we can turn to the alternative situation in which $D - C < A_1$. Here, the individual must choose between Option 4 and Option 2, and he will prefer the former when its net benefits are greater. Symbolically, Option 4 is preferred when

$$S + B_D + B_E - D - E > B_A - A_1$$

From figure 7, we can see that $A_1 = D - C + E$ and that $B_A = B_D + B_E$. Substitution yields

$$S + B_D + B_E - D - E > (B_D + B_E) - (D - C + E)$$
$$S > C$$

This decision rule is slightly different from the others, but it is easy to see why it should guide behavior for this type of individual. He perceives that, once C is subtracted from his dues, the remainder is profitably applied toward the collective good, and that he makes additional profits through his extra contribution. Of the funds applied for political ends, none is wasted on undesired expenditures. This distinguishes him from the other members, who are "forced" to make inefficient purchases of collective goods. Hence, he does not compare S with $C + d$, as they do, but is simply concerned with whether S is greater than C, since this is all he really pays for the privilege of using selective incentives.

A second point is that, while selective incentives are not required to induce him to contribute, and while he will channel the same amount toward the collective good (A_1; $D - C + E = A_1$) under both options, his total contribution will nevertheless be greater if he chooses Option 4. In particular, he will contribute an amount A_1 under Option 2, but he will supply an amount $D + E = A_1 + C$ under Option 4. Because of the value he places on selective incentives, he is willing to contribute more than he otherwise would (assuming $S > C$) in order to *make up* for the nonpolitical portion presumably kept by the organization.

Finally, we should recognize that this individual's contribution will be based directly on political considerations, regardless of which option he chooses. His level of contributions will be sensitive to the goals and political activities of the group, and will fluctuate with even the most minor perceived changes in such factors. He is the only type of contributor for whom this is true.

Conclusion

This diagrammatical analysis illustrates how selective incentives can be entered into the individual's calculations along with information about the collective good, and it helps to clarify the distinctive role that selective incentives can play in changing both the amount and the political contingency of individual contributions. This role goes beyond that of simply giving individuals a direct benefit in return for their decision to join. When selective incentives are offered, (*a*) any individual, regardless of his initial incentives with respect to the collective good, can be induced to contribute at least as much as he otherwise would, (*b*) some individuals can be induced, for nonpolitical reasons, to make extra (and inefficient) purchases of the collective good, and (*c*) contributions that the organization applies toward political ends can be wholly or partially shielded from changes in political circumstances.

This last point, especially, underlines the important organizational role that dues play in conjunction with selective incentives. Dues are important not only because they set required payment levels, but also because they represent stabilizing components of an organization's income. For members of all sizes, paying a set dues fee—no more, no less—can be rational, even in the face of varying political circumstances and, in some cases, even if political benefits loom large in the individual's calculations. Thus, dues and selective incentives jointly operate to solidify an organization's financial base, helping to inhibit the likelihood of large fluctuations in receipts—while at the same time generating a (potential) surplus that can be put to political use.

*Representational Structures
and Internal Politics*

It might seem at first glance that representational structures pose major problems for the analysis of internal politics as we have chosen to develop it. For, clearly, we have made no allowances for voting mechanisms, leadership by elected officials, nor any other formal trappings of democratic decision making; and, if these have important consequences for group goals, as is commonly believed, then we have simplified away a crucial structural determinant of internal politics. This can only appear all the more problematical in view of the fact that, empirically, most economic interest groups do indeed have representational structures.[1] We will show in this section, however, that these problems are actually of little significance; whether or not a material association has a representational structure, the principles underlying internal politics are the same.

We can begin by noting that the decision to set up a representational structure is a policy decision for the entrepreneur and is made according to the same criteria as any other policy decision: he will move in this direction if he believes it is materially advantageous for him to do so. The adoption of formal democracy can have nothing to do with normative notions of fairness, equality, or other values bearing on the "goodness" of such a structure, but is motivated by a concern for its instrumental value in bringing about greater material gain. How, then, can democratic forms prove instrumental in this respect?

The most basic answer is already a familiar aspect of our analysis: in the entrepreneur's political relations with legislators, administrators, public agencies, and even private groups and organizations, the quality of representativeness often has a definite and substantial *value*. If the group is recognized by these participants as representing an affected sector of society or the economy, political access is facilitated, opinions are more easily influenced, favored status is more easily obtained, and the group is thus better able to employ its resources in achieving political and economic objectives. In fact, for many groups, the claim of representativeness may be absolutely essential for the effective pursuit of a wide range of goals.

At bottom, the value of representativeness is a cultural phenomenon, particularly characteristic of Western democratic political systems, and due primarily to certain attitudes that are commonly held by decision-making elites—most notably, by governmental officials who hold the key to political success. This added punch that accrues to an association because of its representational status has long been a recognized fact of political life. E. Pendleton Herring, in one of the early studies of interest group activities in public arenas, remarks on the advantages that representativeness can contribute to a group's cause.

> Where an association represents a recognizable and clearly defined membership, it is welcomed. If the Washington lobbyist can speak authoritatively for a given number of voters upon a definite issue, the legislators find it easier to arrive at some conclusion as to what the people want . . . Such statements are regarded as helpful and valuable. Leaders in the House and Senate representing many different points of view admit that this is true.
>
> In committee hearings, congressmen are very insistent to learn the nature of the organization the lobbyist represents, the composition of the membership, and the methods used in adopting policies. The nearer the association approaches the state of being an authentic and reputable spokesman for an apparent class, industry, profession or well-defined social group, the more does Congress attend.[2]

This is at least as true today as it was then. Given that representativeness can have considerable value, the question becomes What actions must the entrepreneur take, and what costs must he incur, to obtain the benefits involved? Since there is no absolute set of criteria defining representativeness, the answer is that the entrepreneur is required to take certain actions that convince the "right" people that the association's policies are indeed representative of its membership, for it is from these people that the benefits of representativeness must ultimately be obtained. The entrepreneur's task therefore is to make the association *appear* representative, although whether it "really is" representative is beside the point. The evidence strongly suggests, as David Truman indicates, that he can do so by structuring decision-making along lines that conform at least superficially to consensual democratic attitudes defining the "democratic mold." "The attitudes themselves are vague, but they usually involve approval of such devices as periodic elections of key officials, broad participation by the membership in the group's policy making, either directly or through a system of elected representatives, written constitutions, and the like. These, in fact, become elements without which an organization cannot achieve 'respectability' and 'legitimacy' in the community."[3]

Just as cultural attitudes underlie the value of representativeness, then, so they also determine what the entrepreneur must do in order to stake his claim. Generally speaking, associations that adopt this broad form of representation are considered by elites (the people who count) to be democratic, and thus eligible for the benefits associated with representativeness. This structural form clearly gives acceptability, however, to a fairly wide range of specific representational structures falling under its rubric, some of which will cost the entrepreneur less than others in terms of the constraints they place upon his ability to realize his own goals. Therefore, if he follows this course, the rational entrepreneur will choose to adopt a representational structure that will conform to the generally accepted structural form and will choose the specific type of democratic structure that minimizes his own costs. In this way he can endeavor to gain the benefits of representativeness at least cost.

The decision is ultimately up to the entrepreneur. But, from our analysis of internal politics, we know that there may be a number of other actors whose bargaining positions enable them to have a say in the outcome. Thus, as with other sorts of policy decisions, the adoption of a representational structure is the result of a bargaining process in which a set of individuals, the entrepreneur among them, press for the best possible realization of their own interests. It is this full constellation of interactions that determines whether there will be a representational structure at all and, if so, what specific type is most acceptable. The group will therefore adopt formal democratic procedures if the entrepreneur, after considering the relevant range of rewards and sanctions, decides that this direction promises enhanced material benefits.

What about internal politics, then—does the group become democratic? Relying upon the logic of our earlier analysis, we can conclude with some confidence that, when a material association actually does adopt a representational structure, it is *not* transformed into a group that is qualitatively different from the kind of group we have been analyzing all along. One important reason is that, because of the incentives involved, the adoption of formal democratic procedures should not in itself radically alter the relative weights of participants in internal politics, regardless of who the group's elected officials are.

We can see this by recognizing, first, that this sort of structural transition means that an "unaccountable" entrepreneur no longer controls the group's revenues and policies; instead, according to the democratic mold, the association's elected officials take over entrepreneurial roles (although they may delegate their performance to staff members). What criteria will determine *their* policy choices? The answer is that, because they are economically self-interested, decision makers will attempt to use the group as a vehicle for their own material gain—just as the entrepreneur did—and will therefore be sensitive to the preferences of those members, staff personnel, and outsiders who can make material values contingent upon official policy choices. In other words, the new decision makers will have material incentives to respond to the rewards and sanctions wielded by bargaining participants, rather than incentives to allow group policies to be a function of egalitarian voting procedures.

Thus, a larger member who can threaten the maintenance of the group by dropping out will have a strong basis for affecting group goals, even though the group may be controlled by elected officials. To take a more general example: if a number of decision makers insist upon winning in a policy dispute by combining their votes, without regard for the bargaining strengths of others, the result could easily be declining contributions, a smaller membership, fewer political and communications services, the secession of subgroups, the emergence of rivals, and so on. When voting processes take precedence over bargaining processes, material sanctions will be carried out, rewards will be withheld, and the organization will be less able to generate benefits of any kind, political benefits in particular. To the extent that group officials are aware of the material consequences of their decisions, then, the underpinnings of internal policies should not be significantly different when the group has a representational structure.

There are, however, a few notable qualifications which, if not taken into account, could lend importance to voting processes. First, bargaining positions will continue to be the dominant considerations only if the number of officials directly responsible for group policy is kept small. In such cases, the demands and bargaining positions can be made known to the officials in charge, the consequences of various decisional alternatives can be weighed in light of this information, and policy choices can be made accordingly. When large numbers of decision makers are responsible for the final choice, however, there is no longer any real bargaining situation in which this process occurs. If, for instance, policies are decided by the direct vote of thousands of members, then the demands and bargaining positions of "important" individuals generally will not be taken into account by voters, nor will the full range of material consequences associated with policy alternatives; group policies will presumably reflect the "will of the membership." But informed participants will recognize this process as dangerous and disruptive to the group's survival and to its prospects for economic and political success. Accordingly, it is important from their point of view that the number of responsible officials be kept small so that all material considerations can be rationally weighed.

A second qualification is that, when group officials depend upon member votes for their positions of leadership, they may be led to appeal to the membership on an issue basis in efforts to maintain their positions—thereby, to some extent, shaping policies according to patterns of electoral support. This, of course, is the classical mechanism of accountability in any democratic system; but, in material associations, it threatens the generation of benefits by failing to link policies with bargaining strengths. There is, however, a means of neutralizing this problem, the key to which is leader security. If leaders can somehow be shielded from the vicissitudes of competitive, closely fought elections and, in effect, guaranteed official positions, then they will be free of electoral constraints in shaping group policies.

We should also recognize one other relevant factor at this point. Even if these qualifications are taken care of, and thus even if bargaining positions remain the fundamental determinants of group policy, it nevertheless makes a difference who the officials are that exercise formal control of the group. In effect, they constitute a new entrepreneur. And, just as we saw for different entrepreneurial goals, different goals on their part will have an impact on group policies and on strategies of formation and maintenance. This is true not only because there is some flexibility in policymaking, but also because such resources as the communications structure can be employed toward different ends and with far-reaching effects. Thus, those with high material stakes in group policies will not be satisfied simply knowing that their bargaining positions will be taken into account by officials—they will have an incentive to try to determine which individuals get to be officials in the first place.

All of these points suggest characteristics that a representational structure should tend to have in a material association if it is to be adopted. For the representational structure is not decided upon by all members acting in equal capacities, but is designed and imposed by those who are already powerful. Far from being a mechanism for distributing and equalizing control over decision making, and thus for handing over a degree of power to the powerless, it is instead a tool for legitimizing the policies of those who are already in effective control. For those making the structural decisions, it is simply a strategic problem: they must design a representational structure that is consistent with the formal requirements of the democratic mold but that continues to guarantee them an acceptable amount of control over the group's policies. Their task is to take the necessary steps to ensure that the number of responsible officials is indeed small, that officials are shielded from electoral insecurity, that bargaining positions rather than votes are therefore the controlling forces, and that only acceptable individuals occupy official roles.

These same considerations apply for the entrepreneur himself, of course, since he will not allow a democratic transition that relieves him of his material surplus. The representational structure, then, will not only reflect the bargaining strengths of participants, but it will also contain an appropriate "place" or reward for the entrepreneur. If he is a nonmember and a single individual, this may take the form of a deal or contract with other participants, guaranteeing him a formal position of control (e.g., the chief executive of the association), and this might be bolstered over time by certain skills, expertise, knowledge, or resources that he can offer. In short, he might be both formally secure and practically indispensable. On the other hand, the entrepreneur might consist originally of a number of group members—in particular, larger members who are so politically motivated that they incur the costs and risks of setting up an association. Here, the subsequent adoption of a representational structure presents no problem at all since, by design, some or all of the official positions can be occupied (if need be) by individuals who had previously constituted the entrepreneur. Control remains in the same hands. There are additional ways in which the entrepreneur might undergo such a transition as well. The general point which these examples illustrate is that the transition to formal democracy need not remove the entrepreneur from the picture. The person or persons comprising him can remain significant actors, without being "democratized out."

In sum, then, the entrepreneur and other powerful participants can endeavor to gain certain values—which, as Truman notes, are actually critical to the group's effective operation in the political system—by setting up a representational structure. While they must conform to the democratic mold in doing so, they are only willing to accept structures with certain characteristics: the number of officials directly responsible for policy must be kept small, officials must be electorally secure, the influentials should be able to determine who occupies official roles, and, in general, the structure should allow for the expression of underlying bargaining strengths rather than voting strengths. We can now take a brief look at several specific means by which an appropriate system of formal democracy might be brought about.

Through a constitution outlining the representational structure, official roles can be delineated and specific authorities attached to each in such a way that effective policy control rests in a small number of hands. The actual number of elected positions is not important and may be quite high; it is only those with significant control over policy that must be kept low. As for their election by members, one very useful mechanism is a formal device often called the nominating committee—which, empirically, is broadly in accord with the democratic mold. Such a committee functions, as the name implies, to make nominations for elected posts within the association; elections then consist of choices among candidates who are nominated by the committee. The critical choices are therefore made by the members of the committee and not by the mass of members voting in the election. Influential individuals need simply ensure that the committee consists of knowledgeable and informed members, who either have strong bargaining positions themselves or are well aware of the demands and bargaining positions of others. In this way, nominations can be "hammered out" so as to reflect the underlying balance of power and so as to ensure that the resulting elections yield acceptable group officials. The nominating committee is thus a device that operates to eliminate surprises and to enable rational bargaining processes to govern election outcomes even if large numbers of members are voting.

Another critical device is the control over information of relevance to the membership's electoral choices. Especially in large groups, information about the interests and activities of certain members can be downplayed, highlighted, distorted, or simply ignored in an effort to shape member perceptions about who might make a "good" candidate. In particular, acceptable elected officials and staff members can be given highly favorable coverage (as active, resourceful, concerned, etc.); and other individuals can be "built up" through similar media treatment, preparing the way for their future appearance in leadership roles. Outside of the focus on specific individuals, the media can also be employed to shape perceptions about what the group stands for, its activities, its success rate, its concern for representing different points of view, and so on, all of which have a bearing on how members view their elected officials. Hence, even without a nominating committee, nominations and elections could be partially controlled through the control of information. For obvious reasons, this is particularly compelling in large groups whose members are not in frequent interaction and must rely heavily upon organizationally generated information.

Still another mechanism is that campaigns among the membership can simply be forbidden—by the association's constitution, by statute, or by decree—on pain of dismissal from the organization or some other penalty. When this device is adopted, potential candidates are threatened with sanctions if they attempt to publicize their cause or air certain disputes in an effort to recruit electoral support from other members. This is another way of limiting and shaping the information available to members—ensuring that, in respect to certain internal matters, as much information as possible reaches members through official channels. It is also a way of ensuring that structured bargaining processes, rather than voting processes, will determine outcomes.

Without carrying this discussion any further, it should be clear that there are a number of devices available for minimizing the democratic aspects of formal democracy. Indeed, in view of these structural mechanisms and in view of the material and strategic advantages possessed by critical individuals, the adoption of a representational structure does not appear to be an exceedingly difficult strategic problem. Elections can be held at frequent intervals, all members can be allowed (even encouraged) to vote, candidate qualifications can be publicized, and firm democratic links can be claimed between group policies and member preferences—all of which are strongly in accord with the environmentally approved democratic mold, and all of which have very little to do with the true nature of associational policy. An acceptable representational structure, imposed by the entrepreneur and individuals having strong bargaining positions, will be designed to highlight its democratic and electoral trappings—but to ensure that bargaining processes, not voting processes, are the real determinants of policy. The result is an association that *appears* representative, because satisfying certain cultural requirements, but whose policies are explained according to the same principles that apply to any material assocation.

We have touched upon the major issues involved in understanding how and why a representational structure is adopted. Before concluding, however, we should note that there are other uses, in addition to those suggested above, to which such a structure might be put. It need not serve as a superfluous organizational appendage, functionless except for appearance's sake. Rather, it might be integrated in certain ways with other aspects of the organizational structure. This is particularly attractive when the representational structure can be broken down into geographical or special-interest "units of representation." For example, the structure might be used for

1. an indirect system of communications, allowing for messages to and from identifiable segments of the membership. Elected officials in the various units might serve as middlemen.

2. a system for the organized recruitment of new members (from geographical areas, from functional subsectors).

3. a system for encouraging members to generate their own selective incentives through mutually beneficial interactions.

4. a system for stimulating certain kinds of political activities (in legislative districts, in specialized issue areas).

Because of these and other uses to which it can be put, the representational structure need not be "purely electoral" or "separate" in any important sense from other aspects of the organization. As a consequence, outsiders may be led to see organizational structure primarily in representational terms—when in fact the structural units are only superficially for that purpose, their real importance deriving from the communications, administrative, and bargaining behaviors that they facilitate. Hence, by meshing the representational structure and other organizational behaviors, leaders might be able to clothe a whole range of internal strategies in legitimacy and respectability, making it appear that the organization structures its activities for the purpose of representing its members, when this is actually not the purpose at all.

Economic Size and Political Membership

For conceptual and empirical reasons, it is best to relegate the size variable to an appendix. It involves a number of complicating considerations, and to have discussed these in the text would have distracted from the basic points that needed to be made.

Other things being equal, we have reason to believe that the inducement value of politics will increase with economic size. Conceptually, however, the size variable is an "underlying" factor that is not of immediate relevance to the membership decision. In an ideal research design, the impact of size would be captured in a precise measurement of each member's cost-benefit calculus and thus in a much more sophisticated version of our perceptual variable, efficacy. While economic size should obviously play a role (along with other factors) in shaping perceptions of efficacy, it is the perceptions themselves that are of immediate relevance for the decision to join.

Empirically, moreover, special characteristics of the groups we are studying suggest that the link between size and political reasons for joining will not be as consistently strong as we would otherwise expect, and that it will vary across groups.

1. The two farm groups have mass memberships, huge budgets, and very low dues charges (about $40 per member annually) that are not pegged to a member's economic size. The fact that some members have more to gain from group success than others is

swamped by the fact that all members, regardless of size, are making extremely small marginal additions to a tremendous pool of resources. To the extent that any member thinks his contributions make a difference for group success, the explanation is less likely to rest with his economic size than the various psychological and social influences on his perceptions.

2. The Hardware Association is a large group (about 900 members) with a very large budget. While it does peg dues to member size, annual dues charges vary from $25 to only $75, and the size variation within the membership is minimal. The group is essentially comprised of small, independent hardware stores, and even the "large" stores are fairly small enterprises by ordinary business standards. As in the farm groups, then, all members are making very small contributions to a large pool of resources, and differences in member size are not likely to be of much consequence.

3. The Retail Federation is dramatically different. Group members range from small shoe stores to huge department stores, and annual dues charges range from $50 to somewhere in the neighborhood of $20,000, depending upon the member's economic size. The distribution of size within the membership is skewed toward the small end of the continuum, and the vast majority pays less than $200 each in annual dues. At the other end of the continuum, however, are several "special," financially huge members who pay more than $9500 each in dues every year, and, one notch below them on the size scale, another select set of members who contribute between $2500 and $9500. These members carry much of the cost burden for the organization as a whole. Striking variations in size and dues, combined with the group's budgetary dependence on large contributions, suggest that member size should be clearly linked with political reasons for joining in the Retail Federation.

The data on size and political involvement bear this out. (See tables 16 and 17.) In the Retail Federation, size makes a real difference in political involvement—but only at the upper reaches. Beyond a certain "threshold" of size and dues, *all* members make politically contingent contributions. Below it, size variations are not associated with variations in political involvement, and an average of 65 percent join at least partially for political reasons. The farm groups and the Hardware Association, on the other hand, have no special sets of large contributors, and size does not markedly affect their political bases for membership. There is, nevertheless, a weak relationship between size and political involvement in each group, with the larger members somewhat more likely to join for political reasons.[1]

Table 16. Economic size, by the pivotal role of incentives (%)*

Incentive	Retail					Hardware			Farm Bureau				Farmers Union			
	1	2	3	4	5	1	2	3	nf	1	2	3	nf	1	2	3
Services only	32	39	35	0	0	49	43	38	58	43	41	38	25	25	26	19
Politics some- how pivotal	68	61	65	100	100	51	57	62	42	57	59	62	75	75	74	81
Total	100	100	100	100	100	100	100	100	100	100	100	100	100	100	100	100
(N)	(131)	(143)	(43)	(9)	(6)	(125)	(132)	(118)	(155)	(143)	(163)	(123)	(115)	(213)	(149)	(91)

*Size measured by gross revenues, in 1000s.
Retail: 1 = under $100; 2 = $101–$500; 3 = $501–$2500; 4 = $2501–$9500; 5 = over $9501
Hardware: 1 = under $50; 2 = $51–$125; 3 = over $126
Farm Bureau: nf = not an active farmer; 1 = under $30; 2 = $31–$60; 3 = over $61
Farmers Union: same as Farm Bureau

Table 17. Economic size, by the major reason for joining (%)*

Incentive	Retail					Hardware			Farm Bureau				Farmers Union			
	1	2	3	4	5	1	2	3	nf	1	2	3	nf	1	2	3
Services			(NA)			80	74	73	85	68	53	58	39	53	41	33
Lobbying						20	26	27	15	32	47	42	61	47	59	67
Total			(NA)			100	100	100	100	100	100	100	100	100	100	100
(N)			(NA)			(128)	(129)	(120)	(149)	(133)	(158)	(122)	(111)	(208)	(151)	(89)

*See table 16 note.

By extending the probit analysis of chapter 8, we can evaluate the impact of size on political involvement while controlling for efficacy and responsibility. We can also check to see whether the relationships between the latter variables and political involvement are altered when size is controlled. The results are set out in table 18. The figures indicate that size maintains its positive impact on political involvement for every group and for both measures of the dependent variable, although its coefficient is often not significant at the .05 level. Efficacy and responsibility, by contrast, retain their positive relationships throughout, and, with but one slight exception, their coefficients are uniformly significant. Had we gone through all this in chapter 8, then, we would have been led to the same conclusions about the politicizing impact of responsibility and efficacy—and, from a theoretical standpoint, these were the questions at issue.

Table 18.   Probit results: political involvement against efficacy and responsibility

			Retail (N=309)	Hardware (N=332)	Farm Bureau (N=511)	Farmers Union (N=497)
Pivotal role of politics	Responsibility:	coefficient	.13	.18	.23	.16
		(significance)	(.04)	(.01)	(.00)	(.00)
	Efficacy:	coefficient	.21	.31	.44	.19
		(significance)	(.07)	(.01)	(.00)	(.03)
	Size:	coefficient	.14	.14	.16	.07
		(significance)	(.07)	(.06)	(.00)	(.14)
Major reason	Responsibility:	coefficient	NA	.18	.31	.11
		(significance)		(.01)	(.00)	(.01)
	Efficacy:	coefficient	NA	.25	.33	.30
		(significance)		(.03)	(.00)	(.00)
	Size:	coefficient	NA	.09	.28	.11
		(significance)		(.18)	(.00)	(.03)

None of this implies that size is an unimportant organizational variable. Its weak connection to political involvement in the two farm groups and the Hardware Association is due to their special characteristics—huge budgets and memberships, low dues. These are not typical of the average interest group. Moreover, even when member size is not a major determinant of political reasons for joining, it should still be a major determinant of participation within the organization—since larger members ordinarily have a variety of resource and incentive advantages over smaller members. This is borne out, in fact, by additional data from the Minnesota survey (not presented here), which indicate that larger members are much more active in group affairs.

Notes

Introduction

1. For a review of interest group research, see Harmon Zeigler and G. W. Peak, *Interest Groups in American Society.* 2d ed. (Englewood Cliffs, N.J.: Prentice-Hall, 1972); and Carol S. Greenwald, *Group Power* (New York: Praeger Publishers, 1977).

2. The major exceptions, and probably the two best books yet written on interest groups generally, are David B. Truman, *The Governmental Process: Political Interests and Public Opinion* (New York: Knopf, 1951); and James Q. Wilson, *Political Organizations* (New York: Basic Books, 1973).

3. See, for example, the various works cited in Sidney Verba, *Small Groups and Political Behavior* (Princeton, N.J.: Princeton University Press, 1961); David Horton Smith, Richard D. Reddy, and Burt R. Baldwin, *Voluntary Action Research, 1972* (Lexington, Mass.: Lexington Books, 1972); and Constance Smith and Anne Freedman, *Voluntary Associations* (Cambridge, Mass.: Harvard University Press, 1972).

4. Some might argue that political scientists have also shaped their explanations with reference to Robert Michels's "Iron Law of Oligarchy." Robert Michels, *Political Parties,* trans. Eden and Cedar Paul (New York: Free Press, 1958). Michels's argument can be viewed as contradicting pluralist notions, suggesting that group policies are determined by self-perpetuating, self-interested leadership cliques and not by a faithful reflection of member interests. Be this as it may, it appears that political scientists have generally accepted both the Iron Law *and* pluralism but without viewing their inconsistencies as very important. To some extent, this is understandable. The degree of

internal democracy can be treated, from a pluralist standpoint, as something that does not really affect the more fundamental congruence between group goals and member goals—since congruence is guaranteed by the pluralist logic of membership. If individuals join (quit) interest groups because they agree (disagree) with their policies, then the question of oligarchy is in some sense beside the point.

5. The major pluralist works of relevance to interest groups are Truman, *The Governmental Process;* Arthur F. Bentley, *The Process of Government* (Chicago: University of Chicago Press, 1908); and Earl Latham, *The Group Basis of Politics: A Study in Basing-Point Legislation* (Ithaca, N.Y.: Cornell University Press, 1952). For a critique of pluralist theories and ideas, see William E. Connally, ed., *The Bias of Pluralism* (New York: Atherton Press, 1969); Theodore J. Lowi, *The End of Liberalism: Ideology, Policy, and the Crisis of Public Authority* (New York: Norton, 1969); Grant McConnell, *Private Power and American Democracy* (New York: Knopf, 1966); and Henry Kariel, *The Decline of American Pluralism* (Stanford, Calif.: Stanford University Press).

6. Mancur Olson, Jr., *The Logic of Collective Action* (Cambridge, Mass.: Harvard University Press, 1965).

7. Ibid., p. 2.

8. Olson has been criticized on essentially these bases by various writers, and efforts have been made to improve upon and extend his analysis. Informational criticisms are stressed by Norman Frohlich and Joe Oppenheimer, *Modern Political Economy* (Englewood Cliffs, N.J.: Prentice-Hall, 1978), and "I Get By with a Little Help from My Friends," *World Politics* (October 1970); Norman Frohlich, Joe Oppenheimer, and Oran Young, *Political Leadership and Collective Goods* (Princeton, N.J.: Princeton University Press, 1971); D. Marsh, "On Joining Interest Groups," *British Journal of Political Science,* vol. 6 (1976). The relevance of individual values beyond economic self-interest is argued by Brian Barry, *Sociologists, Economists, and Democracy* (London: Collier-Macmillan, 1970); Wilson, *Political Organizations;* Michael Taylor, *Anarchy and Cooperation* (Cambridge: Cambridge University Press, 1976); Robert H. Salisbury, "An Exchange Theory of Interest Groups," *Midwest Journal of Political Science,* vol. 13 (February 1969); and William A. Gamson, *The Strategy of Social Protest* (Homewood, Ill.: Dorsey, 1975). For efforts to go beyond Olson, see John Chamberlin, "Provision of Collective Goods as a Function of Group Size," *American Political Science Review* 68 (1974): 707–16; Wilson, *Political Organizations;* Taylor, *Anarchy and Cooperation;* Frohlich et al., *Political Leadership and Collective Goods;* and the several works cited in Frohlich and Oppenheimer, *Modern Political Economy.* Despite these contributions, however, there has emerged no cumulative or even very well integrated body of work on the nature of interest groups, and little progress has been made toward a more comprehensive theory.

One   Elements of the Analysis

1. Discussions of rational behavior are legion. For a useful explication with applications to politics, see William H. Riker and Peter C. Ordeshook, *An Introduction to Positive Political Theory* (Englewood Cliffs, N.J.: Prentice-Hall, 1973).

2. Economists do not usually assume that individuals are motivated entirely by money. Most commonly, individuals are allowed to possess a whole range of unspecified values; but complexities are submerged under the summary notion of utility and fitted into an economic analysis by assuming that individual preferences (as depicted, for example, in indifference schedules or utility functions) always conform to certain mathematically and economically desirable properties. In virtue of the way individual values are structured and conceptualized, economists need not—or at least they do not—worry about such disparate considerations as ideology, status, and altruism, and how these variously affect economic behavior. While the utility approach is apparently general, a rational utility maximizer can be shown to prefer more money to less, other things being equal; and, on basic theoretical issues, the analysis can conveniently center around money values (prices, wages, income, profits, etc.) rather than the more general and more fundamental concept of utility.

3. Here we are speaking of those works that attempt to deal in a fairly comprehensive manner with the organization as a whole. Most prominent are the following: Herbert Simon, *Administrative Behavior* (New York: Macmillan, 1957); R. M. Cyert and James G. March, *A Behavioral Theory of the Firm* (Englewood Cliffs, N.J.: Prentice-Hall, 1963); James G. March and Herbert Simon, *Organizations* (New York: John Wiley and Sons, 1958); Anthony Downs, *Inside Bureaucracy* (Boston: Little, Brown, 1966); Peter C. Clark and James Q. Wilson, "Incentive Systems: A Theory of Organizations," *Administrative Science Quarterly*, vol. 6 (September 1961); James Q. Wilson, *Political Organizations* (New York: Basic Books, 1973). For a comprehensive review of a great many works on organizational decision making, see Julian Feldman and Herschel Kanter, "Organizational Decision Making," in James G. March, ed., *Handbook of Organizations* (Chicago: Rand McNally, 1965).

4. For heuristic purposes, this discussion will be contrasting the "economic approach" with the "major analyses of organizational decision making." By the economic approach we are referring to the use of models comprised of highly restrictive assumptions (e.g., perfect information, economic self-interest)—and this, of course, is a stereotype that overlooks a great deal of methodological diversity within economics. It is, nevertheless, an approach "typical" of economics, especially in comparison to the other social sciences. Our contrasting reference to the major works on organizational decision making is also a simplification, since it explicitly refers to a certain set of core works (listed in note 3, above), but not to others that would ordinarily have been included under the same general heading (for example, those listed in note

9, below) in a review of the organizational literature as a whole. While some readers may be uncomfortable with this kind of simplified comparison, it is useful for the limited purposes of this chapter, and it is not meant to be taken too far.

5. Downs, for example, singles out nine different goals as particularly important motivators of bureaucrats: power, money income, prestige, convenience, security, personal loyalty, pride in proficient performance of work, desire to serve the public interest, and commitment to a specific program of action. He simplifies matters further by defining five ideal types of bureaucratic officials, each of which is assumed to possess a distinct subset of the nine listed goals. His theory of bureaucratic behavior is then developed with reference to these five types of officials, rather than bureaucrats as they "really are." See especially chapter 8 in *Inside Bureaucracy*.

6. The classic discussions of information are found in Simon, *Administrative Behavior*, and March and Simon, *Organizations*.

7. For proposals regarding the analytical value of the entrepreneur concept, see Robert H. Salisbury, "An Exchange Theory of Interest Groups," *Midwest Journal of Political Science*, vol. 13 (February 1969); Richard Wagner, "Pressure Groups and Political Entrepreneurs: A Review Article," *Papers on Non-Market Decision-Making*, 1966; Norman Frohlich and Joe Oppenheimer, "I Get By with a Little Help from My Friends," *World Politics* (October 1970). For efforts to use the concept in comprehensive political analyses, see Norman Frohlich, Joe Oppenheimer, and Oran Young, *Political Leadership and Collective Goods* (Princeton, N.J.: Princeton University Press, 1971); and Warren F. Ilchman and Norman Thomas Uphoff, *The Political Economy of Change* (Berkeley, Calif.: University of California Press, 1971).

8. The best examples of this shift in perspective are Simon, *Administrative Behavior*, and Wilson, *Political Organizations*. In this regard, we should also mention Chester I. Barnard, *The Functions of the Executive* (Cambridge, Mass.: Harvard University Press, 1958). While Barnard's pioneering work was not a decision-making analysis in the same sense as the others, it foreshadowed future theoretical developments, among them a focus on the "executive" and the requirements of organizational maintenance.

9. This is not meant to disparage attempts at formal theory, but is simply offered as a fair appraisal of their present scope of application. One of the best and most promising formal theories is William A. Niskanen, *Bureaucracy and Representative Government* (Chicago: Aldine-Atherton, 1971). Niskanen deals quite successfully with the supply of goods and services by bureaus, but purposely limits his attention almost entirely to this single dimension of organizational behavior. For reviews and illustrations of formal theories of organizations, see the following essays in James G. March, ed., *Handbook of Organizations:* T. Marschak, "Economic Theories of Organization"; William H. Starbuck, "Mathematics and Organization Theory"; and Starbuck, "Organizational Growth and Development."

Two   *The Decision to Join*

1. For more technical definitions and discussions of the various dimensions and "degrees" of collective goods, see Paul A. Samuelson, "The Pure Theory of Public Expenditure," *Review of Economics and Statistics* 36 (November 1954): 387–90; "Diagrammatic Exposition of a Theory of Public Expenditure," Ibid., 37 (November 1955): 350–56; "Aspects of Public Expenditure Theories," Ibid., 40 (November 1958): 332–38; Richard Musgrave, *The Theory of Public Finance* (New York: McGraw-Hill, 1959); John G. Head, "Public Goods and Public Policy," *Public Finance* 17, no. 3 (1962): 197–219.

2. We are assuming, with Olson, that various levels or amounts of the collective good can be achieved, and that the provision of the good is not simply an all-or-nothing proposition. Were we to assume the latter, a slightly different analysis would be required.

3. Some of the more technically oriented readers would doubtless prefer a mathematical presentation and will consider this sort of diagrammatical exposition too primitive. An adequate mathematical analysis, however, would eventually become quite involved. One suitable method, given the kinds of substantive issues we are concerned with in this book, would be to interpret the decisional problem as one of maximization subject to nonlinear constraints and to arrive at optimal solutions by applying the Kuhn-Tucker conditions. An analysis along these lines is set out in Terry M. Moe, "A Calculus of Group Membership," Working Paper No. 7, Public Policy and Political Studies Center, Michigan State University, November 1978. Because most readers would probably find such approaches too technical to be very enlightening, it seems preferable simply to illustrate diagrammatically how Olson's model can be employed and modified to generate conclusions about individual behavior. In this way, at least, it is quite apparent why we have certain expectations about the bases for membership, since it is actually possible to "see" the various theoretical components at work.

4. Solely for purposes of illustration, the implicit assumption here is that fixed costs are zero; were they nonzero, the area under the marginal cost curve would not represent the entire amount necessary for supplying any specified level of X. This simplification does not affect the general conclusions that follow.

5. For simplicity, income effects are assumed to be zero and multiple time periods are not considered. Were these two factors taken into account, the ceiling on provision would be somewhat greater than x_2 and the precise sharing of costs between j and k would be affected. But the basic conclusions outlined in the text would still hold. For a dynamic analysis of collective action that incorporates income effects, see, e.g., John Chamberlin, "Provision of Collective Goods as a Function of Group Size," *American Political Science Review* 68 (June 1974): 707–16. See also Mancur Olson and Richard Zeckhauser, "An Economic Theory of Alliances," *Review of Economics and Statistics* 43 (August 1966): 66–79.

6. Olson develops these parts of his analysis with the aid of a three-fold typology of groups: privileged, intermediate, and latent. These categories are unnecessary and we will not rely upon them here.

7. Olson also seems to assume that Large Members will emerge only in small groups and that this, too, gives them advantages over large groups. What makes someone a Large Member, however, is the relationship between his marginal cost and benefit curves, and neither of these logically depends on the size of the group. Thus, it seems preferable to say that Large Members can be present in groups of any size and to stress that the advantages of small groups derive from strategic interaction.

8. Olson, *The Logic of Collective Action,* pp. 2–3.

9. Two general points about x_{om}, the amount that any individual m expects others to supply. First, the individual's estimate x_{om} is not necessarily altered when others contribute, since he may be entirely unaware of their behavior. Second, the relationship between x_{om} and contributions will be attenuated when income effects are taken into account: a decrease in x_{om} will have a less positive impact and an increase in x_{om} will have a less negative impact. (In effect, his marginal benefit curve becomes contingent upon x_{om} and shifts when the latter shifts.)

10. On political efficacy, see, e.g., Gabriel A. Almond and Sidney Verba, *The Civic Culture* (Princeton, N.J.: Princeton University Press, 1963); Sidney Verba and Norman H. Nie, *Participation in America: Political Democracy and Social Equality* (New York: Harper and Row, 1972); David Easton and Jack Dennis, "The Child's Acquisition of Regime Norms: Political Efficacy," *American Political Science Review* 61 (March 1967): 25–38; Robert Weissberg, "Political Efficacy and Political Illusion," *Journal of Politics* 37 (May 1975): 469–87; and, for a review of studies of efficacy, Paul R. Abramson, *The Political Socialization of Black Americans: A Critical Evaluation of Research on Efficacy and Trust* (New York: Free Press, 1977).

Three   Organizational Formation and Maintenance

1. Throughout the remainder of part 1, we will be developing an organizational analysis which, while taking various aspects of the real world into account, is certainly not based in any direct way upon empirical studies. In view of this, it is not necessary to try to embed our examination of communications, administration, internal politics, etc., in the literatures of organizational and political research, and there will be no attempt to do so. Readers interested in empirical analyses along these lines can find an excellent and comprehensive treatment in James Q. Wilson, *Political Organizations* (New York: Basic Books, 1973). For an "economic" approach see Albert O. Hirschman, *Exit, Voice, and Loyalty* (Cambridge, Mass.: Harvard University Press, 1970).

2. On the entrepreneur concept, see the various works cited in chap. 1, n. 7.

3. For a discussion of the interesting question of favored tax treatment, see Samuel F. Berger, *Dollar Harvest* (Lexington, Mass.: Heath Lexington Books, 1973).

4. Certain legal requirements will also play a structural role. In the United States, for instance, the pursuit of collective goods through electoral campaigns often calls for the creation of political action committees, and the tax laws (as interpreted by the Internal Revenue Service) put constraints on how politicized the organization can be if it is to retain its tax-exempt status.

5. The requirements and facilitators of success will vary from one political system (or even agency, committee, etc.) to the next, and will vary over time within any given context. The points listed here best reflect the American political environment and may not be entirely adequate for others. In Norway, for instance, lobbying and the "politics of access" are much less important than they are in the United States, while organizational expertise and research capabilities are probably more important. See Robert B. Kvavik, *Interest Groups in Norwegian Politics* (Oslo: Universitetsforlaget, 1976).

6. The analysis here is similar in essential respects to economic analyses of barriers to entry and effective competition. See, for instance, Joe S. Bain, *Barriers to New Competition: Their Character and Consequences in Manufacturing Industries* (Cambridge, Mass.: Harvard University Press, 1956).

Four   Internal Politics

1. In the general literature on organizations, the best and most insightful theoretical treatment of organizational goals is to be found in Richard M. Cyert and James G. March, *A Behavioral Theory of the Firm* (Englewood Cliffs, N.J.: Prentice-Hall, 1963). Instead of assuming that fixed goals are the raison d'être of an organization or that goals are independent variables that explain aspects of organizational behavior—perspectives that are very common— Cyert and March understand goals as products of a bargaining process among organizational participants.

2. See Olson, *The Logic of Collective Action,* chap. 6.

3. Olson recognizes but does not emphasize this last-mentioned implication of the theory.

Five   Departures from the Economic Ideal

1. For a useful discussion of these complications as they apply to voluntary associations, see James Q. Wilson, *Political Organizations* (New York: Basic Books, 1973), chap. 2.

2. Usually, these sorts of motivational complications are assumed away (or glossed over) in order to facilitate formal analysis. For efforts to take them

explicitly into account, see, for example, Michael Taylor, *Anarchy and Cooperation* (Cambridge: Cambridge University Press, 1976); Gary S. Becker, "A Theory of Social Interactions," *Journal of Political Economy* vol. 82, no. 6 (November–December 1974); Thomas R. Ireland and David B. Johnson, *The Economics of Charity* (Chicago: Public Choice Society, 1970); Norman Frohlich, "Self-Interest or Altruism, What Difference?" *Journal of Conflict Resolution* 18, no. 1 (March 1974): 55–73; David Collard, *Altruism and Economy* (Oxford: Martin Robertson, 1978).

3. Regarding empirical work on such questions, see the review of the small-group studies in chapter 6.

4. The analysis of this section is formally developed in Terry M. Moe, "A Calculus of Group Membership," Working Paper, Public Policy and Political Studies Center, Michigan State University, November 1978.

5. Peter B. Clark and James Q. Wilson, "Incentive Systems: A Theory of Organizations," *Administrative Science Quarterly*, vol. 6 (September 1961). We will often be relying upon this typology because it is simple and its categories are theoretically interesting. But the dividing line between these two types of incentives is not always crystal clear—just as the dividing line between material and nonmaterial, economic and noneconomic, is not always clear. (An individual who seeks a higher salary, for example, may do so out of love for his family and a sense of responsibility to provide for them. Is this "economic" or "noneconomic" in nature?) This problem is intrinsic to the subject matter, however—motivations are complex, and there is really no way to talk about the variety of human motives and their behavioral consequences without putting up with a degree of conceptual ambiguity.

6. Empirically, there may sometimes be a relationship between a sense of responsibility (or other purposive dimensions) and individual efficacy. The greater a person perceives his impact to be, the more he may feel a responsibility to contribute or participate. This relationship should vary from person to person, however; and there is no logical reason why purposive benefits require an underlying perception of efficacy.

Six   *The Traditional Background*

1. For critical discussions of the theoretical dominance of pluralism, see Theodore J. Lowi, *The End of Liberalism: Ideology, Policy, and the Crisis of Public Authority* (New York: Norton, 1969); Grant McConnell, *Private Power and American Democracy* (New York: Knopf, 1966); William E. Connally, ed., *The Bias of Pluralism* (New York: Atherton Press, 1969); Henry Kariel, *The Decline of American Pluralism* (Stanford, Calif.: Stanford University Press, 1961); Peter Bachrach, *The Theory of Democratic Elitism: A Critique* (Boston: Little, Brown, 1967).

2. Alexander Hamilton, James Madison, and John Jay, *The Federalist Papers* (New York: Mentor Books, 1961), especially no. 10.

3. Alexis de Tocqueville, *Democracy in America* (New York: Random House, 1955), vol. 1, p. 178. See especially vol. 1, chap. 12 and vol. 2, chap. 5.

4. Theodore J. Lowi, *The Politics of Disorder* (New York: Basic Books, 1971), pp. 32–33.

5. For the distinction between "philosophical pluralists" and "analytical pluralists," see Earl Latham, "The Group Basis of Politics: Notes for a Theory," *American Political Science Review*, vol. 46 (1952).

6. Harold Laski, *A Grammar of Politics*, 4th ed. (London: George Allen and Unwin, 1939), p. 67.

7. See Truman, *The Governmental Process;* Arthur F. Bentley, *The Process of Government* (Chicago: University of Chicago Press, 1908); Earl Latham, *The Group Basis of Politics: A Study in Basing-Point Legislation* (Ithaca, N.Y.: Cornell University Press, 1952).

8. Truman, *The Governmental Process*, p. 33. We should stress that Truman is not talking in terms of broad or vaguely defined attitudes that members share, but in terms of "shared attitudes *toward what is needed or wanted in a given situation*, observable as demands or claims upon other groups in society" (italics added).

9. Ibid., p. 34.

10. Ibid., p. 36.

11. For a critique of "group theory" as a broad analytical framework for understanding politics, see Robert Golembiewski, "The Group Basis of Politics: Notes on Analysis and Development," *American Political Science Review* 54 (December 1960): 38–51; Stanley Rothman, "Systematic Political Theory: Observations on the Group Approach," *American Political Science Review* 54 (March 1960): 15–33.

12. We will be referring to the scheme developed in the introduction to Gabriel A. Almond and James S. Coleman, eds., *The Politics of the Developing Areas* (Princeton, N.J.: Princeton University Press). This is not, of course, the only way that structural functionalism has been applied to interest groups, or to politics generally. For a broader perspective, see William Flanigan and Edwin Fogelman, "Functional Analysis," in James C. Charlesworth, ed., *Contemporary Political Analysis* (New York: Free Press, 1967).

13. There is a vast literature on small groups. For reviews of the major perspectives, studies, and findings, see Paul B. Applewhite, *Organizational Behavior* (Englewood Cliffs, N.J.: Prentice-Hall, 1965); Sidney Verba, *Small Groups and Political Behavior: A Study of Leadership* (Princeton, N.J.: Princeton University Press, 1961); Paul A. Hare, *Handbook of Small Group Research* (New York: Free Press, 1960).

14. Fritz J. Roethlisberger and William J. Dickson, *Management and the Worker* (Cambridge, Mass.: Harvard University Press, 1939).

15. Truman, *The Governmental Process,* p. 193.

16. Verba, *Small Groups and Political Behavior,* pp. 159–60.

17. This body of literature is also vast. For reviews, see David Horton Smith, Richard D. Reddy, and Burt R. Baldwin, *Voluntary Action Research, 1972* (Lexington, Mass.: Lexington Books, 1972); Constance Smith and Anne Freedman, *Voluntary Associations: Perspectives on the Literature* (Cambridge, Mass.: Harvard University Press, 1972).

18. Arnold M. Rose, *The Power Structure: Political Process in American Society* (New York: Oxford University Press, 1967), chap. 5.

19. Arnold S. Tannenbaum and Richard Bachman, "Attitude Uniformity and Role in Voluntary Organizations," *Human Relations,* 1966.

20. Gabriel A. Almond and Sidney Verba, *The Civic Culture* (Princeton, N.J.: Princeton University Press, 1963), chap. 10.

21. See Richard D. Reddy and David H. Smith, "Personality and Capacity Determinants of Individual Participation in Organized Voluntary Action," in Smith et al., *Voluntary Action Research, 1972.*

22. David Horton Smith, Richard D. Reddy, and Burt R. Baldwin, "Types of Voluntary Action: A Definitional Essay," in Smith et al., *Voluntary Action Research, 1972.*

23. Arthur Jacoby and Nicholas Babchuk, "Instrumental and Expressive Voluntary Associations," *Sociology and Social Research,* 47 (July 1963): 461–71; Wayne C. Gordon and Nicholas Babchuk, "A Typology of Voluntary Associations," *American Sociological Review* 24 (February 1959): 22–29.

24. Several such studies have been carried out, but for our purposes they are of little interest. See, for example, Arthur Jacoby, "Some Correlates of Instrumental and Expressive Orientation to Associational Membership," *Sociological Inquiry,* 35 (Spring 1965): 163–75; Alan Booth, Nicholas Babchuk, and Alan B. Knox, "Social Stratification and Membership in Instrumental-Expressive Voluntary Associations," *Sociological Quarterly* 9 (1968): 427–39.

25. Jacoby and Babchuk, "Instrumental and Expressive Voluntary Associations," p. 469.

Seven   Studies of Economic Interest Groups

1. On these and other general aspects of unions, see Lewis Lorwin, *The American Federation of Labor* (Washington, D.C.: Brookings Institution, 1933); Derek C. Bok and John T. Dunlop, *Labor and the American Community* (New York: Simon and Schuster, 1970); J. David Greenstone, *Labor in American Politics* (New York: Knopf, 1969); Jack Barbash, *American Unions: Structure, Government, and Politics* (New York: Random House, 1967); Richard A. Lester, *As Unions Mature: An Analysis of the Evolution of American Unionism* (Princeton, N.J.: Princeton University Press, 1958).

2. Rose Theodore, "Union Security Provisions in Major Union Contracts, 1948–1959," *Monthly Labor Review* 82, no. 2 (December 1959): 1348–56.

3. Olson, *The Logic of Collective Action,* chap. 3. Two other studies are Higdon Clarence Roberts, "Private Benefits and the Cohesion of Voluntary Associations: A Field Test of the Theory of Collective Action" (Ph.D. dissertation, Ohio State University, 1971); and Philip M. Burgess and Richard Conway, "Public Goods and Voluntary Associations: A Multi-Stage Investigation of Collective Action in Labor Union Locals," *Sage Professional Papers in American Politics* (Beverly Hills and London: Sage Publications, 1973).

4. Olson, *The Logic of Collective Action,* p. 75.

5. Ibid., p. 79.

6. The following studies are among those most relevant. Arnold S. Tannenbaum and Robert L. Kahn, *Participation in Union Locals* (Evanston, Ill.: Row, Peterson, 1958); Joel Seidman et al., *The Worker Views His Union* (Chicago: University of Chicago Press, 1958); T. V. Purcell, *The Worker Speaks His Mind on Company and Union* (Cambridge, Mass.: Harvard University Press, 1953); Hjalmar and R. A. Rosen, *The Union Member Speaks* (New York: Prentice-Hall, 1955); Leonard Sayles and George Strauss, *The Local Union* (New York: Harper, 1952); Richard A. Lester, *As Unions Mature;* Alice H. Cook, *Union Democracy: Practice and Ideal: An Analysis of Four Large Local Unions* (Ithaca, N.Y.: New York State School of Industrial and Labor Relations, 1963). For a useful overview, see Arnold S. Tannenbaum, "Unions," in James S. March, ed., *Handbook of Organizations* (Chicago: Rand McNally, 1965).

7. Seidman et al., *The Worker Views His Union,* chap. 11.

8. Ibid., pp. 243–44.

9. Ibid., p. 245.

10. Ibid., pp. 247–49.

11. Tannenbaum and Kahn, *Participation in Union Locals.* See chaps. 4–6.

12. Roberts, "Private Benefits and the Cohesion of Voluntary Associations...." This finding is a result of asking members to name benefits they receive that nonmembers do not.

13. Tannenbaum, "Unions," p. 740.

14. Cook, *Union Democracy,* pp. 210–11.

15. See, for instance, Seymour Martin Lipset, *The First New Nation: The United States in Historical and Comparative Perspective* (Garden City, N.Y.: Anchor Books, 1967), chap. 5.

16. Tannenbaum, "Unions," p. 754.

17. See, for instance, Tannenbaum and Kahn, *Participation in Union Locals,* chaps. 4–6.

18. Lipset, *Political Man,* p. 409.

19. Tannenbaum and Kahn, *Participation in Union Locals,* p. 230.

20. Ibid., p. 148.

21. See Tannenbaum, "Unions,"

22. See Lipset, "The Political Process in Trade Unions," in *Political Man;* also, "Trade Unions and the American Value System," in *The First New Nation.*

23. There are a great many works of relevance here. See for instance, Selig Perlman, *A Theory of Labor Movement* (New York: Augustus M. Kelley, 1949); Louis M. Hartz, *The Liberal Tradition in America* (New York: Harcourt, Brace, 1955); Walter Galenson, ed., *Comparative Labor Movements* (New York: Prentice-Hall, 1952); Leon D. Epstein, *Political Parties in Western Democracies* (New York: Praeger, 1967), chap. 6.

24. See Epstein, *Political Parties in Western Democracies,* chap. 4.

25. See the discussion in James Q. Wilson, *Political Organizations* (New York: Basic Books, 1973), chap. 7.

26. See, for example, D. Lockwood, "The New Working Class," *Archives Europeennes de Sociologie,* no. 2 (1960); F. Zweig, *The British Worker* (London: Pelican, 1960); F. Zweig, "The New Factory Worker," *The Twentieth Century* (June 1960); John H. Goldthorpe et al., *The Affluent Worker: Industrial Attitudes and Behavior* (Cambridge: University Press, 1968); Mark van de Vall, *Labor Organizations: A Macro- and Micro-Sociological Analysis on a Comparative Basis* (Cambridge: University Press, 1970). For those analyses that are not published in English, see the footnotes in van de Vall, pp. 34–41.

27. van de Vall, *Labor Organizations;* and Goldthorpe et al., *The Affluent Worker*. We should point out that the latter study focuses on the "upper" blue collar workers (making at least 17 pounds per week in 1962)—but this is not likely to exaggerate the extent of privatization for the British workers generally. In the first place, an increasingly large portion of the labor force has over the years risen out of the "lower" blue collar category. And, in the second place, van de Vall's study shows that the upper blue collar and white collar union members are *less* likely to exhibit privatization than the lower blue collar members. Thus, the Goldthorpe focus on the "affluent worker" should not overstate the phenomenon.

28. van de Vall, *Labor Organizations,* p. 131.

29. Ibid., p. 122.

30. Ibid., pp. 136–37.

31. Ibid., p. 146.

32. Goldthorpe et al., *The Affluent Worker*. The first passage is from pp. 107–8, the second from pp. 113–14.

33. Ibid., p. 111.

34. For a general treatment of farm groups see V. O. Key, *Politics, Parties, and Pressure Groups,* 4th ed. (New York: Thomas Y. Crowell, 1958), chap. 2; Lowi, *The End of Liberalism,* chap. 4; Truman, *The Governmental Process,* chap. 4; Harmon Zeigler, *Interest Groups in American Society* (Englewood Cliffs, N.J.: Prentice-Hall, 1964), chap. 6.

35. Olson, *The Logic of Collective Action,* chap. 6.

36. Samuel R. Berger, *Dollar Harvest* (Lexington, Mass.: Heath Lexington Books, 1971).

37. John A. Crampton, *The National Farmers Union* (Lincoln, Neb.: University of Nebraska Press, 1965).

38. For information of this sort on the development of the Farm Bureau, see Orville M. Kile, *The Farm Bureau Through Three Decades* (Baltimore, Md.: Waverly Press, 1948); and Grant McConnell, *The Decline of Agrarian Democracy* (Berkeley: University of California Press, 1953).

39. Berger, *Dollar Harvest,* chap. 4. The information that follows is a brief summary of the points that Berger makes throughout the book, and most will not be individually footnoted.

40. On tax matters, see especially Ibid., chap. 6.

41. Ibid., p. 26.

42. Besides Crampton, *The National Farmers Union,* not much is written on this group. For general information on its development, see Theodore Saloutos, *Farmer Movements in the South, 1865–1933* (Berkeley: University of California Press, 1960); Theodore Saloutos and John D. Hicks, *Agricultural Discontent in the Midwest, 1900–39* (Madison: University of Wisconsin Press, 1951). Most of the discussion below is based on Crampton.

43. Ibid., p. 148.

44. Ibid., p. 150.

45. Ibid., p. 149.

46. Ibid., p. 87.

47. Ibid., p. 125.

48. However, the survey data in the next chapter also suggest that, at least for the two Minnesota groups studied, politics is indeed more important as a membership inducement in the Farmers Union than in the Farm Bureau.

49. Brown and Bealer, "Value Orientations and Behavioral Correlates of Members in Purchasing Cooperatives," *Rural Sociology* (M 1957).

50. James A. Copp, "Perceptual Influences on Loyalty in a Farmer Cooperative," *Rural Sociology* (June 1964).

51. Ibid., p. 171.

52. Angus Campbell et al., *The American Voter,* abridged ed. (New York: Wiley, 1964), p. 217.

53. W. Keith Warner and William D. Heffernan, "Benefit-Participation Contingency in Voluntary Farm Organizations," *Rural Sociology* 32 (June 1967): 139–53.

54. E. E. Schattschneider, *The Semi-Sovereign People: A Realist's View of Democracy in America* (New York: Holt, Rinehart, and Winston, 1960), p. 30.

55. Ibid., p. 32.

56. They may, however, heavily rely upon large contributors that are not single individuals—cooperatives, insurance companies, county subunits, and so on—and these may play internal political roles analogous to those of large firms in business associations.

57. Key, *Politics, Parties, and Pressure Groups,* p. 96.

58. See, for example, Opinion Research Corporation, *Members Appraise Associations* (Washington, D.C.: Association Service Department, Chamber of Commerce of the United States, 1966).

59. On the NAM, see Wilson's discussion in *Political Organizations*, chap. 8. See also Richard W. Gable, "Birth of an Employers' Association," *Business Historical Review*, vol. 33 (Winter 1959); and Alfred S. Cleveland, "NAM: Spokesman for Industry?" *Harvard Business Review*, vol. 26 (May 1948).

60. Olson, *The Logic of Collective Action*, pp. 141–48.

61. Wilson, *Political Organizations*, p. 156.

62. Ibid., p. 160.

63. Ibid., pp. 157–61.

64. On associations of small businesses, see Ibid., chap. 8; Joseph Palamountain, *The Politics of Distribution* (Cambridge, Mass.: Harvard University Press, 1955); Harmon Zeigler, *The Politics of Small Business* (Washington, D.C.: Public Affairs Press, 1961).

65. Zeigler, *The Politics of Small Business*, p. 66.

66. See Opinion Research Corporation, *Members Appraise Associations*.

67. David Marsh, "On Joining Interest Groups," *British Journal of Political Science* 6 (July 1976), p. 265.

68. Ibid., p. 262.

69. J. Roffe Wike, *The Pennsylvania Manufacturer's Association* (Philadelphia: University of Pennsylvania Press, 1960). The discussion that follows is based on Wike's account.

70. Ibid., p. 37.

71. Ibid., p. 69.

72. Schattschneider, *The Semi-Sovereign People*, p. 35.

73. Olson, *The Logic of Collective Action*, p. 145.

74. Ibid., p. 143.

75. Opinion Research Corporation, *Members Appraise Associations*; Temporary National Economic Committee, *Trade Association Survey*, monograph 18 of *Investigation of Concentration of Economic Power* (Washington, D.C.: Government Printing Office, 1941), p. 376.

76. Wilson, *Political Organizations*, p. 152.

Eight   Some New Data

1. For the three business groups, a proportionately small number of "associate" members was omitted from the sample. These are members who are not really in the group's economic sector (for example, associate members of the Hardware Association are not hardware stores, although some are suppliers of hardware stores). Moreover, it is typically the case (according to group leaders) that most of these members do not join to use economic services or because they support group goals—but, instead, to make business contacts, curry favor, make their names known, and otherwise enhance their business prospects in the economic sector. Via a mail survey, it is difficult to get members to admit motives of this sort—and likely that they will claim to join in

"support" of group goals. In view of this problem, and in view of their fairly small numbers, it seemed best simply to omit associate members. The situation is different for the farm groups—in which significant proportions of members are not active farmers, and in which organizational services (political and nonpolitical) are of direct value to these individuals. They are accordingly included in our samples.

2. For neither the Farm Bureau nor the Farmers Union was a random sampling procedure feasible—due to the ways that organizational records are kept, the costs of using these records to achieve a random sample, and the unwillingness of leaders to be bothered by such complications. An effort was made, accordingly, to arrive at an adequately representative sample, by methods that were both relatively inexpensive and acceptable to leaders. For the Farm Bureau, this was accomplished by singling out six representative county organizations, obtaining their membership lists (which state headquarters does not have on file), and using these as the member sample. For the Farmers Union, whose state headquarters does have a complete membership list, blocs of about 100 names were chosen in a random fashion from the list of over 20,000 names (arranged according to zip code). In both groups, the final sample came to approximately 1750 members.

3. See Terry M. Moe, "An Economic Theory of Interest Groups," Ph.D. dissertation, Department of Political Science, University of Minnesota, 1976).

4. In all cases, at any rate, the response rates are sufficiently high to indicate that we are studying a broad range of members, and not just a special subset. This is supported by member responses to questions on participation (not presented here)—which show that most respondents participate only rarely or not at all in group activities. This is just what we would expect from "average" members.

5. This question was not asked to the Retailers, which was the first group to be surveyed.

6. The pivotal role of incentives is a more discriminating measure of political involvement than the major reason for joining. In order to illustrate the apparent generality of the relationships, however, figures on both measures of the dependent variable are presented. Their average intercorrelation (τ_β) is about .40.

7. The Printers are omitted from this table as well as the others. Because the number of respondents is fairly small in this group, and because their answers are highly homogeneous (almost everyone joins for services), we would find ourselves trying to explain variations that derive from very few members.

8. The use of dichotomous dependent variables threatens to violate basic regression assumptions. The probit model is similar in many respects to the regression model, but is specifically designed to correct for such problems. See John Aldrich and Charles Cnudde, "Probing the Bounds of Conventional Wisdom: A Comparison of Regression, Probit and Discriminant Analysis." *American Journal of Political Science*, vol. 19, pp. 571–608.

9. We should also point out that this is a sample of organizational members and does not tell us anything about why nonmembers fail to join. It may be that Olson's model does a better job of explaining the behavior of nonmembers than members—and that, for group constituencies in their entirety, its success rate is higher than our data imply. If so, this would underline the model's utility as a theory of collective action, in the broader sense. But it would *not*, at the same time, establish the model's utility as a theory of interest groups, since the key to an understanding of interest organizations rests with why their members join and how they behave as organizational participants.

Nine   *Conclusion*

1. Peter H. Odegard, *Pressure Politics: The Story of the Anti-Saloon League* (New York: Columbia University Press, 1928); Oliver Garceau, *The Political Life of the American Medical Association* (Cambridge, Mass.: Harvard University Press, 1941).

2. E. E. Schattschneider, *Politics, Pressures, and the Tariff* (New York: Prentice-Hall, 1935).

3. David B. Truman, *The Governmental Process* (New York: Knopf, 1951).

4. Seymour Martin Lipset et al., *Union Democracy* (Garden City, N.Y.: Anchor Books, 1962); James Q. Wilson, *Political Organizations* (New York: Basic Books, 1973); Mancur Olson, *The Logic of Collective Action* (Cambridge, Mass.: Harvard University Press, 1965).

5. See, for instance, Norman Frohlich et al., *Political Leadership and Collective Goods* (Princeton, N.J.: Princeton University Press, 1971); Robert L. Bish, *The Political Economy of Metropolitan Areas* (Chicago: Rand McNally, 1971); William H. Riker and Peter C. Ordeshook, *An Introduction to Positive Political Theory* (Englewood Cliffs, N.J.: Prentice-Hall, 1973), especially chaps. 3, 9, 10; Randall Bartlett, *Economic Foundations of Political Power* (New York: Free Press, 1973); Mancur Olson and Richard Zeckhauser, "An Economic Theory of Alliances," *Review of Economics and Statistics* 43 (August 1966): 266–79.

6. Methodologically, this approach is quite similar to those employed by Simon and Downs. See Herbert Simon, *Administrative Behavior* (New York: Free Press, 1957) and Anthony Downs, *Inside Bureaucracy* (Boston: Little, Brown, 1966).

Appendix A

1. See Terry M. Moe, "A Calculus of Group Membership," Working Paper, Public Policy and Political Studies Center, Michigan State University, November 1978.

2. This is assumed in order to avoid complications that arise due to fixed costs, but the same general conclusions could ultimately be derived without it.

Appendix B

1. See discussions in David B. Truman, *The Governmental Process* (New York: Knopf, 1951), part 2; and James Q. Wilson, *Political Organizations* (New York: Basic Books, 1973), chap. 12.

2. E. Pendleton Herring, *Group Representation Before Congress* (Baltimore: Johns Hopkins University Press, 1929), pp. 49–50. On the general value of representativeness, see also Truman, *The Governmental Process*, chaps. 11–14; and Wilson, *Political Organizations*, chap. 15.

3. Truman, *The Governmental Process*, p. 50.

Appendix C

1. The only deviations of consequence are the "not an active farmer" members in the Farm Bureau and the Farmers Union. A more detailed analysis would suggest that, in the Farm Bureau, these members join overwhelmingly to get the group's insurance while, in the Farmers Union, they are especially interested in politics and score quite high on feelings of responsibility. Apparently, these two groups attract "outside" members on quite different bases, with the Farm Bureau again banking of the nonpolitical. See Terry M. Moe, "An Economic Theory of Interest Goups," (Ph.D. dissertation, Department of Political Science, University of Minnesota, 1976).

Index